The Manship School Guide to
POLITICAL COMMUNICATION

The
Manship
School
Guide to

Edited by

POLITICAL
COMMUNICATION

DAVID D. PERLMUTTER

LOUISIANA STATE UNIVERSITY PRESS
BATON ROUGE

08 07 06 05 04 03 02 01 00 99
5 4 3 2 1

Designer: Laura Roubique Gleason
Typeface: Trump Mediaeval text with Gill Sans display
Typesetter: Coghill Composition
Printer and binder: Thomson-Shore, Inc.

Library of Congress Cataloging-in-Publication Data

The manship school guide to political communication / edited by David
    D. Perlmutter.
        p.   cm.
    Includes index.
    ISBN 0-8071-2480-X (cloth : alk. paper). — ISBN 0-8071-2481-8
(paper : alk. paper)
    1. Campaign management—United States.   2. Electioneering—United
States.   3. Political consultants—United States.   I. Perlmutter,
David D., 1962—   .
JK2281.M36   1999
324.7'0973—dc21   99-23661
                                                                CIP

To my wife, Christie

CONTENTS

ILLUSTRATIONS

| Raymond D. | FOREWORD |
| Strother | |

As this book explains, political consultants have been around for a long time but were best known as being among an inner circle of political activists. That has changed. Sometime in the middle 1980s, the press focused a strong light on a small band of professionals who helped candidates communicate, organize, and win elections. Movies, books, editorials, and an avalanche of mentions in newspapers and appearances on television gave these obscure players almost folk hero status. The notoriety, however, was accompanied by problems. The consultants came to be blamed for the decline of political parties, voter apathy, the lower quality of candidates, and the high cost of campaigns. And in truth some of the criticism is valid—perhaps more so now than ever.

The publicity also encouraged an increasing number of people who called themselves political consultants clamoring to win the fame and fortune they read about. There soon were more consultants than available candidates, and the newcomers were forced to dip down to races as small as those for state legislatures and local judgeships. It is not unusual these days for a mayor of a town of one hundred thousand people to hire consultants.

As campaigns grew more sophisticated, specialties developed. Consultants now provide services specifically in fund-raising, direct mail, research, computer campaigning, scheduling, press, speech coaching, media production, and campaign management. There are people who sell lists of voters and focus group leaders who probe voters' reaction to nuances that would once have been ignored by political candidates as recent as John Kennedy. The era of the "general consultant" is fading fast.

Many of these trends are not unique to American enterprise: ours is a maturing business suffering from the many problems associated with unchecked growth and an absence of professional standards. Though each consultant grapples daily with ethical considerations, there is no rule book to guide him or her. No standards gauge competence. No tests must be passed to qualify for the title of political consultant. As a result, a few bad actors influence the public image of the profession.

We now see a generation of sons and daughters entering our business in the footsteps of their parents. Young people are leaving college with ambitions of becoming campaign professionals. Unfortunately, their perception of how consultants conduct themselves is taken from movies and stories attributed to a group of bottom-feeders who bring discredit to a group of bright, well-meaning, and talented men and women who have achieved success in a most honorable manner.

It is time for political professionals to reach out to younger people. It is time for us to police ourselves. We are gears in the apparatus of democracy, and we must admit that there are stripped and broken cogs in the machinery.

This book is a collection of ideas and practices, traditions and innovations about political communication by those largely responsible for political communication in our time. Just to scan the chapters is to understand that consultants are not simply cowboys who ride airplanes and connive to trick voters. Art and science are represented here. Better yet, there is honor and integrity. And that should be the loudest message of all.

ACKNOWLEDGMENTS

This project was funded with a research professorship generously granted by the Manship family. I would also like to thank Maureen Hewitt and LSU Press for their interest in and encouragement of the book. Gratitude is extended to Ted Windt, whose response to the manuscript considerably improved it. I also thank Michelle Cobas and Casey Laws, my conscientious and hard-working assistants. Most of all, I want to thank my wife, Christie, whose tireless editing, organization, and advice made a project of this size and complexity possible and publishable.

The Manship School Guide to
POLITICAL COMMUNICATION

David D.   INTRODUCTION
Perlmutter

It is generally agreed that the political process today is consultant driven: where once party bosses were kingmakers, now political consultants determine much of campaign and election strategy and are even influential in the making of public policy. This phenomenon is hardly new. The courts of Rameses II, Julius Caesar, Charlemagne, and Elizabeth I swarmed with counselors offering tips on how to improve public goodwill and secure power. What is different today (at least from the precedent of American history) is that instead of being background confidants, political consultants are public—some even say independent—players. Their appearances come in many forms, from the Hollywood screen to the CNBC studio, from the op-ed pages of the *New York Times* to the "results" sections of academic papers. Perhaps more ominously, thousands of young women and men are setting out from college each year hoping to place the title "political consultant" on their business cards.

Hence the task of this book: to go beyond the blarney and blather and to discuss what consultant-driven political communication for campaigns and elections is and can be at the turn of the millennium. Although some of the essays criticize aspects of the process, most simply try to explain what it is, what it is not, and how it is done; we invite the reader to retain a critical eye in this light. The contributors range from academics to journalists to political professionals; they are concerned with such diverse enterprises as recounting the history of political consulting in the republic, obtaining free media for their cause or candidate, designing television ads, profiling the Hispanic voter, understanding how the Constitution covers paid political speech, and diagnosing the sometimes tender, sometimes testy relationships between consultants and clients. (Some topics—for example, political debates, the Asian American vote, women as consultants—because of the exigencies of time, space, and submission difficulties, were not included; they may be addressed in a later edition of this volume.) The essays were solicited from people who have demonstrated considerable expertise in their subjects. Each contributor was mandated to explain in brief but also in detail how a *process* works. We hope that even so-called experts in any one part of politics might learn something from

1

another writer's piece. Keep in mind, however, that the opinions expressed and the methods advocated are those of the individual authors. The reader is encouraged to research any particular topic further before coming to a definite conclusion.

But this book is not solely a how-to primer. A goal (not necessarily shared by all who participated) was to try to establish some facts and truths in an arena of argumentation that often lends itself to hyperbole and fantasy. All would agree that many Americans of varying political persuasions have lost faith in the political system. Simply put—something needs to be done. But before reforms can move forward I think it necessary to ascertain what actually are the problems we face. Unfortunately, inhibiting the process of problem solving are several myths about politics and media. Most are at their core false, but like all tall tales their really interesting feature is their widespread currency.

The first myth is that of the political money-monster. Once upon a time, in this hoary tale, American politics was driven by virtue and reason. Then came the bad money men, and now politics, especially campaigns and elections, is weighed down by filthy lucre. Politicians spend huge sums on television and other media, and special interests have bought control of the government. The ordinary person can no longer influence political events or hope to seek office.

Indeed, there is some truth here. It is extremely difficult to run for higher office in America without an enormous war chest filled with one's own money or that of wealthy friends and partisans. In almost all other aspects, however, the myth is groundless. First, there are more than five hundred thousand elected officials in the United States, probably a higher ratio of elected officeholder to citizen than in any other country in the history of the world. To run for offices that matter to a great number of people—school board representative, for example—most definitely does not take a venture capital fortune. Moreover, that any man or woman cannot on a whim run for the United States Senate and stand a good chance of being elected is hardly unfortunate. The ballots are already clogged and confused; if for each office we were asked to choose among hundreds of our neighbors, democracy would soon descend into Babel. Nor is it disastrous that Nazis, Know-Nothings, and Leninists cannot find media time and ballot prominence equal to those for Democrats or Republicans.

The problem is that when people assert that mass-mediated politics costs too much, they do not consider the *relative* amount we do spend. In 1998, it is said, a billion dollars was spent on campaigns and elections. We allot more annually to many other consumer products, both indispensable and incidental. A few are worth reviewing, because one can judge the character of a civilization by where it spends its disposable income: $6.8 billion for video games; $5.8 billion for applying artificial fingernails; $3 billion at movie snack bars; $2.81 billion for Prozac; $1 billion for golf balls; $1 billion for Halloween costumes (65 percent of which are for adults). And so on. We are stingy on our politics even by government spending standards. For example, the Clinton administration spent more than $8 billion on Operation Uphold Democracy in Haiti.

A more revealing comparative statistic is that each year Americans pay about $10 billion for pornography; thus, we spend about ten times as much every two years on porn as on campaigns and elections. As Nadine Strossen of the American Civil Liberties Union has wittily noted, this spending does not represent ten perverts shelling out $1 billion a year. In contrast, at most about a third of the billion dollars annually spent on campaigns is directly donated by individuals, which means that the average American gives no more than $2 a year to the political process. In addition, as Ed Zuckerman points out in his essay, many of the spending restrictions that politicians and consultants work under do not account for twenty-five to thirty years of inflation; the spending power of one dollar in 1972 is now about a quarter. We the people are, in a word, underfunding democracy.

Why, in an age of a vastly expanded population that can be reached only through mass media channels, do we still think that candidates can campaign with a couple of dimes, a buckboard, and a barrelhead? The answer is that we have a homespun conviction that politics shouldn't cost anything. A cultural historian might trace this notion back to the Revolutionary era and even before; the frugal American colonists revolted as much at the expenses associated with aristocracy as at unreasonable taxes. Similarly, we have bridled at Richard Nixon's overdressed White House doorkeepers and Nancy Reagan's new china; we display equal ire at the expense of $40 million required to run for a California seat in the United States Senate.

In being outraged, we forget that we are no longer a nation concentrated along the East Coast in thirteen lightly populated states. Mass communication, likewise, no longer consists of the bulk printing of broadsides and their distribution by donkey. We are also slow to see how changes in campaigning (for example, campaign seasons starting ever earlier, super-combined primaries at the national level, demands by media to pay up-front costs for placing ads) have forced candidates to raise more money, sooner. We expect democracy to exist on the cheap, although we should know that it is lack of money that causes the most desperation and corruption. Ironically, political consultants bring ruthless efficiency to this impoverished process. They are able, for example, to create a television commercial with not unpleasing aesthetic properties for about one one-hundredth the money the publicists of Toyota and Revlon expend.

That said, politics is and always has been about personality. In most campaign races, at least those not involving ballot referendums, people vote for people, not for policies. The second-century Greek writer Dio Cassius observed that "all crowds judge measures by the men who direct them." If you tell, for example, a die-hard Bill Clinton supporter that "President Clinton recently proposed this," he or she will be more inclined to think favorably of the proposal—whatever it is—than if you introduce it as originating from Rush Limbaugh.

But another myth—the "Mr. Smith Goes to Washington" fantasy drawn from the deeper well of the Cincinnatus ideal—holds that these candidates should be what were once called "men of the soil" or "born in a log cabin," that is, unpolitical, unshaped, unconsulted. Being natural folks, they should eschew modern media trickery and manipulations. That we do not impose such primitivism and unprofessionalism on any other occupation seems not to matter. The basic problem is that we live in a mass-mediated age, so compromise must be made with technology to be able to communicate politically. Ronald Reagan, for example, had a made-for-the-screen persona, but he always understood the need for memorizing the script, walking through the performance beforehand, and testing the lines. He knew that success in front of a camera was possible only because of the labor and organization of all the elements behind the camera. No one is "natural" on TV. Someone has to be director, gaffer, and best boy.

Then there is the myth of the "out of touch" politician who is beholden to the lobbyists and pays no attention to his or her constituents. Reading these pages, and observing the inner workings of political campaigns, suggests that exactly the opposite is the case—although the consequences are equally dire. Bill Clinton is the best example of the new model politician: he listens. In fact he does not (it is said) make any decision without consulting polls and focus groups. Indeed, consultants and officeholders are very much concerned with what the people think and want. The result—leaders who will not jump ahead of the curve and will not lead in the old-fashioned sense—is problematic. Many important innovations in American democracy, like civil rights for citizens of sub-Saharan African descent, would have never occurred if many politicians of the time had paid attention only to polls and the weight of constituent mail.

But in expressing cynicism that all politicians are corrupt, and in painting political consultants as viscous opportunists, we are not just casting aspersions but flattering ourselves. Of course consultants are to blame for much of what is wrong with politics, but to say in turn that the populace are victims is to subscribe to another myth that is perpetuated by the whole spectrum of American politics. Moralists on the right claim that Washingtonian immorality stands in stark contrast to the down-home virtues and honesty of the ordinary American. (Recent White House chicaneries and the resulting public indifference have not supported this theory.) Those on the left contrast "the people" with corrupt politicos and corporate fat cats, as if greed and sloth were traits held only by the powerful. Politicians themselves will also play along, criticizing each other, even running against their own species with insincere anti-Washington rhetoric. Finally, the American press contributes to the demonizing of political players and their advisers and promotes a commensurate uplifting of the electorate.

In short, nobody dares turn the finger of accusation away from our leaders, journalists, and spinmeisters—the usual suspects—and back toward the ordinary citizens. As the literary scholar and cultural historian Paul Fussell once noted in the debate about high auto insurance rates, blame will be cast against "greedy" insurance companies, lawyers, politicians, and so on, but no one will boldly suggest that people might try driving more safely. In many public issues, from Social Security to the environment, we demand solutions without sacrifice.

This unwillingness to fault "the people" is traditional and ubiquitous. Charles Mackay, writing in the nineteenth century, described the South Sea "Bubble," the speculative frenzy that had seized his country of England a hundred years previously. Masses of people, from dukes to butchers, had thrown away their life savings on the promises of unlimited wealth in gold and beaver pelts to be gathered from expeditions to the New World, without any evidence whatsoever that those riches were immediately obtainable. When the bubble collapsed and Parliament began its inquisition, the directors of the South Seas Company were vilified. But as Mackay put it so acidly, "Nobody blamed the credulity and avarice of the people—the degrading lust of gain, which had swallowed up every nobler quality in the national character, or the infatuation which had made the multitude run their heads with such frantic eagerness into the net held out for them by scheming projectors. These things were never mentioned. The people were a simple, honest, hard-working people, ruined by a gang of robbers, who were to be hanged, drawn, and quartered without mercy" (*Extraordinary Popular Delusions and the Madness of Crowds*, 1841). Demonization was (and is) preferable to self-criticism.

We live in analogous circumstances and hold similar prejudices today. Almost all the problems of politics that we decry and which political consultants seem to perpetuate could be solved in a fortnight by an invigorated and self-ennobled American people. If each of us gave $100 a year to the politicians and political causes of our choice, the so-called special interest money would be washed away in the tide, and the fat cats would grow lean on slim pickings. Even twenty hours a year of our time devoted to politics would make a difference when multiplied by the size of the voting population. (More people have attended at least one sporting event than have read a news editorial or voted.) Or, better yet, what if we all took democracy seriously and became an educated electorate, actually thinking about and researching our voting choices? This is not utopia, this is what we say we want; this is the way it is supposed to be.

If we expend only a little money, thought, and time, perhaps we might have people running for office who took virtue, fiscal and personal, seriously. The famous lament of Cicero was, "Oh, happy Marcus Cato, whom no one dares to try to corrupt!" The Roman senator he envied was legendary for his uprightness, an anomaly in his own time. But such exemplary men and women have always existed, and they can be found both in boardrooms and in bowling alleys. Their rectitude will only be nurtured, however, and their presence in political life encouraged, by a mass movement of public sentiment and private dollars.

This book, then, can be seen as a corrective to the many myths about modern political campaign communication. We discover in these pages that it is a business run mostly by serious and sober people. But we find something else, too. The reader will note the high level of enthusiasm these men and women have about their particular specialties, to the point of "my constituency is the crucial swing vote," or "my campaign communication technique is the most effective." As editor, I toned down such boosterism but did not eliminate it; after all, the reader may judge the wares in this collected marketplace of ideas.

In fact, these people *believe* in what they do: whatever their age, political philosophies, or area of expertise they are aggressive partisans of their methods and the people they serve. Indeed, from the survey discussed at the end of the book we found that consultants tend to work only for candidates of one party and mostly for candidates with whom they agree on the issues. These people are not guns for hire, nor do they engage in campaign practices that are simply the means to collecting exorbitant fees. As one consultant pointed out, "All the really good political consultants could probably be making a lot more money marketing Furbies."

It is, of course, difficult to claim idealism in politics without inviting laughter. But in these pages you will find civic-minded ideas and commitment, and this is a social good. The solution to the problems of politics and media, if there is one, will not be from the top down. We cannot expect the powers that be to make things better for us, because their urge to satisfy our unreasonable cravings is largely the cause of the present difficulties. No popular movement for political reform can exist, however, without a vanguard of experienced political workers who understand the process and its problems and are willing to collaborate and change for the better. From among the ranks of political consultants, reformers will find opponents, but they will also find their greatest allies.

Finally, this book has a more prosaic agenda item. As several writers here mention, and others explore in detail, the pop culture myth of the political consultant includes images of fame, sex, and cash obtained simply by being spontaneously clever. A quick tongue seems to buy CNBC guest spots and invitations to Glenlivet-and-cigar parties with the rich and powerful. But what these essays emphasize is that whatever rewards come to successful political consultants they are based on the human activity most absent on television: *work*. In sitcoms about aspiring twenty-somethings in the big city, a preponderance of time seems to be spent chatting in coffeehouses. Likewise, political consultants on TV and in movies are largely represented as bullshit artists. They are talented artists whose medium is bullshit, that is, spin. And spinning seems to be easy—short hours, no heavy lifting.

In outlining here in copious and comprehensive detail some of the varieties of campaign activities, a blow is struck against this myth. What is apparent is how much labor and thought must go into the vast minutiae of political campaign communication. Even if one disagrees with the style and substance of the result, the sweat of the process deserves notice and respect. No one who wastes August, September, and October indulging in the excesses of the seraglio could possibly retain the mental acuity and physical stamina necessary to win a race for one's candidate on the first Tuesday in November. If the reader recognizes this point, that consulting for political campaign communication is a business and that this business requires industry, economy, concentration, preparation, deliberation, and discipline, then the *Manship School Guide*'s mission is accomplished.

UNDERSTANDING THE INDUSTRY

Robert V.
Friedenberg

A PREHISTORY OF MEDIA CONSULTING FOR POLITICAL CAMPAIGNS

We will never know for certain the identity of the first political consultant. Perhaps it was the individual who, in 1758, suggested to a candidate for the Virginia colonial assembly that he purchase refreshments for the voters. That candidate staged a pseudo-event when he bought 160 gallons of beverages at a cost of 39 pounds to help his constituency celebrate his candidacy. He won his election. His name was George Washington. Though we will never know who was the first political consultant, we can safely surmise that those early consultants, most likely friends and relatives of the candidates, who volunteered their suggestions, time, and effort, were on the scene during the first elections.

In the years following the American Revolution, the new nation witnessed the birth of political campaigning. Several factors gave rise to political campaigning in young America. First was the obvious fact that there were differing interests and factions among citizens. Although these interests had existed before the Revolutionary War, they were largely ignored or temporarily patched over to facilitate a unified war effort. With the end of the war, however, those differences began to manifest themselves.

From the end of the Revolutionary War to 1787, in state after state, two factions emerged. The urban faction, centered in the eastern seacoast cities, was composed of relatively wealthy businessmen and professionals who had a broad national outlook and favored a strong central or federal government that would protect wealth and facilitate the growth of trade, manufacturing, and business. In the South, many large plantation holders whose economic interests were similar to those of urban businessmen also shared these views. The rural faction, centered in the less settled inland communities, was composed primarily of small farmers and had a more local outlook. They favored a weaker central government that placed local agricultural interests ahead of trade and business interests. Issues such as the use of paper money and tariffs often divided these groups.

Many of these concerns coalesced in the summer of 1787, when the Constitutional Convention met to establish a new central government. The fight over ratification of the newly written Constitution was a first: a truly national political battle. The campaigns for and against ratification of the Constitution involved coordinated efforts that crossed state boundaries. Arguments that proved successful in one state were quickly communicated to the ratifying conventions of other states. Votes were delayed or rushed in some states to facilitate their having the most impact on other states. Newspaper articles and editorials, as well as other printed materials, were reprinted from one state and used in other states. In effect, the advocates in the first states to debate ratification became consultants to those who debated ratification later.

After a strenuous three-week debate, in December 1787 Pennsylvania became the second state to ratify the Constitution. Though the Antifederalists in Pennsylvania failed to prevent ratification, they produced the "Dissent of the Minority," which ultimately had more impact on the new government than any materials developed for these debates. The Pennsylvania "Dissent of the Minority" reflected Antifederalist objections to the proposed Constitution based on its failure specifically to affirm that the rights of individual citizens would be guaranteed under the new Constitution. Though Federalists argued that all rights not specifically treated by the new Constitution were reserved for individual citizens, the Pennsylvania Antifederalists wanted those rights enumerated.

During the remaining ten months of debates, the widely circulated Pennsylvania "Dissent of the Minority" influenced many of the later state ratification debates. Taking their lead from Pennsylvania's Antifederalists, opponents attacked the proposed Constitution for its lack of a bill of rights. In many of the subsequent ratification conventions, including those in Massachusetts, New York, and Virginia, the Federalists won over undecided delegates by promising that the first Congress would enact a bill of rights. Several of the state ratification conventions even went so far as to submit proposed amendments containing bills of rights at the time they ratified. Those proposals were used as the basis for the first ten amendments to the Constitution, commonly called the Bill of Rights, passed by the first Congress in 1789.

In addition to creating a national political campaign, the ratification controversy gave rise to yet another campaign "first." In late 1787, Federalist ratification advocate Theodore Sedgwick and his Antifederalist opponent, John Bacon, both running for a seat in the Massachusetts constitutional ratifying convention, debated the merits of the new

Constitution. Thus they engaged in what may well have been the first political campaign debate in the nation's history. Although Sedgwick and Bacon are long forgotten, the precedent of their debate was soon followed in other early campaigns, perhaps most notably the 1789 debates between two future presidents, James Madison and James Monroe, which took place during their campaign for a seat in the first House of Representatives.

By the time of the first political campaign that was national in scope—the constitutional ratification campaign—political consulting was a fact of American political life. Though the advisers and boosters to candidates of the time may have been largely volunteers, they often served the functions of contemporary consultants by providing help with pseudo-events, speechmaking, and printed materials.

As the nation developed under the new Constitution, campaigns became commonplace. The growth of campaigns gave rise to candidates calling on friends and political associates to help. The most accomplished and prominent early political operative in the United States was John Beckley.

Beckley worked in a variety of appointed political positions, most notably as the first clerk of the Virginia House of Delegates and as the first clerk of the United States House of Representatives. He is best remembered, however, as America's first political campaign manager. An intimate of Thomas Jefferson, Beckley learned his craft in Jefferson's 1796 run for the presidency. Beckley launched the first "media blitz" in American campaigning, flooding what he perceived to be the critical swing state of Pennsylvania with thirty thousand sample ballots and thousands of political handbills extolling Jefferson's virtues. The extensiveness of this effort is evident by the fact that only twelve thousand Pennsylvanians voted in the election. Moreover, Beckley attempted to organize what today would be called "opinion leaders" throughout western Pennsylvania to serve as surrogate speakers for Jefferson. He analyzed Jefferson's speeches and distributed many of them in those parts of the state where he felt they would be best received. Though Jefferson was defeated by John Adams in 1796, he did carry Pennsylvania.

In the presidential election of 1800, Beckley again worked ardently on Jefferson's behalf, extending his field of operations to encompass not only Pennsylvania but also parts of New York, Connecticut, and Maryland. Among his contributions to Jefferson's campaign was a widely circulated biographical pamphlet in which Beckley claimed that Jefferson was "a man of pure ardent and unaffected piety; of sincere and genuine virtue; of an enlightened mind and superior wisdom; the adorer of our God; the patriot of his country; and the friend and benefactor of the whole human race." This time Jefferson proved victorious.

If Beckley was the first prototype of today's political consultants, the 1828 campaign of Andrew Jackson was the earliest prototype of today's media-driven campaigns. New York senator Martin Van Buren ran the Jackson effort, putting together a national campaign drawing on his own personal network of political leaders. Van Buren melded Jackson's support in Tennessee and the West with his own New York organization. He then won over leaders in Georgia, parts of Virginia, and the Carolinas. Working from the top down, drawing primarily on state leaders like Thomas Hart Benton of Missouri and urban leaders such as Alan Campbell of Louisville, he crafted a national political organization on Jackson's behalf. In effect, Van Buren was the forerunner of both the modern general consultant and the field operation consultant.

Once a local or state leader had committed to Jackson, the members of his organization became Jackson's local "hurrah boys." These precinct-level workers dropped literature throughout the community, managed rallies, and, perhaps most important, in villages and towns, staged the first national get-out-the-vote—or GOTV—campaign on election day.

Jackson's campaign harnessed the mass medium of the day, the printing press, in two ways. First, it made heavy use of sympathetic newspapers. Campaign representatives worked ardently to secure favorable stories about the hero of New Orleans. Second, the Jackson campaign produced an enormous number of pamphlets, handbills, broadsides, and other printed literature, which was distributed throughout the nation. Jackson rallies were staged to generate public enthusiasm. In addition to the predictable political speeches, these events involved food, drink, parades, songs, and the distribution of campaign literature. Moreover, tying into the candidate's nickname of "Old Hickory"—because, like the hardwood tree, he had proved his toughness to his troops during the War of 1812—every Jackson rally gave away hickory brooms, canes, and sticks. On city streets and in small town squares, Jackson supporters erected large hickory poles. Like the buttons, bumper stickers, and yard signs of today, these symbols were tangible signs of support for the candidate.

Traditionally, from George Washington forward, presidential candidates were reluctant campaigners. Believing that it was unseemly to campaign for the nation's highest office and that the office should seek the man, Washington, and fifty years worth of presidential candidates who followed him, did not give campaign speeches. In 1840, William Henry Harrison, a sixty-seven-year-old former Indian fighter, with a limited record as the territorial governor of Indiana and a member of the House and Senate from Indiana, was nominated by the Whigs. Although Harrison was chosen in part because he held a blameless record, the Democrats soon attacked him as incompetent and perhaps senile. His silence seemed to reinforce these assertions, and the Democrats soon took to calling him "General Mum." But on June 6, 1840, General Mum spoke. Breaking with tradition, Harrison addressed a crowd from the steps of the National Hotel in Columbus, Ohio. It was the first of twenty-three speeches that he delivered throughout the fall. Ranging in length from one to three hours, Harrison's speeches effectively refuted the charges that he was incompetent or senile. It is not clear whether Harrison had help in preparing his speeches. Certainly it would have been available because the Whigs flooded the nation with surrogate speakers. William Ogden Niles, using the name of the little village where Harrison won his most significant military victory over the Indians, published a ninety-five-page *Tippicanoe Text Book* explicitly to provide Harrison surrogates with materials for their speeches.

Improvements in transportation and communication technologies following the Civil War dramatically affected political campaigns in the late nineteenth century. In 1896, William Jennings Bryan, then only thirty-six years old, displaying energy rarely found in presidential candidates, traveled eighteen thousand miles by rail to deliver over six hundred speeches in twenty-seven states to a total audience of over five million people. His opponent, William McKinley, did not try to maintain such a schedule. Instead, McKinley benefited from the organizational skill of his manager, Mark Hanna, who established a speakers' bureau operation that eventually had fourteen hundred surrogates speaking on McKinley's behalf.

Totally ignored in the excitement of the McKinley-Bryan race, that same year the post office initiated rural free delivery, bringing mail service to the most remote areas of the country. Since its establishment, campaigning by mail has continued to grow in importance. In recent decades, with computerized mailing lists, direct mail consultants have become vital players in American campaigns. Yet just as the extension of mail service to the entire nation was largely ignored in 1896, a hundred years later, in the television-dominated campaigns of 1996, few observers remarked on the fact that America's 513,000 elected officials and their opponents spent more money on direct mail than on any other form of campaign media.

Perhaps the first true forerunner of contemporary political consultants was Edward Bernays. One of the first publicity agents in the nation, Bernays was called on by President Woodrow Wilson to help mobilize public opinion in support of American involvement in World War I. A nephew of Sigmund Freud, Bernays attempted to bring scientific principles to the practice of public relations. Virtually every president, between Calvin Coolidge and Dwight Eisenhower asked Bernays for advice. Bernays summarized his theories of political consulting in his last major book, *The Engineering of Consent*. The title exemplifies his beliefs, suggesting that government and political leaders can win consent in a rational, scientific, precise manner. As early as the 1920s, Bernays was a strong advocate of polling and in a host of other ways foreshadowed contemporary campaigning.

If Edward Bernays prophesied the future, it remained for a California husband-and-wife team, Clem Whitaker and Leone Baxter, to form the firm that served as a model for the contemporary political consulting business. Whitaker came to political consulting after first working as a political reporter in Sacramento and then opening his own news bureau to distribute articles about California politics to that state's seven hundred newspapers. His early experiences convinced him that a simple theme, frequently repeated, was the key to a successful campaign. In the language of today's consultants, Whitaker preached the importance of constantly staying "on message." He met his wife and business partner, Leone Baxter, an organizer for the Redding, California, Chamber of Commerce, when they worked together on a successful local referendum campaign. From 1934 to 1958, Whitaker and Baxter ran seventy-five campaigns in California, winning seventy of them. Among their clients were California governors Frank Merriam, Earl Warren, and Goodwin Knight.

Whitaker and Baxter would thoroughly research their client, the opponent, and the issues. They would then develop an overall strategy keyed to a simple theme. They would help their candidate develop speeches and advertising consistent with that theme. They would help schedule their candidates' speeches and place advertising, first in newspapers and later in radio and television, to ensure that targeted California voters would be exposed to their candidate's message.

As Whitaker and Baxter were winding down their careers in the 1950s, a new medium and a new era were emerging. Though television had been used in Senate races in 1950, it was not until the presidential election of 1952 that this medium began to play a crucial role in electoral politics. In that year, both major party presidential candidates used consultants to help them harness the new medium. Much attention has been paid to the content and techniques used to produce a series of spot commercials, "Eisenhower Talks to America," that helped Republican Dwight David Eisenhower triumph over his Democratic foe, Illinois governor Adlai Stevenson. Often overlooked is that, in 1952, just as in every campaign that has used television extensively since that time, an equally valuable service provided by television consultants is to buy television time strategically so that a candidate's message is seen by targeted voters.

The contemporary era of political consulting, with its heavy stress on television, is often dated to the 1960 presidential election. Yet this examination of the prehistory of media consulting has illustrated that today's media-oriented political consultants stand on the shoulders of predecessors who date back to our nation's earliest moments. Democracies reward effective persuaders. Democracies resolve domestic strife through the ballot box. The men and women who seek office in democracies such as the United States must necessarily place a premium on the ability to persuade. It should not surprise us that those individuals who can master the techniques of political persuasion—whether those techniques be the turning of a clever phrase, the successful execution of a torch-light rally, the creation of a massive speakers' bureau, the development and distribution of effective mail pieces, the production and placement of television commercials, or the designing and maintaining of an effective Internet site—have always been found behind the candidates for whom we vote.

SUGGESTED READINGS

Friedenberg, Robert V. *Communication Consultants in Political Campaigns: Ballot Box Warriors*. Westport, Conn.: Praeger, 1997.

Jamieson, Kathleen Hall. *Packaging the Presidency*. New York: Oxford University Press, 1984.

Mickelson, Sig. *From Whistle Stop to Sound Bite: Four Decades of Politics and Television*. New York: Praeger, 1989.

Thurber, James A., and Candice J. Nelson (eds.). *Campaigns and Elections American Style*. Boulder: Westview Press, 1995.

Trent, Judith S., and Robert V. Friedenberg. *Political Campaign Communication: Principles and Practices*. 3d ed. Westport, Conn.: Praeger, 1995.

Joseph Napolitan

PRESENT AT THE CREATION
(OF MODERN POLITICAL CONSULTING)

A week before I sat down to write this chapter, my colleague Matt Reese, one of the founding generation of political consultants, died after a long illness. In my last conversation with Matt, he told me that he intended to write an article deploring the deterioration of our business. All of us would have benefited from Matt's wisdom. These words, therefore, are expressed in his spirit and in his name.

Political consultants have been around ever since we have had political campaigns. But the business as we know it today, with its myriad specialists, high visibility, and multi-million-dollar campaign budgets, did not really get started until the early 1960s. I was there; to the best of my knowledge I was the first person ever to describe myself as a "political consultant."*

I got into the business almost by accident. In November 1956, after working for ten years as a reporter for the *Springfield* (Mass.) *Union*, I resigned from the newspaper and opened a public relations office in Springfield. About two weeks after I opened my doors, a thirty-one-year-old state representative named Tom O'Connor walked into my office, said he wanted to run for mayor, and asked if I would be interested in running his campaign. I said sure—and tried to figure out what to do.

My political experience up to that point had consisted of covering political news for the *Union*. My search for information about how to run political campaigns led me to read *Professional Public Relations and Political Power* by Stanley Kelley of Princeton University.** Professor Kelley's main point was that professional public relations techniques, including heavy use of media, would change the way political campaigns are run in the United States.

My next step was to visit Dan Brunton, the incumbent mayor, whom Tom O'Connor was running against in the Democratic primary

---

*As detailed in Robert Friedenberg's chapter, the techniques of political consulting were first used in California in 1933, when Clem Whitaker and Leone Baxter pooled their talents to defeat the massive Pacific Gas & Electric Co. in a referendum. After the election, Whitaker and Baxter formed their own firm, Campaigns, Inc., which pioneered the procedures so common today.

**It continues to be the best guide to the early years of our business and played a major role in my decision to become a political consultant.

and a friend from my newspaper days. Brunton was completing his sixth consecutive two-year term and was a heavy favorite for reelection. I told him I had been asked to do O'Connor's campaign. The mayor figuratively patted me on the head, told me that if I didn't take O'Connor's money someone else would, but that Tommy had no chance of winning.

We campaigned aggressively, used television more effectively than ever before in a local election in Springfield, and capitalized on O'Connor's good looks and impressive speaking skills. O'Connor defeated Brunton in every one of the sixty-four precincts in Springfield. He became mayor, and I became, without knowing it, a political consultant. The next year I did a campaign for district attorney for Matthew J. Ryan, who won a nine-man primary and went on to serve for thirty-two years before retiring undefeated.

I was on my way. An incident that occurred a few years later—I ran a campaign *against* Tom O'Connor for mayor, and my candidate, Charles V. Ryan, defeated him—convinced me that maybe advisers really did have some influence in winning elections. I won my first thirteen campaigns and considered myself invincible. Then I lost a primary election but still was proud that none of my candidates had lost to a Republican. That record was shattered soon afterward, and since then, although I have had many more winners than losers, I've known the pain of defeat as well as the pleasure of victory. (Many years later, I asked Matt Reese about a new consultant I didn't know who had won eight or nine elections in a row and was much in demand. "Is this guy any good?" I asked Matt. "He's pretty good," replied Reese, "but he'll be a lot better after he loses a few campaigns.")

My first experience in national politics, in 1960, was when I joined John F. Kennedy's campaign staff as an assistant to the director of organization, Larry O'Brien. One of my assignments was to screen television spots that had been produced for Kennedy's campaign. In those days no one specialized in producing political television; the spots were usually produced by advertising agencies. By today's standards, our spots were simplistic and naïve, especially considering the telegeneity and eloquence of our candidate. Most of the ads were simply lifts from Kennedy's speeches, often with poor lighting, bad sound, and little or no use of visuals or graphics.

There was one producer, however, who was beginning to specialize in political television: Charles Guggenheim, who pioneered the thirty-minute political documentary. Guggenheim's early efforts in a gubernatorial election in Arkansas attracted national attention, and he has made some of the all-time best thirty-minute political biographies, including "Man Against the Machine" in Pennsylvania in 1966, which allowed my candidate, an unknown named Milton Shapp, to score an astonishing upset in the Democratic primary for governor. The film was highly emotional and made an asset out of Shapp's being Jewish, which in those days in Pennsylvania was regarded as a major liability. The documentary was a work of art, a great leap from simply filming a candidate speaking.

After the Kennedy election in 1960, I was faced with the choice of joining the administration, as most of my friends from the campaign were doing, or remaining in private business. I was still a kid, thirty-one years old, my business was going well, I loved the challenge of campaigns, and I decided to concentrate on advising candidates how to win elections.

In those days, most campaigns (presidential elections excepted) were run by people who lived in the state (or city) where the election was held. Some of these campaign managers were politically active lawyers, some were advertising or public relations people, and too often they turned out to be the candidate's brother-in-law. I quickly realized that there weren't enough elections in Massachusetts to provide me with the income I'd like to have and that if I were to be successful it would be necessary for me to seek campaigns in other parts of the country.

A few political advisers traveled to various states to advise candidates, most of whom worked for the Democratic or Republican Senate campaign committees. One of the best was Joe Miller of Washington, who was dispatched as far away as Hawaii to help Democratic candidates.

When I made the decision to "go national" in 1961, I also had to decide *how I would describe myself and the kind of work I did*. Until then, I had been calling myself a public relations specialist, but I thought I needed something more specific for this new endeavor and so settled on the title "political consultant."

From the beginning, I was a generalist who concentrated on defining strategy and messages, designing (but not producing) media, designing and analyzing survey research, and providing counseling on all phases of campaigns that involved communicating with voters. I had no special skills. I knew nothing about film or television production or time buying or any of the many arcane specialties of today's consultants.

What I felt I could do was to select the best producer for a specific candidate and to assemble the right team for a campaign.

I was a pure consultant. I gave advice, usually in the form of written memorandums. Except for one brief and ill-considered attempt, I never charged a commission, never demanded a share of the media time buy (which has become the most lucrative income-producing area in our business), never sought any compensation except the fee I charged the client. In this way I felt I could provide my candidates with my best advice without compromising my position or subconsciously favoring one firm or one technique because by doing so I would share in the profits.

In short, I put campaigns together and tried to make them work.

It was a pleasant surprise to learn that there was a demand for my services. I and the other new "political consultants" brought to campaigns outside the areas where we lived experience, knowledge of new techniques and technology, familiarity with specialists who could be used for certain functions, a willingness to spend a lot of time traveling, and the ability to shift gears and focus on the campaign at hand.

From time to time in the early days I would *manage* a campaign rather than just *consult* in the campaign. I did this for Endicott (Chub) Peabody, former governor of Massachusetts, and Milton Shapp, two-term governor of Pennsylvania. The problem with managing a campaign is that it takes *all* of your time; you can manage only one campaign at a time, and I preferred to be involved in several campaigns simultaneously.

Today no one thinks twice if a campaign in Iowa uses a television producer from Washington, a direct mail specialist from Sacramento, an organizational expert from Boulder, and a radio producer in New York. But in the early days I don't know how many times I was told a version of "Well, that might work in New York but it won't work here in North Carolina." After forty-two years in the business I've learned that no matter what state or country you are working in, the object is always the same: *figuring out a way to persuade a voter to mark his X after one name instead of another on the ballot.*

My role varied from campaign to campaign, usually depending on how good the candidate's own staff was. If the campaign staff was competent and well organized, I would often concentrate on "broad strokes" such as designing strategy and messages. If the campaign staff was inexperienced or not very good, I found myself writing memos on everything from organizing a coffee hour to how to decorate the head-quarters.

Things were simpler in the early days. The major difference was that the cost of campaigns was so much less, even in today's dollars. Often we didn't begin television advertising until three weeks before the election; now in most major elections one or more of the candidates is on the air six months before election day. For all practical purposes, negative advertising had not yet been invented (at least not on televi-sion, and not with the viciousness in vogue today). Polls were con-ducted in face-to-face interviews, and it often took several weeks to get results. The pace was slower, the intensity level lower.

Although I can't even run a minicam, I became an avid student of the impact of television on voting behavior and followed its develop-ment to the point at which it was the dominant medium in most cam-paigns; there are still many campaigns today in which hundreds of thousands of dollars that would be better spent on other approaches are pumped into television, often (but not always) because the lead consul-tant in the campaign also happens to be a television producer. I have seen campaigns lost because too much money was spent on television and not enough in other areas, such as direct mail, personal voter con-tact, and organization.

I usually worked with producers by describing the strategy of the campaign, the problem we wanted to address in a particular spot, and the message we wanted to convey. Then I would get out of the way and let the producer or director do his or her job. Obviously, we screened all spots before they went on the air and, when warranted, made rec-ommendations on how they could be improved.

One of the problems in dealing with television producers, then and now, is that too many of them get so carried away with the need to be "creative" that they lose track of the objective, which is to advance the strategy of the campaign. One New York producer, Sally Hunter, put this problem into perspective a few years ago with the perceptive com-ment, "Strategy first, creativity second."

Another challenge was the skepticism and resistance members of the permanent campaign staff felt toward outside consultants. More than thirty years ago I developed a little talk that I still use when join-ing a campaign for the first time. It goes something like this: "I'm not here to tell you about politics in this state [or, in later years, more often 'this country']; all of you here know more about local politics than I do. And I'm not looking for a job after the election. I don't want to be the governor's chief of staff (or 'the senator's administrative assistant'). All I want to do is help you win the election and go home." As soon as the staff realized I was no threat to any position they might covet, relations improved considerably.

All campaigns begin with the candidate, and candidates come in all forms, sizes, shapes, and degrees of intelligence. Most, however, are intelligent and competent and willing to listen to a consultant's advice (even if they don't always follow it). Some tilt too far in the other direction. David Garth, another political pioneer, tells the story of meeting with a candidate and asking him why he was running and what he hoped to accomplish for his state. "I haven't the slightest idea," the candidate said. "That's why I'm here."

To which Garth retorted, "Get the hell out of my office."

I choose my candidates carefully. Unless the right chemistry exists between candidate and consultant, the relationship will be contentious and unrewarding. This rapport helped in developing repeat business.

By the early 1970s, I realized there was a large world outside the United States that I wanted to be part of, so I began actively soliciting campaign assignments in other countries. I began spending a week or two in Europe every three months, calling on political party leaders, polling companies, advertising agencies, and others involved in the political process, so that when parties in those countries felt it might be time to bring in an American consultant, in many cases I was the only one they knew. In that manner I got a lot of the early overseas work.

I quickly learned that regardless of the language or the culture or the climate, there aren't many differences in advising candidates abroad and advising them in the United States. It's all a question of what you can do to persuade voters to mark their X after one name instead of another.

Surprising as it may sound, another aspect of the early days of consulting was its lack of competitiveness. When only a handful of us were in the business, we usually weren't out competing against each other to get candidates but simply trying to persuade candidates that someone from out of town really could help in their campaign. It wasn't until the early or mid-1970s that virtually all major campaigns used outside consultants of one kind or another.

By the late 1960s, I began to believe we needed to take some measures to organize our business, to try to develop some professional standards. To this end, Michel Bongrand of Paris and I founded the International Association of Political Campaign Consultants (IAPC) in Paris in November 1968, and two months later I invited every political consultant I knew of in the United States, regardless of party, to a meeting at the Plaza Hotel in New York and created the American Association of Political Campaign Consultants (AAPC). (The word *campaign* was dropped from both titles a couple of years later because members felt it was too restrictive.) AAPC now has over 600 members and IAPC about 125 from more than twenty countries. They are the two largest organizations in the world for political professionals and have spawned sister organizations in Europe and Latin America.

Naturally, there have been some dramatic changes in political consulting over the past forty years, none greater than the trend toward specialization. Unfortunately, I think, there are few general consultants left. Most of the strategy design and message definition work performed by generalists in the early years has been assumed by television producers. Quite a few producers do a good job in these areas, but many others know much more about production values than they do about political strategy, and consequently their campaigns suffer. Television people tend to overfavor television as the medium of choice—even though other media may be more suitable to the campaign.

Another recent development is that while for many years the press ignored political consultants, now it has gone to the opposite extreme: consultants are becoming celebrities (or "polebrities," as someone wryly noted). While I concede that especially in the early days I was flattered to be featured in *Life* or the *New York Sunday Times Magazine* or interviewed on *60 Minutes*, for the past twenty years or more I have adopted a policy of never giving interviews on campaigns in progress. I don't mind discussing the campaign *after* the election but won't do so until the votes have been counted. Perhaps my "generation gap" is showing, but I think the focus of attention in a campaign should be on the candidate and what he or she has to say and not on the consultant.

Partly because of the success of organizations like AAPC and partly because of the greater acceptance of consultants as a fixed feature of major campaigns, the media have come to rely on us as sources for information about politics, including developments, trends, and incidents that reflect on the business. We have even begun to try self-regulating. A few years ago, AAPC held a press conference featuring prominent pollsters from both parties who took a strong position against "push polling." This was the first time AAPC had taken such an action; may it not be the last.

In recent years, political consulting has become (at least in the minds of those who know little about it) a "glamor" business glorified by such films as *Power* and *Wag the Dog*. I cringe when I see consultants write "kiss and tell" books that reveal embarrassing information about their candidates. Any of us who have spent a lot of time in the business know things about our candidates they would rather not have revealed. Most important, a consultant owes a certain amount of loyalty to his candidates—even after the election.

Indeed, it's proper that, in any campaign, the real power lies with the candidate, not with the consultant. It is, after all, the *candidate's* campaign; all I can do is recommend what I believe should be done. If the candidate chooses to ignore my advice, he is free to do so; it is his money, his career, and his neck on the line. If we disagree frequently on major points or sharp differences develop in how we believe the campaign should be run, I simply step aside.

So here we are: an industry awash in notoriety and money, hands on the rudder of political power—but all is not well. Many people are concerned that political consulting (and consultants) have gotten out of hand, that campaigns have become obscenely expensive, that campaigns now appeal to people's worst instincts instead of their best ones, that standards have deteriorated and more effort is spent trying to evade campaign regulations than trying to live up to them. In truth, all good consultants worry about these same conditions and are increasingly apprehensive about the future of the political process.

SUGGESTED READINGS

Chagall, David. *The New Kingmakers*. New York: Harcourt Brace Jovanovich, 1981.

Kelley, Stanley. *Professional Public Relations and Political Power*. Baltimore: Johns Hopkins University Press, 1956.

Napolitan, Joseph. *The Election Game and How to Win It*. New York: Doubleday, 1972.

Sabato, Larry J. *The Rise and Fall of Political Consultants: New Ways of Winning Elections*. New York: Basic Books, 1981.

Darrell M.
West

A BRIEF HISTORY OF POLITICAL
ADVERTISING ON TELEVISION

Television advertising in presidential campaigns got its start in 1952. Though simplistic by contemporary standards, early political spots often took the form of footage from press conferences or testimonials from prominent citizens. Many were "talking head" reels in which the candidate (or his supporter) looked straight into the camera and spoke for thirty or sixty seconds without any cuts, graphics, animation, or mixing of many shots from different locations and events.

Contemporary ads, in contrast, are visually exciting. Technological advances allow ad producers to use colorful images and sophisticated editing techniques to make spots more compelling. Images can be spliced together to link one visual image with another. Animated images can visually "morph" one person into another in a split second. It is the norm to use catchy visuals, music, and color to capture the viewer's attention and convey political messages.

These changes have generated a dramatic growth in the use of advertising as a communications tool. Ads now constitute about 60 percent of the budget for major presidential candidates. Not only are television spots the largest single expenditure in campaigns, they are a major source of information for voters and a tool for influencing the way reporters cover political races.

Ads can be used for a variety of purposes, from undermining political opponents by associating them with unfavorable visual images to enhancing the candidates' appeal by associating them with positive images such as flag and family. In addition, ads influence patterns of media coverage. One of the most striking developments of the contemporary period has been the increasing coverage of political advertising by reporters. The network news executive William Small described this as the most important news trend of recent years, noting, "Commercials are now expected as part of news stories." Many news outlets have even launched "Ad Watch" features. These segments, aired during the news and showed in newspapers, present the ad, along with commentary on its accuracy and effectiveness. The most effective ads are those whose basic message is reinforced by the news media.

The increase in news coverage of advertising has blurred or even eliminated the past division between the free (news) and paid (advertisement) media representations of campaigns and elections. It is now common for network news programs to rebroadcast ads that are entertaining, provocative, or controversial.

Ads that are broadcast for free during the news or discussed in major newspapers have several advantages over those aired purely as commercials. First, viewers traditionally have trusted the news media—far more than paid ads—for fairness and objectivity. William McGuire has shown that the credibility of the source is one determinant of whether the message is believed. The high credibility of the media gives ads aired during the news an important advantage over those seen as overt commercials. Roger Ailes explained it this way: "You get a 30 or 40 percent bump out of [an ad] by getting it on the news. You get more viewers, you get credibility, you get it in a framework."

Second, ads in the news guarantee campaigners a large audience and free air time. Opinion polls have documented that nearly two-thirds of Americans cite television as their primary source of news. This is particularly true for what Michael Robinson refers to as the "inadvertent audience," those who are least interested in politics and also among the most volatile in their opinions.

Airing ads during newscasts can, however, have some drawbacks. When ads are described as unfair to the opposition, media coverage undermines the sponsor's message. The advantages of airing the ad during the news can also be lost if reporters challenge the ad's factual accuracy. Favorable coverage is not assured, and the way that reporters cover ads affects how people interpret them.

JOHNSON'S "DAISY" AD IN 1964

Nothing illustrates the emergence of advertising as an effective political tactic better than the 1964 "Daisy" spot, arguably the most infamous ad in television history. The ad, designed by Tony Schwartz, opens with a little girl standing in a meadow plucking petals from a daisy. After she counts "1, 2, 3, 4, 5, 6, 7, 8, 9," an ominous voice begins its own countdown: "10, 9, 8, 7, 6, 5, 4, 3, 2, 1, 0." At zero, the picture of the child dissolves and a mushroom cloud fills the screen. President

Lyndon Johnson closes the ad by warning: "These are the stakes. To make a world in which all of God's children can live, or to go into the dark. We must either love each other or we must die."

This ad aired only once, during NBC's "Monday Night at the Movies" showing of *David and Bathsheba* on September 7, 1964. Condemnation of the spot came almost immediately. Bill Moyers, then Johnson's press secretary, recounted: "The president called me and said, 'Holy shit. I'm getting calls from all over the country.' Most of them said that it was an effective ad. Others said they didn't like it." Press reaction was swift. According to Lloyd Wright, an advertising strategist for Johnson, "The first night it aired, it created such a media flap that the next night it was used in its entirety on the newscasts on all three networks."

Even though the spot was never rebroadcast as a commercial, news reporters included it in news stories and thereby assured it a wide audience. In conjunction with other Democratic ads suggesting that Barry Goldwater, the Republican candidate for president, was an unstable extremist not to be trusted with America's future, the "Daisy" ad helped Johnson achieve a landslide victory. The effort dramatically demonstrated the emerging new era of campaign communications.

BUSH'S "REVOLVING DOOR" AD IN 1988

George Bush's "Revolving Door" ad illustrates how, in conjunction with clever stage management, commercials can take an issue at the edge of public concern and make it the focal point of a campaign. Visually, the ad was simple but striking: criminals entering and then immediately exiting a prison through its revolving door. CBS first covered this commercial in its broadcast on October 7, 1988 (news stories about convicted criminal Willie Horton—who had been released on a prison furlough program and shortly thereafter arrested for a newly committed crime—had been broadcast September 22). The story described the commercial as an ad that would highlight the prison furlough policy of Governor Michael Dukakis. Clifford Barnes and Donna Cuomo, victims of an assault by a convict who had been released on a weekend furlough, were reported to be participating in a speaking tour with a pro-Bush group. Bush, meanwhile, was shown campaigning with police officers.

A related story followed on October 20, this time showing in great detail Horton's crime record and supplying background on the Bush ad. Bush was shown campaigning in New York City at a police union rally. It was not until October 24 and 25—almost three weeks after the commercial appeared—that opponents appeared on the news to claim that the "Revolving Door" ad contained racist undertones. But in keeping with the horse race mentality of the media, a second story on October 25 also quoted Tony Schwartz as saying that Bush's ads were successful and that the "Revolving Door" was particularly effective.

The contrast with the coverage of Johnson's "Daisy" ad was stark. Whereas the 1964 ad was immediately condemned and removed from the airwaves, reporters in 1988 treated the furlough ad as a genuine news story. Criticisms came late and were never solidly addressed; the spot was not pulled off the air. More important, news stories during that election season emphasized the effectiveness of negative ads or commented on how they were increasingly acceptable to the public. Finally, some analysts even attributed Bush's lead in the polls to the success of his negative commercials and the lack of an appropriate and timely response by Dukakis.

This tolerance of negativity, combined with the grudging respect reporters accorded to effective GOP ads, created a pattern of coverage that assisted Bush. Whereas reporters in 1964 had condemned the "Daisy" ad, journalists in 1988 did not complain when the "Revolving Door" commercial stayed on the air. They even rebroadcast the ad repeatedly throughout the last month of the campaign. This treatment gave Bush more air time and therefore lent him more credibility than any campaign organization alone could have managed. The news media helped make Bush's 1988 advertising campaign one of the most effective efforts of the past twenty years.

CLINTON CONTRAST ADS IN 1996

By the 1990s, after several elections filled with attack ads, voters were growing weary of campaign negativity. Ever sensitive to changing voter sentiments in this regard, the Bill Clinton campaign made effective use of "contrast" ads, which both criticized the opponent and explained how their own candidate would address voters' concerns.

Both Clinton and Robert Dole, each having wrapped up his party's nomination, aired commercials throughout March, April, May, and June attacking each other. Clinton tied Dole to Newt Gingrich and accused the pair of gutting Medicare, Medicaid, education, and the environment. Dole, for his part, questioned the president's trustworthiness in light of the Whitewater allegations concerning Clinton's real estate and financial transactions in Arkansas.

Clinton won the spring phase of this campaign. By June 1996, according to a CBS News/*New York Times* poll, he had a lead of 54 to 35 percent among registered voters and was viewed more favorably than Dole. Whereas 48 percent viewed the president favorably and 33 percent saw him unfavorably, Dole had a favorability rating of 29 percent and an unfavorability rating of 35 percent. By early October, Dole's unfavorability rating had risen to 41 percent, while his favorability rating remained at 29 percent. Clinton was viewed favorably by 47 percent and unfavorably by 36 percent. His lead was 53 to 36 percent.

But more surprising was how well Clinton did on the blame game. When asked in May 1996 whether the candidates were spending more time explaining their views or attacking the opponent, 32 percent of voters perceived that Dole was explaining his views and 48 percent believed he was attacking his opponent. In Clinton's case, 53 percent thought he was explaining his views and only 28 percent felt he was attacking his opponent.

By the last week of the campaign, 55 percent felt Dole was attacking his opponent, 21 percent believed Clinton was doing so, and 21 percent thought Reform Party candidate Ross Perot's ads were attacking his opponents. When asked who was most responsible for the negative campaigning that year, 52 percent cited Dole, 13 percent Clinton, and 6 percent Perot.

As they had done successfully in 1992, the Clinton team used an inoculation strategy to warn people that Republicans would launch "a relentless attack" of negative advertising and misinformation. Speaking before a thousand Democratic women at Emily's List (a women's pro-choice political caucus), First Lady Hillary Clinton predicted: "Get prepared for it and don't be surprised by it. When you've got no vision of how to make the world a better place for yourself or your children, then you go negative." After Dole went negative in the fall, Clinton adviser George Stephanopoulos explained Dole's public persona to a newspaper reporter: "All you ever see him doing on TV is carping, attacking, whining."

The Clinton staff shielded themselves from the backlash against negative campaigning by employing contrast ads. Recognizing that voters do not approve of negative advertising, the Clinton ads combined negative and positive appeals. An example is an ad Clinton ran as a response to Dole's attack on Clinton's drug record. The ad criticized Dole for opposing the creation of a drug czar and Congress for cutting monies for school drug prevention programs but then went on to explain that Clinton had sought to strengthen school programs and that he had expanded the death penalty to include drug kingpins. By using attack ads as a surgical tool, not as a sledgehammer, the Clinton campaign attached negatives to the opponent while sheltering itself from blame by voters upset about highly critical ads.

SUGGESTED READINGS

McGuire, William. "Persuasion, Resistance, and Attitude Change." In Ithiel de Sola Pool, ed., *Handbook of Communication*. Chicago: Rand McNally, 1973.

Robinson, Michael. "Public Affairs Television and the Growth of Political Malaise." *American Political Science Review* 70 (1976): 409–32.

Runkel, David, ed., *Campaign for President: The Managers Look at '88*. Dover, Mass.: Auburn House, 1989.

West, Darrell M. *Air Wars: Television Advertising in Election Campaigns, 1952–1996*. 2d ed. Washington, D.C.: Congressional Quarterly Press, 1997.

West, Darrell M., and Burdette A. Loomis. *The Sound of Money: How Political Interests Get What They Want*. New York: Norton, 1999.

Amy Keller | POLITICAL CONSULTANTS AS NEWS

The strange caller with the thick British accent asked me what I could tell him about a Republican political strategist named Roger Stone. As a reporter who regularly covered political consultants, would I, he asked, describe Stone as a staunch conservative who publicly advocated "family values"? It was in the heat of the 1996 presidential campaign cycle when I received that phone call; the curious fellow on the other end of the line was a Florida-based reporter working for the *National Enquirer*.

Only a few weeks earlier, the press had unveiled the tawdry details of presidential consultant Dick Morris's relationship with a $200-per-hour call girl whom he allowed to eavesdrop on his telephone conversations with President Bill Clinton. This time, the tabloids had set their sights on Stone. Seizing on his somewhat loose affiliation to then-presidential hopeful Bob Dole's campaign, the *Enquirer* was about to make similarly salacious allegations about Stone's and his wife's personal life.

It had been less than a year since *Roll Call* had decided to begin aggressively covering the political consulting industry (see Fig. 1). Now it seemed that the supermarket tabloids had discovered political consultants too—with a vengeance. In later conversations I had with sources close to Stone, some accused the *Enquirer* of staking out his home, badgering his mother, and digging through his trash to get their "story." Other "friends" of Stone, meanwhile, seemed to blame the strategist himself. One colleague casually confided that Stone loved "being the Prince of Darkness" and recalled that Stone had proudly distributed copies of a 1985 *New Republic* article about himself titled "State-of-the-Art Sleazeball."

But exhibitionist or victim, Stone and his story serve as a stern reminder that the high-stakes game of political consulting has become an unavoidably conspicuous way to make a living. Some political consultants even view negative publicity as a sort of rite of passage. "Any consultant of quality is likely to have had a few attacks against them," GOP opposition researcher Gary Maloney observed when Stone was making headlines four years ago. On the flip side, heightened publicity

Figure 1.

Courtesy Amy Keller, Roll Call

has also helped a few lucky individuals in the consulting community attain a celebrity status once reserved for the candidates they served.

Yet while political consultants themselves have not always dominated the spotlight, the solid relationship between reporters and strategists is hardly recent. The fact is, any political reporter worth his salt knows the importance of cultivating political consultants as sources. Truly good campaign coverage depends on being able to get inside the nuts and bolts of the campaign operation and being familiar with all its myriad specialists. It means interviewing the pollster and picking the brain of the media consultant. It requires talking to the person who's designing the direct-mail pieces and finding out who's handling the candidate's fund-raising.

The relationship between reporter and consultant is a symbiotic one—or parasitic depending on the circumstance of the moment. The journalist finds access to valuable "inside" campaign information. The strategists running the campaign have access to a mouthpiece, and in this day and age of multi-million-dollar media campaigns, a free sound-byte is priceless. During the 1996 presidential campaigns, for example, it was common for media consultants to forward scripts of their latest advertisements to reporters before they were aired on television. Eager to satisfy their copy-hungry editors, most reporters would almost immediately write stories about the most recent stream of advertisements, citing the scripts and reporting on the candidate's latest mode of attack in commercials that sometimes were never broadcast at all. Talk about reduced-rate advertising!

Nevertheless, some consultants flatly refuse to speak with the press. Usually this decision is based on the belief that their clients—not they—should be the subject of news stories. Others consider the circumstances and act accordingly. As one Democratic consultant explains it, "I serve on campaigns where I talk to reporters on the record, and on some campaigns I talk to them on background, and there are some campaigns where I don't talk to reporters at all—because for some reason or another the campaigns don't want people to know there's a consultant involved."

Media-shy or not, consultants are wise to establish terms of communication with a reporter before they begin any exchange. This protects both the reporter and the strategist by helping to prevent confusion over what material can be used in an article. While some reporters have slightly different concepts of what these terms mean, the following are generally safe guidelines:

"On the record." Anything the person says can be used in a story, even as a direct quote by the individual.

"Off the record." The source is providing information for the reporter only; the reporter will not use that information in the form of a direct quote or otherwise. (Warning: reporters will often try to get off-the-record information confirmed elsewhere to make it usable.)

"On background." The reporter may use the information provided, but he or she may not directly attribute it to the providing source; rather, a "prominent Republican consultant" or a "source within the campaign" may be cited. When speaking "on background," consultants should establish in advance with the reporter how they will be referred to. The safest rule to follow is that if you don't want to see it in print, don't say it.

While consultants have long been prime sources for political reporters, with the evolution of the political consulting industry the business itself has proved to be an interesting beat. As we have discovered at *Roll Call*, there is certainly a market for information about the world of political consulting—a market among the consultants themselves, who are eager to read what their colleagues and competitors are doing, and a market among their clients, the politicians who require their services. As the Dick Morrises and James Carvilles of the world have proved, the general public also has demonstrated an appetite for news about political strategists. In the same way that America is interested in Hollywood directors and script writers, the average Joe seems to care about the behind-the-scenes workings of a campaign, the masterminding of the candidate's bid for office.

Playing to the more narrow audience of consultants themselves, I've learned to cover political consulting as any business reporter might cover an industry: telling my readers which firms are hot—and which are not—reporting about new consulting alliances, and delivering the news of bitter breakups. Like any business, consulting is rapidly changing, and the advent of new technology also makes for hot news. In 1996, a consultant working for Senator John Warner (R-Virginia) caught considerable flak for creating a television ad that manipulated a photograph of fellow Virginia senator Chuck Robb (Democrat). Warner's media consultant sought to highlight Warner's Democratic opponent as having close ties to former Virginia governor Doug Wilder (Democrat), but the strategist went a step too far when he substituted the opposition candidate's head for Robb's in a photo taken of Robb and Wilder. Senator Warner won his reelection, but his media firm faced the public humiliation of being fired and having to apologize for its questionable tactics.

One of my favorite "controversy" stories is a short piece I wrote in the fall of 1995 about a Louisiana political consultant named Roy Fletcher. At the time, former Clinton adviser Dick Morris was being denounced by others in the consulting community for committing what many in the business consider a "cardinal sin": working on both sides of the fence. Morris's colleagues were berating him for advising Democrats like Clinton while at the same time working for Republicans like Senate Majority Leader Trent Lott (R-Mississippi). Fletcher did not have the big-name clients that Morris did, but he did take a similar approach to his work. The slow-talking mediameister felt no compunction about advising both Democratic and Republican House members. He even took on then-GOP candidate Mike Foster's campaign for governor, although he had previously been on the bankroll of Foster's Democratic rival, Cleo Fields. "I'm not nearly as big as Dick Morris, and I don't ever intend to be, so that's why I haven't gotten any flak, I guess," Fletcher told me with a hearty laugh when I interviewed him for that story.

Fletcher, however, is hardly the first consultant to come under fire from his colleagues. In the fiercely competitive and ever-expanding political consulting industry, it is not uncommon for consultants to plant negative stories about rival firms to try to sully the reputations of their competitors. This poses a special concern for journalists, who in the course of trying to break a story may become unwitting pawns in a dirty public relations campaign. The key to sorting out fact from fiction and reality from rumor is for the reporter investigating the story to be sure to get both sides.

Following the Republican takeover of Congress in the 1994 elections, for example, several political consultants took aim at a GOP pollster named Frank Luntz, who had been credited with helping conservatives draft their "Contract with America." It was that ballyhooed contract—a point-by-point outline of what GOP candidates promised to accomplish in the House if they were elected—that many believed helped to advance record numbers of Republicans to Congress that year. The contract's success also propelled Luntz from near obscurity to the annals of polling history. The relatively young consultant developed an impressive roster of clients that included several members of the GOP leadership, and he became a frequent face on CNN and other news networks. Luntz's sudden fame, however, also attracted some negative attention from his jealous competitors in the consulting industry who alleged that his role in helping craft the contract had been overstated and who began waging a campaign to discredit the successful strategist. Other pollsters, for example, began attacking Luntz's polling methods and finding fault with his preferred method of surveying via small focus groups; more petty criticism, usually in the form of gossip told to journalists, was even directed at his hairstyle. Perhaps the cutthroat nature of the business and the backbiting finally wearied him. At the end of the 1998 campaign cycle, Luntz announced that he was abandoning the world of political consulting to concentrate on corporate clients.

Feuds between individual consultants also tend to make headlines. One bitter episode of mudslinging resulted from a dispute between two Democratic media consultants—a media strategist and a media buyer—who had worked together on the campaign of Representative Lane Evans (D-Illinois) in 1996. The media strategist involved in the disagreement, Bill Zimmerman, contended that the buyer he had subcontracted to buy airtime for the ads, Jan Crawford, had swindled him out of some money he was due.

Zimmerman eventually sued Crawford in court, but before a verdict was rendered the disagreement became a whirling storm of controversy that kept the Democratic consulting community abuzz for months. Zimmerman's supporters lobbied to have Crawford removed from the board of the American Association of Political Consultants by spreading unverified rumors about her personal life to reporters and other strategists. Meanwhile, allies of Crawford rushed to her defense. Cathy Allen, a Seattle-based Democratic consultant who was interviewed for a story about the public brawl, defended her friend and argued that Crawford was being smeared by the sexist members of the male-dominated consultant community.

In December 1998, a Virginia court finally laid the controversy to rest when it ordered Crawford to pay Zimmerman the disputed fees totaling more than $30,000. The incident, however, provided a stern lesson to the nation's community of political consultants. Noted Allen, "If you see the work consultants do to besmirch candidates, you can only imagine what happens when they turn it on someone they don't like personally."

Phillip L.
Gianos

POLITICAL CONSULTANTS
IN AMERICAN FILM

THE EARLY HISTORY OF POLITICAL
CONSULTANTS IN FILM

The early history of political consultants in film is best seen in the films of Frank Capra, particularly the final two of his Depression-era trilogy of *Mr. Deeds Goes to Town* (1936), *Mr. Smith Goes to Washington* (1939), and *Meet John Doe* (1941). Both *Smith* and *Doe* involve portrayals of political campaigns in which the separate roles of power-seeker, consultant, and media specialist are rolled into one.

In both films, the villain is intent on expanding political power. In *Smith*, his goal is relatively modest—keeping alive a crooked land deal for which he needs Senate approval. In *Doe*, it is vastly more sinister—establishing a nationwide proto-fascist movement. Each villain tries to destroy the opposition's media operation and substitute his own in its place. Capra's villains are wealthy, but their real power lies in using wealth to bend media to their political ends. In *Smith*, the destruction is accomplished by wrecking the pitiful opposition newspaper run by Senator Jeff Smith's (James Stewart) Boy Rangers. In *Doe*, the villain uses his private police force to cut—literally—the power to radio broadcasters covering a huge political rally that threatens to get out of control. In both films, the villain—who is his own consultant—then substitutes his own deceitful message using his own media—newspapers, radio, and billboards.

An important transitional film that links this portrayal of the campaign professional's function with more contemporary versions of political consultants is the John Ford–directed *The Last Hurrah* (1958), based on Edwin O'Connor's roman à clef novel about Boston mayor James Michael Curley. The last hurrah of the title refers not only to the death of Mayor Frank Skeffington (Spencer Tracy) but to the death of a political era in which friends-and-neighbors, ethnically based politics succumbs to television and those who have learned to use it. In a key scene (which may be seen as Ford's parody of Richard Nixon's Checkers speech) Skeffington's callow challenger is coached through a television appearance. Ford constantly reinforces the coming political juggernaut of television and contrasts it with Skeffington's style of politics—noisy, personal, and doomed.

Despite Skeffington's opponent being a nonentity, the challenger does as he is told by his advisers and defeats the more politically substantial incumbent. In *The Last Hurrah*, Frank Skeffington loses because he has lost touch. After Skeffington loses, he dies. In *The Last Hurrah*—unlike the two Frank Capra films—the roles of campaign professional and client are separate. It is the professionals who are now the more knowledgeable about campaigns. The message is clear: adapt or perish.

CAMPAIGN CONSULTANTS IN CONTEMPORARY FILMS

By the time *The Candidate* was released in 1972, the role of political consultant was well established. Books like those in Theodore White's *The Making of the President* series and similar insider accounts revealed the texture of campaigns. *The Candidate* does this as well as any political film made. Much of this success is attributable to the screenplay by Jeremy Larner, who served as a speechwriter in Eugene McCarthy's insurgent campaign for the Democratic presidential nomination in 1968.

The movie begins with a gaggle of consultants comparing notes after an election. They share professional gossip, compare wins and losses, then head off to the next campaign. One of the consultants initiates the events of *The Candidate* by persuading Bill McKay (Robert Redford), an idealistic lawyer doing pro bono work at the Mexican border, to make an apparently hopeless run as the Democratic nominee for U.S. Senate from California. His opponent will be the aging but polished incumbent Crocker Jarmon (Don Porter). The consultant is Marvin "Luke" Lucas (Peter Boyle), whose sales pitch is to assure McKay that he need not fear compromising his principles because McKay is certain to lose. Lucas certifies this for the candidate-to-be by writing "You Lose" on a matchbook and giving it to him. McKay asks the consultant, "Marvin, what's in it for you?" Lucas states his terms—salary, expenses—the deal is struck, and the campaign is born.

A second consultant is introduced—Howard Klein (Allen Garfield), the media guru. Klein is as matter-of-fact as Lucas but tougher and more cynical. It is his character who first introduces the essentially male, sexual conception of politics that underlies much of *The Candidate*. Klein wants to frame the race as one of virility versus impotence. As candidate and consultant talk strategy, Klein pointedly pounds on a bag of nuts with a hammer.

Klein's dialogue is laced with phrases that reinforce his view of politics in general and this race in particular. Jarmon is "soft as an old banana." Klein tells his client that by contrasting the younger McKay with the older Jarmon in their ads, the public will conclude that "the Croc can't get it up any more." Klein is a constant source of combative sexual/political references: "beating his [Jarmon's] meat"; "balls in both hands"; "unzip himself."

The more time McKay spends with his new employee/allies, the further he slips away from the people with whom he surrounded himself in his days as a crusading lawyer. In one scene, director Michael Ritchie places a tired McKay in the center of the frame between two arguing campaign aides, both closer to the camera and therefore much larger visually than McKay. The candidate is visually trapped and diminished by his own campaign. Inevitably, McKay's old allies fall away. McKay has become the candidate, his life has become the campaign, and both are in the hands of strangers.

McKay's journey takes him closer to power even as he attempts to distance himself from it. Much of this ambivalence is expressed stylistically: McKay collapses repeatedly into helpless laughter while trying to tape a television statement; he mocks his own stump speech. But some of McKay's compromise is substantive. Advised to cut his hair, he does. In one of the movie's cleverest bits of dialogue, McKay is cautioned by his campaign handlers to blur his clear pro-choice position on abortion rights by saying when asked that he is "considering my position" on the issue. McKay's response is, "OK, I'll think about it." But does this mean that McKay is only considering whether to take his advisers' counsel or that he has accepted their advice and "I'll think about it" will become his standard response on abortion rights? The audience doesn't know, and we suspect McKay doesn't either.

Consultants in the film represent both expediency and expertise. They have the skills that McKay needs to win, and for the candidate a guaranteed loss is now less attractive than it once was. His circumstance places him between his idealistic lawyer days and the power he seeks. His willingness to compromise in the pursuit of power is roughly measured by the degree to which he heeds his advisers' counsel. McKay's political journey begins with Lucas's plea for him to run and ends with the two of them alone in a hotel room the night of Mc-Kay's win. In the final scene, McKay looks plaintively at Lucas and famously asks him, barely audibly, "Marvin . . . what do we do now?" As this line suggests, much of the charm and verisimilitude of *The Candidate* lies in the fact that neither the candidate nor his consultants dominate events.

As political consultants became more visible, so did the influence attributed to them in movies. The over-the-top high point of such characterizations is *Power* (1986). Indeed, one might change the title of *Power* to *The Consultant* as the stylish and high-powered Pete St. John (Richard Gere) replaces the rumpled, balding men who represent consultants in *The Candidate*. Pete St. John is a stock character, who in this film happens to be a political consultant but who could be any driven, hyper-successful male professional.

St. John divides his time in the film between Washington, D.C., Latin America, Ohio, New Mexico, and Seattle, in all of which he advises clients. Much of the film involves a series of scenes in which St. John practices his art. He skillfully edits a television spot to turn disastrous footage into a triumph; coaches a client on debating technique; produces a response television ad for an embattled gubernatorial candidate; directs spots on location; and has his research specialist tutor a fledgling candidate on the basics of demographic analysis and simulation. These are the most compelling scenes in the film.

When not doing these things, St. John confers with the powerful, spends time in his sleek Euro-style office complex, occasionally has sex with his assistant Sydney (Kate Capshaw), or plays electronic drums accompanying the Benny Goodman orchestra through earphones while flying between jobs. All this makes St. John rich as well as powerful. He tells his clients, "I am in control," and "I'm in charge of all the elements." He makes it clear to them that what they do once they have won is up to them. His job is merely to elect them.

The pace of the film slows considerably by the halfway point. A story line involving Arnold Billings's (Denzel Washington) blackmailing of respected Senator Sam Hastings (E. G. Marshall) is linked to story lines involving the decline in the professional fortunes of aging political consultant—and St. John mentor—Wilfred Buckley (Gene Hackman) and a coming together of St. John with his former wife, journalist Ellen Freeman (Julie Christie). In the end, *Power* reveals itself to be a melodrama with politics as background and the consultant's job merely an exciting thing for St. John to do.

Despite its weakness as a film, *Power* does amplify the Hollywood rendition of political consultants. Most important, it places the consultant in the center of the film and makes him glamorous. *Power* also places the consultant in a position of complete control over his clients, to the point that he has second thoughts (though they are only briefly expressed) about that power. *Power* additionally introduces a first and second generation of consultants; one can imagine the Marvin Lucas character of 1972's *The Candidate* turning up as the down-on-his-luck Wilfred Buckley in 1986's *Power*. In its scenes picturing the work of the consultant, *Power* serves to legitimize and celebrate the role.

The year 1998 saw the release of two high-profile films featuring political consultants, each of which is a spiritual descendant of earlier films. One is the Bill Clinton roman à clef *Primary Colors*. This film has much in common with *The Candidate* and for the same reasons: its source material, the famous novel by Anonymous (Joe Klein), also revels in politics. *Primary Colors* reintroduces three elements to the movies' picture of consultants missing in *Power*. It makes them considerably less slick than Pete St. John and more like the decidedly non-slick consultants of *The Candidate*; it reintroduces the give-and-take between candidate and adviser; and it expands the number of advisers trying to get the candidates' ear. In so doing, *Primary Colors* reintroduces the element of democratic chaos—of politics—to campaigns. It is notable that *Primary Colors* downplays media technology as much as *Power* emphasizes it.

The advisers to presidential candidate Jack Stanton (John Travolta as a Bill Clinton–like southern governor) are stand-ins for advisers in the Clinton primary campaigns of 1992. Billy Bob Thornton plays Richard Jemmons (James Carville); Maura Tierney is Daisy Green (Mandy Grunwald); Kathy Bates is Libby Holden (Betsey Wright); Caroline Allen plays Lucille Kaufman (Susan Thomases). Much of the film is taken up with the relationships among the advisers and their candidate—complex relationships that also involve the candidate's family, his political opponents, the media, and the public whom they all are courting.

These relationships are played out as a series of crises hits the Stanton campaign—a Gennifer Flowers–style revelation, a stand-by-your-man television appearance, a teenage pregnancy, a challenge from another southern governor, an ethical dilemma involving releasing information damaging to an opponent, husband-and-wife flare-ups. The point of view of the film is that of Henry Burton (Adrian Lester), the grandson of a Martin Luther King–like leader who is drawn into the campaign. (The character's name and his role in the film strongly bring to mind the Henry Burden character of *All the King's Men*, though in contemporary terms he is George Stephanopolous.) The dominant political tone of the film lies in the chaotically democratic nature by which all the principals—the candidate, his wife, and the advisers—simultaneously support, oppose, disappoint, infuriate, and depend on each other as they work through these crises.

In this respect, *Primary Colors* is a more comedic version of *The Candidate*, which is also concerned with the comedy and chaos of campaigning. While Robert Redford plays McKay with wry and ironic detachment and Travolta's Stanton is played more broadly, both candidates are charmers. People love them and want to work for them. Candidate and consultants in both films have complex and changing relationships. Unlike *Power*, where the candidate does what the consultant says, the office-seeker in *The Candidate* and especially *Primary Colors* gets told off by his hired hands, though it is the candidate who usually prevails. The model of politics of *Power* is authoritarian, with the consultant in control; the model of politics of *The Candidate* and *Primary Colors* is noisily and messily democratic, with consultants only part of the mix and playing what is, finally, a subsidiary role.

If *The Candidate* and *Primary Colors* are cousins, so also are *Power* and the other 1998 release, *Wag the Dog*. The primary similarity between the latter two is their attribution of great power to consultants. The primary difference is that *Wag the Dog* is a satire while *Power* takes Pete St. John very seriously.

Wag the Dog is (like *Primary Colors*) essentially a series of near-catastrophes in which the consultants (unlike *Primary Colors*) always triumph. The initial catastrophe hits the incumbent president a few weeks before the election when he is accused of a sexual impropriety by a pubescent Firefly Girl. Conrad Brean (Robert De Niro) is brought in by the White House, in the person of presidential aide Winifred Ames (Anne Heche), to handle the situation. The crisis approaches complete meltdown when the president's opponent starts running spots whose soundtrack features Maurice Chevalier singing "Thank Heaven for Little Girls." Brean advises that a presidential trip to China be extended to buy time and suggests that the White House issue denials that the new and entirely imaginary B-3 bomber is being activated ahead of schedule.

Given the enormity of the political threat, movie producer Stanley Motss (Dustin Hoffman) is brought in, forming the film's primary unit: Motss, Brean, and Ames—two spinmeisters and a White House aide, in that order of importance. The three—though primarily Motss and Brean—quickly refine the basic story line: the illusory B-3 activation is linked to illusory Albanian terrorists and an illusory suitcase bomb somewhere in Canada. The White House's chief allies in this improvised screenplay are the media. The spinmeisters' plan is to deny the story they have created. The denials are expected to be—and are—disbelieved by the press though they are in fact true. There is no B-3, no Albanian threat, and no suitcase bomb in Canada. Thus is created the irony of the setup. The spinmeisters are truthful in their denials. The media expect the White House to lie. Therefore the media's disbelief about the truth leads them to spread the lie. It works.

Much of the rest of the film is an elaboration of this premise. Footage is created overnight purporting to show an Albanian girl fleeing the carnage. Patriotic songs focusing on the crisis are instantly written, involving a brief parody of the making of the "We Are the World" video. Athletic shoes are parlayed into a symbol of the made-up crisis. A military hero (Woody Harrelson) is manufactured for the occasion, though through a mix-up he turns out to be a psychotic military convict who murdered a nun. No matter—the triumvirate of media pros fix that problem, too. Essentially, *Wag the Dog* tells the story of media and political consultants who make a war, sell it, then make up a peace and sell that too. In every crisis they turn dross into gold and manage to create profitable commercial tie-ins along the way.

Several political morals of *Wag the Dog* stand out. First, to steal a line from *The Candidate*, "You and I know this is bullshit, but the point is they're buying it." Second, the president for whom all this is ostensibly being done is barely visible and is reduced in several scenes to taking directions off camera from the advisers. One of his few expressed preferences is for a particular type of kitten to be held by the Albanian girl in the bogus war footage. Third, the advisers are thoroughly professional and focused on the job at hand. Professional ego does not get in the way until the very end, to the detriment of movie producer Motss, who really doesn't understand the game—politics is more dangerous than show business—and pays for it with his life. Finally—and this is a throwback to the Frank Capra view of the world—the media and especially the public are complete fools.

SUGGESTED READINGS

Brownstein, Ronald. *The Power and the Glitter: The Hollywood-Washington Connection*. New York: Pantheon Books, 1990.
Crowdus, Gary. *The Political Companion to American Film*. Chicago: Lakeview Press, 1994.
Gianos, Phillip. *Politics and Politicians in American Film*. Greenwood, Conn.: Praeger, 1998.

Matthew
Dowd

CORPORATIONS AS
CANDIDATES

Political communications can take various forms, from efforts on behalf of partisan candidates, to nonpartisan campaigns, to initiative and referendum campaigns. Corporations and companies have found a new way to use public policy debate in political communications to accomplish their external goals.

Although the corporate world is affected by legislative and regulatory government activities, it has kept some distance from direct debate of public policy. In the past, involvement of corporations has been limited to making contributions to political candidates (who use these finances to design their own political communications) and forming political action committees to make future contributions. In addition, companies sometimes hire lobbyists to carry a particular message directly to a decision maker.

These efforts were very direct and were based on established relationships. Corporations and their lobbyists had confidence that a particular decision maker could control debate and public policy action. This political communication is akin to the "old" world of political candidates' communications, when a few influencers decided the candidates in a race, had a strong impact on newspapers, and exerted much more control over the political campaign environment than they now do. But this world has changed. Campaigns began to make use of mass media communication to speak directly to a larger body of voters.

Many corporations are cognizant of the shift in public policy development that has occurred in the last fifteen to twenty years. This shift occurred for a variety of reasons. First, public policy making has become a much more open process. Far fewer agreements are reached behind closed doors with limited or controlled debate. The press (both newspapers and electronic media) is a much more active participant in this process—thus government officials' constituents are more aware of policy development.

Second, the speed at which information is disseminated to the public has increased dramatically and will continue to do so. News sources include not only twenty-four-hour news programs and local cable programs but also the Internet. Such "real-time" information brings voters much closer to decisions that are made, and their input and re-actions can likewise be instantaneous.

And third, governmental bodies have become much more hetero-geneous. In areas that were traditional strongholds of Democratic of-ficeholders, Republicans have gained strength. In formerly solid Re-publican areas, Democrats now hold offices. The number of minority and female officeholders has increased dramatically over the last twenty years as well and will continue to do so. This diversity has broadened the debate and limited the effectiveness of relying on a se-lect number of "old boy" lobbyists to carry messages. Though lobbying is still a necessity, corporations should view that function as only one element of a broader campaign for public approval.

POSITIONING THE CORPORATION

Since the public is now a major part of public policy, corporations must use political communications to make themselves heard. Corporations can use the methods originally adapted for traditional candidate cam-paigns and conduct their own campaigns. These tools include research; mass communication, both broad (media) and narrow (direct mail, bro-chures); field operations; and interaction with the press.

Because the public and information seekers are more attuned to public policy, corporations need to have a firm basis in research so they can gauge voters' sentiment on issues, evaluate the opinions of public policy makers and influencers, create and disseminate proper mes-sages, and position the corporation itself. There are obvious excep-tions, but research enables corporations to assess the position they should take. This research can include focus groups, public opinion polling, message testing, and any number of the other methods used in political campaigns.

Corporations have begun to use broad message communications to affect the public policy debate as well. It is not surprising to see "candi-date-like" spots communicating public policy positions to involve the general public or key opinion leaders. These spots may be positive, negative, or comparative. They can be aired far in advance of the time decisions are made, they can mobilize support on behalf of a particular goal, they can attempt to affect the debate as policy develops, and they can position the public policy "postaction" to prepare for future de-velopments.

In traditional political campaigns, field organizations have been used to deliver messages to or to mobilize particular constituencies. Many statewide campaigns involve county coordinators, precinct workers, and volunteers. Corporations also have these tools at their disposal. In many companies, employees at all levels can deliver messages across all political jurisdictions. Employees recognize the significant impact public policy can have on their corporation's success and are eager to become involved.

Finally, since the press plays a more active role in policy decisions, corporations must work with it just as a political candidate would. Proper messages need to be communicated, at the right times and in the right ways, for corporations to be successful. The press receives input from a variety of sources, and corporations need to play an active role in these communications so their messages will be heard.

THE FUNDAMENTALS OF CORPORATE POLITICAL COMMUNICATION

As corporations use these political campaign tools and begin to assume a role similar to that of a candidate running for office, it is important that they keep in mind some fundamentals of political communication.

Candidates must always stay "on message" and repeat this message similarly in all venues, including television spots, candidate rallies, discussions with the press, communications by volunteers, and any other contact with voters. Similarly, corporations need to stay on message in any communication related to the public policy debate. All broad communications must be consistent with communications directly to decision makers, and the same message must be communicated to the press as to the corporation's employees. Variation from the consistent message will not only reduce overall effectiveness but could negatively affect a corporation's position with key decision makers. Because opponents will seize on inconsistencies or flip-flops, corporations should avoid communicating one message to one audience and another message to a different audience. For example, a corporation communicating a certain message to Wall Street analysts (such as expected higher earnings or reductions in the number of employees to cut costs) and another to opinion makers could alter the public policy debate.

Another fundamental in political campaigns is designing communications to influence the key voters in a race. Corporations should concentrate resources primarily on affecting the decisive "votes" in the public policy debate. Many candidates drain resources in communicating to those who will not get involved (nonvoters) or to voters who have already made up their minds. Corporations need to ensure that communications are not directed toward constituencies that will not affect the public policy debate or toward decision makers who are already firmly resolved about an issue.

A campaign's resources must be planned so they will have the maximum impact when a voter goes to the polls. The media schedule, press hits, candidate travel, voter mobilization—all should be laid out to reach culmination on election day. Many times candidates peak too early, too late, or not at all. Corporations in political communication must also identify the "election day," which could be a vote at a city council meeting on zoning, a legislative committee vote on a particular amendment, or any event at which the public policy debate will culminate in a decision. Corporations need to plan the campaign communications to peak on these particular election days.

CORPORATIONS AND PUBLIC POLICY

Corporate involvement with political communications in public policy debates is similar to traditional efforts by candidates, but there are differences as well. While certain tools and processes can be adopted from the candidate political consulting world, certain dissimilarities need to be acknowledged.

First, corporate campaign efforts are not driven by historical voting patterns that affect candidates' campaigns. In the latter, certain demographic and geographic elements follow historical election patterns. For example, African American voters normally support Democratic candidates overwhelmingly, while upper-income white voters traditionally support Republican candidates. Though there have been exceptions to this rule and others, historical voting patterns exist. Most political candidate campaigns are ultimately decided by 20 to 30 percent of the electorate, normally designated as "swing" voters. Thus the majority of the electorate usually follows historical voting patterns. In corporate campaign efforts, coalitions of voting or decision blocs cut across nearly all geographic and demographic bounds. Since public policy debates can affect constituencies and locations very differently, it is not unusual for there to be very diverse coalitions.

Further, since there are many emerging industries and corporations that did not exist or were not envisioned ten or twenty years ago (for example, Internet providers, high-tech firms), there are no historical voting patterns. The days in which—or so pundits said—Republicans supported business interests and Democrats were consumer advocates are long over, if they ever existed.

A second difference for corporate "candidates" is that while for traditional political candidates the opposition consists of one player, in corporate public policy campaigns there usually are multiple opposing interests involved in the campaign. This opposition list could include other corporate entities with different public policy goals, associations or coalitions of certain direct consumer interests, labor unions, and other worker groups. Thus the lines are not always clearly divided into two separate and distinct political camps. Sometimes the public policy debate is framed and divided into two separate efforts. Usually these are coalitions with multiple decision makers who have different public policy interests and different long-term business or positioning goals. This factor makes the political communications much more difficult and often more reactive. Because of these multiple opposing interests, compromises in public policy are usually forged, which sometimes cause the "winners" and "losers" to be indistinct. In traditional political campaigns, it is very clear who won on election day.

In corporate campaigns, election day can be difficult to pinpoint, and there is usually more than one. Sometimes the election days for corporate political efforts are imposed from outside sources and are readily apparent: for example, a legislative body designates a day a vote will be taken on a particular piece of legislation. But many times these election days are moving targets (for example, committee votes) and often have to be imposed or selected by the corporate candidate itself. A corporation could, for instance, determine that a particular meeting of opinion leaders is an election day that must be "won." Yet in practice, in corporate campaigns, there are almost always multiple election days, as, for example, when a legislative committee votes several times on parts of the same bill.

Finally, corporate campaigns usually don't end at the last election day; certain public policy issues will be revisited, and regulatory bodies will continue to monitor activities. Whereas a political candidate's campaign ends definitively in victory or defeat, corporations are generally unable voluntarily to enter and exit the public policy debate. It is an ongoing process that can have a dramatic effect on a corporation's business life.

| Rick | INTERNATIONAL POLITICAL |
| *Rick* | |

Rick
Ridder and INTERNATIONAL POLITICAL
Luther CONSULTING
Symons

Political consultants operating outside the United States have existed for a long time, but American-style consulting has become much more prevalent in the 1990s.* An increasing number of political parties and candidates throughout the world are seeking professional guidance from international consultants in all phases of campaign operations: research/polling, communications, and management.

American consultants and their methods have met with mixed success internationally, however. Some clients have embraced American strategies and have eagerly engaged prominent U.S.-born and trained consultants in their campaigns. Most notable among recent major elections in this regard was Boris Yeltsin's presidential campaign in Russia in 1996, which featured American consultants in principal roles in all major party structures. At the other end of the spectrum, some parties and candidates have shunned U.S. consultants, fearing that open association with "Yankees" would hurt their chances with their electorates. Generally, American consultative roles have fallen in the middle of the two extremes. U.S. consultants are routinely retained to perform a variety of political services and often operate inconspicuously. The result has been an increasing use of American techniques in foreign campaigns and elections.

At the same time, the idea that international consulting is limited to U.S. consultants traveling abroad and exporting American political methods is outdated. Although American consultants may work in a greater number of countries than their international counterparts, many non-U.S. consultants are building impressive client lists outside their home countries. This is especially true in Europe, where consul-

---

*Various trade organizations exist for political professionals operating outside of the United States. The International Association of Political Consultants (IAPC) is the oldest and largest of these groups, having just celebrated its thirtieth anniversary with a membership roster of nearly one hundred from over twenty countries. There are also consultant organizations in Europe (the European Association of Political Consultants) and Latin America (Asociación Latino Americana de Consultores Politicos).

tants routinely work in numerous countries, and Latin and South America, which have thriving consultant communities.

Whatever their origin or bases of initial experiences, cross-border or international consultants (meaning those who operate in a policy-level role in major campaigns in more than one country) face major challenges. Each must be overcome with research, hands-on application, local contacts, and a sensitivity to native political, social, and cultural rules and folkways.

THE VARIETY OF POLITICAL SYSTEMS

Very few nations in the world have electoral systems similar to the dual-party, federal republic system in place in the United States. One of the biggest differences lies between democracies with presidential forms of government and those with parliamentary structures. Within each of these broad categories there are numerous variations among countries. For example, the parliamentary systems in Great Britain and Italy bear little resemblance to each other. Additionally, there are huge differences in the means of determining winners of elections in various nations. Some have a "first past the post" system whereby the winner is the candidate who receives the greatest number of raw votes in a given race. Other systems use proportional representation, allotting seats to parties based on their overall showing in a given election.

For consultants serving clients in more than one nation, creativity and flexibility are extremely important job skills. Adapting techniques to fit the variations in electoral models is critically important for international consulting. Success comes from the ability to provide strategic advice that fits the particular constraints imposed on the candidates or parties by the systems in which they operate.

DIFFERING POLITICAL CULTURES

There are also significant deviations in the political culture of different nations. Many have short campaign periods with elections coming two to three weeks after being called. Others have no particular schedule for elections but rather hold elections at the will of parliaments or prime ministers. These systems contrast with the American model, where campaigns operate in full mode for a year or longer on budgets of hundreds of thousands or millions of dollars. Clearly, the strategic planning and advice given to international clients must be structured to fit the temporal and other restrictions of the election system in which they operate.

Consultants operating in multiple nations must also confront the obstacles posed by the wide variety of campaign finance strategies used in different parts of the world. At one extreme are the government-financed elections in numerous European nations and at the other the "dog-eat-dog" atmosphere that pervades fund-raising in U.S. campaigns. In countries where candidates or parties finance their own operations, consultants must face the reality that increasing amounts of time must be devoted to raising money.

Consultants operating outside the United States also have to accept wide variations in cultural and political customs and norms. Campaign services must be tailored to fit the particular cultural needs determined by the social and political mores of a given nation. Behavior that is acceptable for a candidate in a Western European nation might be totally inappropriate for a candidate running in South America, and vice versa. For instance, in the United Kingdom, candidates wear party ribbons while campaigning. Such adornments in other nations—the United States, for example—would be perceived as silly or an overly lavish display of party allegiance.

Additionally, consultants must structure the advice they give their clients to meet the particular social consequences of multiparty fields in which opposition candidates belong to the same coalition government as the client's candidate. If, for instance, the consultant represents a candidate from a center-left party operating in coalition with a green party, it is often not socially or politically expedient to criticize a green candidate even though he or she is—technically—the direct opposition in the race.

DIFFERING MEDIA AND CONTENT

Perhaps the biggest area of deviation in political operation, and therefore a considerable dilemma for consultants, concerns the communication devices used by candidates and parties in various nations. Whereas television is the undisputed champion in American political communication, it is not an available option in some nations (for example, Sweden prohibits political advertising on television). Consultants thus have to be well versed on media not heavily used in their home country. Newspaper advertising, posters, and other print media, for instance, are much more heavily used outside the United States.

Other communications techniques may or may not be useful in a given country. Direct mail will work well in countries with a reliable postal system and accurate, available lists of voters but is completely ineffective in countries where data on voters are unavailable or postal delivery is unreliable. In one South American nation, for example, consultants were provided with a voter list that lacked addresses or other identifying data for hundreds of thousands of voters. A test sample revealed that fewer than 10 percent of the voters actually received mail at the addresses listed.

Even in electoral systems that allow television advertising for political campaigns, wide differences exist in the nature of the advertising that candidates and parties actually use. Most political television internationally bears little resemblance to the thirty-second spots typically seen in the United States. In many countries, the television spots are longer and many are focused on the party, not the individual candidate. A recent example of a successful media campaign of this type occurred in Germany in 1998, where the Social Democrats ran a sequence of spots that built on the party message of "we are ready" and focused on the themes of security, reliability, and hope. The candidate was not shown in the ads until the final weeks of the campaign. In another instance, recent Brazilian political spots featured scantily clad women and exuded a large dose of sexual energy.

Just as these kinds of ads would not work (or would cause voter backlash) in American elections, typical U.S. issue spots or negative attack ads would be rejected in many foreign countries. For instance, ads attacking a candidate's personal life—which can be successful in the United States—have little effect in countries (e.g., France) where a candidate's personal life is not part of the political dynamic. In all, the lesson is that "cookie-cutter" approaches do not work; the cross-border consultant must understand what forms and content of media are appropriate in each nation.

POLLING AND RESEARCH

In recent years, polling, focus groups, and other forms of qualitative and quantitative research have been increasingly valued in campaigns throughout the world. For consultants providing these services, however, there are once again issues to be faced when confronting various technical and social hurdles that influence the gathering and analysis of data.

While American pollsters can safely assume that virtually every voting household in the nation has an operating telephone, such is not necessarily the case in other parts of the world. Thus pollsters have to adapt data-collection techniques to the methods that work best in the country they are working in. These variations also play a role in communications and field strategies. If there are no accurate voter lists in a country, the difficulties for mail communications and get-out-the-vote efforts are magnified. Additionally, using phone banks to contact voters is not a viable option in countries with spotty phone coverage or unreliable phone lists.

Research can be a particularly trying exercise in Third World areas. One American researcher resigned from a campaign in Papua, New Guinea, because the campaign's research methodology consisted of counting the number of posters for candidates on specific varieties of trees.

MESSAGE DEVELOPMENT

Consultants working worldwide must also recognize the importance of language. These professionals are not only faced with communicating with clients who speak a different language than their own but also with the peculiarities of regional dialects, slang, and other subtleties in crafting political communication in a foreign language. These consultants often have to hire consultants themselves (translators) to serve their foreign clients. These translators must be able to advise not just on wording but on all the nuances of tone, style, metaphor, and allusion that mark effective verbal communication.

Thus perhaps the greatest challenge for any political consultant operating outside his or her home country and culture is to recognize social and cultural norms in each country and to make sure that these broader societal issues are integrated into political strategy and advice. Gender roles, ethnic and regional factions, and other societal determinants must be considered when political professionals supply advice in all strategic areas of any campaign. Examples abound: in Japan, men and women speak in a different tone and vocabulary; in Latin countries, considerable class and regional resentment arises when the "high" speech of government and intellectuals is directed at ordinary people.

Sometimes language can create significant difficulties. For instance, English phrases are not always interpreted consistently in other English-speaking countries. In the United Kingdom, the phrase "knocking up" is used to refer to door-to-door activities, whereas in the United States and Australia, the term has a distinctly different meaning that has little to do with campaign tactics.

Perhaps in no single area of campaign management is the difficulty of using language effectively more apparent than in message development. For a candidate or party to have a winning message, it *must* be tailored to fit the social and cultural fabric of the electorate. The need for a salient campaign message that motivates voters to act affirmatively on behalf of a candidate or party is universal. International consultants are faced with the challenge of helping clients to find that message within the broader social context.

Generally that message is easily recognizable by a good consultant and the campaign management. In 1996, the Australian Democrats needed a slogan to distinguish them from the other two traditional and perceived corrupt parties. After a series of focus groups, the consultant team concluded that the best slogan was one the party used twenty years previously: "We'll keep the bastards honest."

Kim Levine | # GETTING STARTED IN POLITICAL CONSULTING

When someone asks me what I do for a living, an internal dilemma begins. Do I tell them I work for a political consulting firm or a media consulting firm, or do I just cut to the chase and say we make political commercials? Each of these answers provokes a different reaction. If I say "media consulting" I either get a completely blank look or a puzzled smile. I also feel a little deceitful; I am leaving out the word *political.*

In the end, I simply say "political consulting." Politics is the name of our game, it's what we do, it's who we are. But it can cause a person's eyes to glaze over, the smile to turn to a frown or a smirk to appear. Mostly I see the smirk that seems to ask, *"Aren't you people all just a bunch of scoundrels?"*

Usually, I react by asking, "Have you seen those political commercials with candidates asking for your vote on election day?" (The answer is always yes.)

"Well, my firm makes those. Essentially that's what we do."

"No, not all candidates, our firm only works for Democrats."

"No, not all the Democrats. There are a lot of firms that do what we do. We work for various candidates around the country."

"No, not Clinton (at least in the last ten years), and I don't personally know Monica Lewinsky."

At the end of the conversation I am either describing my specific responsibilities or defending my profession. Ultimately, Dick Morris comes up, and I point out he is actually a pollster, not a media consultant. I feel a little bit better.

Inevitably, however, they complain to me about "all those awful attacks" and the "terrible mudslinging" that have become staples of campaign commercials.

No answer I give satisfies them; moreover, I can't really blame them. Television can get pretty ugly during an election season. When you have candidates who have more money than God (our favorite type of client) they can afford to cover the airwaves with positive and negative spots. The tighter a race becomes, the meaner it gets. It can drive a voter mad: mad enough to turn it all off or mad enough to go to the polls and vote for their candidate. Or, as in my case, fascinated enough to want to be a political consultant. In fact, a negative ad made me the woman I am today—but I don't tell the smirkers that.

IN SEARCH OF NEGATIVITY

I spent a semester of college in Washington, D.C., and was required to write a research paper. I had no idea what topic to choose. I was interning at a television station and I was studying politics so I thought, why not take a look at political commercials? I had seen the "Willie Horton" and the "Daisy" ads numerous times in class, and I was interested in learning more about how they affected voters.

Notice it was the two most famous *negative* ads that drew my attention. I couldn't have cared less about Reagan's "Morning in America." I wanted to learn more about mudslinging and opposition research and how to respond to an attack ad. Negative campaign advertising was much more controversial and sexy. Critics maintained that it suppressed voter turnout and cheapened our electoral system, while consultants claimed it could make the difference in a campaign. There was hardly a race in the last few election cycles that didn't use a negative, attack, or comparative spot throughout the campaign. Therefore, I went in search of anyone who could tell me more about the negative ad and its effect on voters.

I read books and trade magazines and talked to political science professors, but it was the consultants I visited and interviewed that drew me to this profession. Their lives and jobs seemed so glamorous. They traveled across the country, and some even did international work as well. They were called to be on political talk shows and quoted in the *Washington Post* and *New York Times*. They knew congressmen, senators, and governors on a first-name basis, and they were part of the Washington elite. I had done a little research in political consulting fees and media buy commissions so I knew political consultants were hardly starving. The industry combined the two things I found most interesting, politics and television (not to mention that my university major and minor were political science and communications, respectively).

I felt I had found my calling. Now, how did I break into it? I had never even worked on a campaign. It was the spring of 1995, only a few states had elections, and I wasn't interested in moving to Louisiana or

Kentucky for the summer. I thought maybe I could just intern with a political consulting firm for the summer. So that's what I did.

It wasn't easy finding a firm that was hiring interns for the summer. I only wanted to work for Democrats, and the shock of the 1994 midterm elections (otherwise known as the year of Newt) was still felt. Newt and his "Contract with America" were at their peak, and Democrats were not happy or looking forward to a prosperous year. It was also the summer of an off-year. This meant there were no federal elections and just a handful of state elections. Most firms concentrated on corporate or international work to pay the bills.

Therefore, in Washington, D.C., the land of free labor, I knew I wasn't going to be making much money. I was right. I worked for a great bunch of guys but was paid only $75 a week. I had to work weekends at a restaurant and baby-sit a couple of nights a week to make ends meet. The firm I worked for didn't have much going on over the summer so I spent a lot of time clipping newspapers and helping reorganize files. But I did learn about television and production and media buying just by being there. I made the most of my time by watching all their demo reels and asking questions, learning who their past clients were and even assisting the media buyer.

I began to get an idea of how the business was run and what a political consultant did. I never had any real hands-on experience, but I learned by watching and listening. Plus, I put the internship on my résumé, and that was the most important thing. I was graduating the next year—1996, a presidential election year. I knew I wanted to be back in D.C. to experience a political consultant's election year, and I can say now, from experience, that it was quite different.

GOING FULL-TIME

Two days after graduation, in the middle of the election season, I started work at another Democratic political consulting firm as an administrative assistant/office manager. My experience the summer before had helped me find a permanent position in Washington. It was entry-level and I was told I was overqualified for the job, but I took it anyway. It was the best thing I ever did.

I walked in on the first day and knew the year was going to be a lot different from the previous summer. The phones were ringing off the hook and everyone seemed frenzied. This was exactly what I was looking for . . . until I was shown the phones, fax machine, travel agent's number, and how to create invoices and make coffee. I was a glorified secretary—at least, that's what I thought at first.

In my first two months I learned three things. Number one, political consulting was a man's world. I worked in an office that was completely male. From the partners to the interns, I was the only woman. It never bothered me, I just took notice and set out to prove myself. I was also the youngest employee. With two strikes against me, I didn't have room to make mistakes. This led me to lesson number two. Anything they asked me to do, I did. And I did it correctly and quickly. From filling out a FedEx form to composing a contract for a new client, I did it without complaining or screwing up. I showed them I could do the easy things efficiently and the difficult tasks correctly. I tried to be the first one there and the last one to leave. I learned to fill vacuums—lesson number three. We are a small firm and sometimes we were short on staff. If I saw that something needed to be done I just did it. I knew that continuing to jump in where I was needed without being asked would lead to opportunities, and within two months it did.

LEARNING THE ROPES

Our commercial shooting schedule in August was a nightmare, and there didn't seem to be anyone available to advance a shoot for our congressional race in Tampa, Florida. Before I knew it I was calling the travel agent to book my ticket to Tampa. I had never advanced a shoot before. I had been on one shoot for Mary Landrieu in Louisiana, but that was just to observe. The partners had enough faith in me to find their locations, round up a crew, build a schedule, and interact with the client. Raymond Strother, the president, came down the night before the shoot, and the next day everything went as scheduled. Before long, I found myself in Wichita, Kansas, advancing a shoot for one of our Senate races.

I was doing two jobs, running the office and advancing shoots. I was able to advance only a couple of shoots because of my responsibilities in the office, but I had gotten a taste of a consultant's life and I liked it.

The next step was learning about postproduction. I started spending more time in post houses, making fixes on TV spots, and producing radio ads. I worked with voice talent, made on-the-fly decisions about script changes, and chose music and special effects. I was still the office manager, but I was learning the ropes. Working in the office allowed me to see the business side of political consulting while working on location and in production facilities introduced me to making television. By election day 1996, I was ready to learn more about strategy, polling, and script writing.

Unfortunately, the next year wasn't really the learning experience for which I had hoped. Those in political consulting know that the business is extremely cyclical, and the year after a presidential election is always slower than a normal off-year. I was lucky enough to have a permanent position at the firm; by January it was just the three partners and me. (To pass the time, I did a lot of surfing on the Internet.) We had a few small races and did some corporate public relations work, but there really wasn't enough business to keep the three partners constantly occupied, let alone me. I'll admit I was frustrated and bored, but 1996 was still fresh in my mind and the guys had promised me great things in 1998. No more invoices or administrative duties. I would be traveling and dealing with clients and their campaigns. Plus, I would be heavily involved in production, from the film/video shoot to the final edit.

In the off-year I saw the steps involved in acquiring new clients. I did a lot of the research in finding out who was running for what and where. I watched the partners reach out to potential candidates and sell themselves. I even went on a couple of pitches (as the token woman). I saw how competitive political consulting had become. Finding races and beating out all the other consultants was not easy. There are so many firms around the country that competition is fierce and can be frustrating. I've heard more than one consultant say he would have to start concentrating on corporate affairs rather than running around trying to find political races. (In the off-year you can hear many consultants grumbling about changing professions.) Fortunately, by the 1997 holiday season we had a great candidate list lined up and things were swinging into high gear.

"YOU'RE GONNA MAKE IT AFTER ALL"

Nothing compares to a political season. It's nonstop action, late nights, and living in airports. And that's just the fun part. In my second political season I accomplished all the things I wanted and more. I actually began to grasp what a political consultant did. Developing a message and sticking to it was just as important as producing television. I discovered what a poll reveals and how that information can help a campaign and its consultants build a message, develop a campaign plan, organize a media buy, and decide what kind of TV spots to run.

My main job was making sure the spots were produced. I traveled around the country over the course of the year. I saw places like Atlanta, Georgia, and Santa Fe, New Mexico, but I also spent my fair share of time in the Arkansas Delta and northern Alabama—not prime vacation spots. The traveling was great but extremely tiring. Arriving at the office with circles under my eyes was a normal occurrence. I put together the shoots on these trips and was under the gun the whole time. If one thing went wrong and a sound person didn't show up or a location became unavailable at the last minute, the shoot could be ruined. Money and time would be lost, and those are two things that are the most sacred and the most scarce in any campaign.

Staying in hotels, eating out, belonging to the Delta Crown Room, and qualifying for million miler status on airlines (I haven't quite made it there yet) can be the perks of the business. But late flights, faulty rental cars, resorting to fast food when on the run, and flaky crew members can drive you insane. It's no wonder election seasons are every other year—we need the off-year to recuperate.

When the shoot is over, the fun begins with hours spent in dark, windowless edit rooms cranking out spot after spot, making sure each one is creative, effective, and different in its own way. Once that's finished and the client and his pollster finally approve the spots (not always an easy process), we have to get them to the stations, making sure they are aired at the right time, during the right program with the right audience. Sometimes by then we've been attacked on air or our opponent has brought up a new issue and another shoot is scheduled. . . . Back to the airport I go.

Political consulting can be brutal. In my two seasons I've seen good people lose and bad people win. I witnessed one client's worst nightmare: finding out midcampaign there was no way to win. Yet I know how good it can feel when your client reaches his or her goal; sharing that goal and working together to achieve it is quite euphoric. (Especially when it dawns on a young consultant that *she* is now starting to know governors, senators, and congressmen on a first-name basis.) It's a tough business for both candidates and consultants. One day you're up and the next day you're down. The rewards are tremendous, but the disappointments are ego-shattering. In the end, your reputation is all you've got. Luckily, the political world we live in is fickle and come-backs happen just as often as personal disasters. There is always an-other election around the corner, and all you have to do is find a candi-date who can win.

Political consulting has become its own industry. Because of the power of TV, the media consultant on a campaign has become some-what of a guru. It doesn't happen overnight. Although it seems many politicos have taken to hanging out a shingle and jumping into the in-dustry, I think it takes more than running a campaign or working for a political group to understand the power of television. The fashion in which I worked my way into consulting is probably rare; most people start out on campaigns or in the press. I just seemed to walk into con-sulting, learning the business side first and then production. I still have much to learn about strategy and the politics of it all. I think as the industry grows larger and consultants continue on the road to political punditville, young people will start out in consulting firms. I am not sure if I recommend my method or means. I was lucky, but one could easily become lost in the administrative shuffle, remaining in a sup-port staff position, laid off every November. Experience a campaign, work for a candidate, and spend an election night when only one race matters. There will be plenty of time to learn the art of producing tele-vision.

And be prepared to deal with those smirkers.

LAWS AND REGULATIONS

Louis A.
Day

POLITICAL ADVERTISING
AND THE FIRST AMENDMENT

During the fall 1998 Sixth District congressional race in Louisiana, Republican incumbent Richard Baker aggressively defended himself against a Democratic Party–sponsored television ad accusing him of voting to cut Medicare and raid the Social Security Trust Fund. Apparently fatigued by such negative campaign tactics, WBRZ-TV in Baton Rouge decided to pull the plug on the ad just before the election. The station cited the lack of adequate response time to last-minute attack ads as justification for the decision.

Although the Democratic Party defended the claims as "absolutely true," even Baker's opponent, Democratic challenger Marjorie Mc-Keithen, applauded the decision and said that she favored changing federal election law to eliminate all such "third-party" attack ads in the sixty days leading up to the election. Such suggestions mirror the perennial debate surrounding government's role in ensuring that the channels of political communication remain uncorrupted and whether such government initiatives are even constitutional. Or to put it another way, has the quality of political campaigns degenerated to such a point that our confidence in the marketplace of ideas (rather than government regulation) as the final arbiter of political truth has been severely eroded? If so, should government have a role in restoring some degree of decorum to political campaigning? How far may government go in regulating false and deceptive political advertising without running afoul of the First Amendment?

Since John Milton proclaimed confidently more than 350 years ago that truth would always trump falsehood in a free and open encounter in the public square, philosophers, politicians, and constitutional scholars have debated the wisdom of that prophecy. Even Justice Oliver Wendell Holmes, who enshrined the Miltonian philosophy in his "marketplace of ideas" metaphor in opposition to government censorship, was skeptical that truth would always prevail. In contemporary democracies in particular, the cacophony of voices is too great, the political competition too intense, and the respect for truth too fragile to assume a laissez-faire posture with regard to the regulation of speech.

As the thirty-second commercial and the ten-second soundbyte

67

have replaced political discourse as the weapons of choice in winning public office, the marketplace analogy now appears to be a philosophical anachronism. The prevalence of negative campaign strategies, sometimes inspired by controversial attack ads, has frequently blurred the distinction between truth and falsehood in the collective mind of the electorate.

Of course, the brutality of American political campaigns did not begin with the current genre of attack ads employed by some campaign strategists. George Washington may have been the father of our country, but that did not impress his political opponents, who accused him of having monarchical aspirations. The attacks on Thomas Jefferson were even more vituperative. His detractors accused him not only of being an atheist and a madman but an *illegitimate* atheist and madman. Abraham Lincoln was described variously in the press as a buffoon, fiend, lunatic, robber, savage, and traitor. Such unflattering portrayals, including false accusations of political malfeasance or moral turpitude, have continued unabated, but modern politicians are less inclined to ignore such attacks than their early predecessors. Some have responded with aggressive campaigns of their own, including attack ads; a few have taken more drastic measures by invoking state libel laws or campaign falsity statutes.

Since censorship is anathema to democratic systems and yet the democratic process depends on a reliable flow of truthful information, how to deal with deliberate falsehoods or other communications strategies within a constitutional framework is a persistent paradox. In the United States, political falsehoods are dealt with primarily through libel laws and state campaign falsity statutes. Although defamatory falsehoods are the stuff of private litigation, and campaign falsity statutes involve government regulation, the two are not entirely discrete venues. As we shall see, the Supreme Court has "constitutionalized" the law of libel, a legal revolution that has informed legislative efforts to deal with false campaign rhetoric.

DEFAMATORY FALSEHOODS IN POLITICAL ADVERTISING

Defamation is defined as a false statement of fact that is likely to injure someone's reputation. To prevail in a defamation suit, a candidate must prove, among other things, that the charges are false and that they involve questions of fact, not mere opinion. In addition, the accusations or representations must be of a kind that are not merely critical of a candidate's performance, political views, or voting record but are likely to injure the candidate's reputation.

Until 1964, defamation was essentially an equal opportunity tort. The common law of libel did not distinguish between public officials and private parties in establishing the burden of proof. But the landmark decision of *Sullivan v. New York Times*, handed down in 1964, raised the barriers significantly against libel suits by public officials. The case began when a committee of civil rights activists in the South placed a full-page political ad in the *New York Times* accusing police in Montgomery, Alabama, of carrying out a "wave of terrorism" against peaceful student demonstrators. It also charged authorities with the bombing of the home of Martin Luther King, Jr., and harassing him with several arrests for minor offenses. The ad contained a number of inaccuracies, however, and L. B. Sullivan, the commissioner responsible for the police department, sued the *Times* for libel. A jury awarded Sullivan $500,000 in damages and the Alabama Supreme Court affirmed. In 1964, however, the U.S. Supreme Court reversed, holding for the first time that the First Amendment limits the authority of states to award libel damages to public officials unless they can prove that the defamatory falsehoods are published with actual malice, that is, the knowledge that they are false or demonstrate/display a reckless disregard for the truth of the publication. This ruling was later extended to public figures.

The *Sullivan* case was the opening salvo in what would become a revolution in the application of the First Amendment to civil litigation against the media, but it is particularly relevant to the topic under discussion. Under *Sullivan*, the media have been practically immunized against defamatory falsehoods contained in political advertisements unless they know the claims are false or "publish" with reckless disregard of whether the information is false. In legalese, this is known as "actual malice."

But what about the candidates themselves? The weight of opinion suggests that candidates who sue their opponents for defamation must also prove actual malice. In other words, they must show that their opponent's ad included a statement about the plaintiff that was factually false and that the other candidate either knew it was false or published (or broadcast) it with a reckless disregard of its falsity. The line between a fact and an opinion, from a legal perspective, is not always a bright one, however, and courts are inclined to interpret statements, even those that to the average person appear to be provably true or false, to be expressions of opinion, thus removing them from the sanction of state libel law.

GOVERNMENT REGULATION OF POLITICAL ADVERTISING

Campaign Advertising: Political or Commercial Speech?

Any meaningful discussion of government regulation of false political advertising must begin with the realization that political ads are really a hybrid of the two most prominent forms of speech in American society: political speech (that which informs our public debate) and advertising, or as the Supreme Court refers to it, "commercial speech." In their most noble moments, such ads can service the political system by providing valuable information on a candidate's views and platform and can enrich the voters' arsenal of political knowledge during a campaign. Yet there is an unmistakable resemblance between commercial and political advertising in their format and techniques—so much so that political ads are frequently referred to derisively as the "packaging" of candidates.

From a legal perspective, whether political ads, which are designed to "sell" candidates to the electorate, are considered commercial or political speech is significant. In the United States, false political speech, even defamatory falsehoods, receives some constitutional protection. On the other hand, states and the federal government are free to regulate false advertising without any serious constitutional consequences. The selling of toothpaste, it seems, doesn't command the same respect as the day's political intelligence. But when political speech is combined with commercial speech—or, to put it more indelicately, when candidates are packaged like shaving cream or Hormel sausage—some interesting legal questions are posed, the most significant of which is, For the purpose of government regulation, should campaign ads be treated like political speech or commercial advertising?

Commercial advertising is constitutionally protected only when it embodies a truthful message for a lawful product. The regulation of false advertising by the Federal Trade Commission (FTC) poses no *serious* First Amendment issue. On the other hand, false political speech is fully protected under the First Amendment as long as it is done without "actual malice," as defined in the *Sullivan* decision.

The Supreme Court has left little doubt as to where political ads fall in the constitutional scheme of things. As early as 1964, in the *Sullivan* decision, the Court rejected the argument that speech that communicates information of public interest loses its constitutional protection simply because it is conveyed in the form of an advertisement. Thus a voter who believes that he or she has been misled by a political ad has no recourse before the courts, the FTC, or the Better Business Bureau.

Nevertheless, campaign reform is perennially attractive to voters, and some state legislatures have not awaited the Supreme Court's benediction in attempting to impose some decorum on the political process. In so doing, they have had to walk a tightrope between regulating the most egregious abuses of political advertising and protecting the public square from the oppressive hand of government regulation.

State Regulation of False Political Advertising

About a third of the states (seventeen) have statutes that prohibit or regulate deceptive campaign speech, which of course includes false political advertising. These laws differ significantly in their scope and purpose. For example, statutes in nine states apply to both written and oral communications. The other eight states regulate only false political speech in written form. Three specifically limit the type of written statement covered. For example, Minnesota's statute restricts only paid political advertisements, campaign material, and letters to the editor. North Dakota limits false political ads and news releases, whereas Tennessee covers only campaign literature. The remaining campaign falsity statutes make no distinction as to the type of written false statement prohibited.

In addition to a threshold showing of falsity, several statutes demand proof of additional elements as a prerequisite to a violation. Both the Nebraska and Oregon laws, for example, require that the false statement relate to a *material fact*. In Alaska, Mississippi, and Montana statutory violations are limited to those that are defamatory under the common law, that is, those that are injurious to reputation. A majority of the states with campaign falsity statutes (ten) require that the false statement be designed or have the tendency to affect the vote on a candidate or ballot question. The sanctions for statutory violations, as might be expected, vary from state to state. For example, in Louisiana, in addition to a misdemeanor penalty, an affected candidate or voter is entitled to an injunction against future violations of the law. Several states provide for the invalidation of an election or removal from office of the winning candidate if he or she is found to have knowingly made a false statement during the campaign. Even here, however, there is one significant exception. Every state has a constitutional provision similar to Article I, Section 5, of the U.S. Constitution, which provides that the legislature is to be the sole judge of the qualifications of its members. Thus courts have no jurisdiction in this area because of the separation of powers doctrine.

Despite what appears to be an impressive regulatory scheme for false political speech, the overall effectiveness of such statutes is dubious. The case law in this area is limited to fewer than three dozen cases in six states. Based on the reported cases, however, two trends have emerged. First, appellate courts have applied a rule of strict construction to campaign fraud statutes, thus resisting the temptation to expand the coverage beyond the specific language of such statutes. At the same time, they have frequently interpreted allegedly false campaign statements in such a way as to place them beyond the reach of state law. For example, since all of the statutes are directed at false statements of fact (rather than opinion or commentary), some courts have gone to extraordinary lengths to construe political statements as opinion or commentary rather than assertions of fact. A case in point is a decision from the Wisconsin Supreme Court. When a candidate for sheriff suggested that his opponent was a "love pirate" and a "demoralizer of homes" (because he allegedly had written a questionable letter to a married woman), the court decided the statements fell within the field of political commentary.

When statements are ambiguous—they might be interpreted as fact or opinion—courts are unlikely to find campaign falsity violations. For example, when a *former* elected official, in challenging an incumbent for a different office, used the slogan "Return a Proven Leader," the Oregon Supreme Court found the slogan susceptible of two inferences: one false (that the candidate was the incumbent) and one true (that the candidate had served before in public office). The court held that the ambiguous statement was not false as long as any reasonable and truthful inference could be derived from it.

Nevertheless, the line between fact and opinion and truth and deception is not always clear, from a legal perspective, and for this reason courts have been sensitive to the dangers of censorship under state campaign falsity statutes. The inescapable conclusion is that the effectiveness of such statutes has been severely limited or even eviscerated through judicial construction.

Statutory construction aside, opponents of state regulation of false political speech (including advertising) argue that such statutes are unconstitutional. Although the U.S. Supreme Court has never specifically addressed the issue, there is no direct precedent for the notion that banning the deliberate misrepresentation of facts in political communication is, in itself, unconstitutional. Besides, all the statutes appear to conform, in one way or another, to the standard set forth in the *Sullivan* decision that defamatory falsehoods against political candidates are constitutionally protected unless they are uttered with *actual malice*, that is, knowledge of falsity or reckless disregard for the truth of the statements.

State Regulation of Truthful Ads

The regulation of truthful political ads, of course, does implicate core First Amendment values, and state laws and municipal ordinances that serve to regulate the *content* of political messages violate the First Amendment. For example, the Mississippi Corrupt Practices Act, designed to control election eve accusations, prohibits the making of any charge against a candidate, *whether true or false*, during the five-day period before an election. The inclusion of *truthful* communications, no matter how intemperate they might be, strikes at the core of the First Amendment and, if tested in court, would probably be quickly dispatched as a regulatory mechanism for political speech.

Mandates that regulate the time, place, and manner of distribution are constitutional, as long as they are content-neutral and serve some significant governmental objective and as long as there are alternative venues for candidates to express their views. For example, a ban on all billboard advertising to preserve the beauty of the community would withstand constitutional scrutiny as long as the ban was not directed just at political ads.

Anonymous Ads

Some states have attempted to promote rational voting behavior by requiring that candidates disclose additional information. For example, under the banner of the "public's right to know," many states have banned anonymous political ads. Such initiatives are predicated on the asserted government objectives of deterring both false attacks on candidates and falsely attributed statements, facilitating rebuttal by candidates to false statements, and providing voters with sufficient information to assess campaign appeals. The California Supreme Court, in rejecting a challenge to that state's campaign disclosure statute, probably reflected the views of most state courts in observing that there is no constitutional right to hoodwink voters.

As early as 1960, however, the U.S. Supreme Court, in a case that also originated in California, held that anonymous speech is constitutionally protected, and in 1995, in *McIntyre v. Ohio Elections Commission*, the Court extended that principle to state regulation of anonymous *political* speech. "The right to remain anonymous may be abused when it shields fraudulent conduct," declared the Court in invalidating an Ohio statute that prohibited the distribution of anonymous campaign literature, "but political speech by its nature will sometimes have unpalatable consequences, and, in general, our society accords greater weight to the value of free speech than to the dangers of its misuse." This principle *does not* apply to the broadcast media, which are governed by federal sponsorship.

Political Advertising and Media Access

State legislatures have focused most of their attention on campaign falsehoods rather than ensuring a candidate's access to the public square through advertising. While such statutes would appear to "enhance" rather than "abridge" the First Amendment's intent of ensuring an unfettered political marketplace, in 1974 the Supreme Court held that a governmentally mandated right of access to the print media is unconstitutional. A different constitutional paradigm is applied to the electronic media, however, which are governed by the Federal Communications Act of 1934, as amended. Section 315 of the act requires that, when a broadcast licensee allows a "legally qualified" candidate for a given office to "use" his or her facilities, the licensee must provide "equal opportunity" to *all* other candidates for that office. Section 315 applies to all appearances by a political candidate except during bona fide news programs and interviews. The exact meaning of equal opportunity has been the subject of adjudication by the Federal Communications Commission (FCC), but it essentially means that all candidates for the same office must be treated alike. For example, if state senatorial candidate "A" purchases fifty minutes of airtime on Channel 10, all other candidates must be provided with the *opportunity* to buy an equal amount of time (hence the common reference to Section 315 as the "equal time" law, although the term never appears in the statute). Similarly, if Candidate "A" seeks maximum exposure by scheduling all of his spots in prime time, all of Candidate "A's" opponents must be afforded the same opportunity. And so on.

Section 315 does *not* obligate a broadcast licensee to sell or otherwise provide time to candidates for any given race at the state and local levels, but Section 312 of the act requires broadcasters to provide "reasonable access" for candidates for *federal* elective office. In other words, a broadcaster may not, as a matter of policy, refuse to make time available (either through commercial spots or otherwise) to candidates for Congress or president and vice-president.

Does the "equal opportunities" requirement apply to supporters of political candidates? In 1970, in response to an inquiry from a congressional staff member, the FCC declared that when a station provides time to supporters of a candidate during a campaign, the station is obligated to offer equal opportunities to supporters of opposing candidates. Two years later, however, the commission limited this requirement to the major party candidates, thus relieving broadcasters of the obligation to accommodate requests from supporters of minor party or fringe candidates. Interestingly, while the FCC requires that groups who do "issue ads" (such as supporters of candidates) must document the accuracy of their claims, candidates themselves are not subject to such restraints.

Voter apathy continues to be the Achilles' heel of the world's most democratic nation. Voter turnout for the 1998 midterm elections, for example, was among the lowest in history. Critics attribute much of the political cynicism to increasingly negative campaigns that rely almost exclusively on emotional rather than rational appeals, the most egregious manifestation of which is the attack ads. Although the reasons are certainly more complex than just the tone of political ads and commercials, some states have attempted to reverse the trend through simplified registration procedures or the use of mail-in ballots (e.g., in 1995 Oregon became the first state to conduct a statewide election for federal office solely by mail ballot). While such initiatives are commendable from the standpoint of increasing the number of ballots cast, they do not guarantee a better informed citizenry or one that is less cynical about the political process or the candidates who aspire to public office.

Some states have attempted to instill a certain amount of virtue into political campaigns through various regulatory devices, but for the most part government oversight has been either ineffective or of dubious constitutional validity. Perhaps the most reasonable solution is self-regulation, with sanctions imposed by the court of public opinion rather than a court of law. For example, a few states already employ voluntary codes of fair campaign practices. Under such arrangements, a voluntary code is established and candidates agree in advance to abide by this code or perhaps just particular sections of the code. Citizens' committees can serve as a clearinghouse for complaints from aggrieved candidates. The committees evaluate the complaints and release their findings to the news media to ensure maximum coverage.

For those states searching for strategies to impose some degree of ethical decorum on the political process, a worthy prototype (or at least a point of departure) can be found in the Code of Professional Ethics of the American Association of Political Consultants. There are nine points to this code, but two are particularly relevant to the present discussion. An association member pledges not to "indulge in any activity which would corrupt or degrade the practice of political campaigning." More specifically, an association member promises to "refrain from false or misleading attacks on an opponent or a member of his or her family and [to] do everything in my power to prevent others from using such tactics."

Although self-regulation is not a panacea for cultivating the moral virtue of political campaigns, it can serve as a formidable alternative to government regulation, as well as an effective public relations instrument in restoring the voters' confidence in the political process.

SUGGESTED READINGS

Fueroghne, D. K. *Law and Advertising*. Chicago: Copy Workshop, 1995.

Hall, J. A. "When Political Campaigns Turn to Slime: Establishing a Virginia Fair Campaign Practices Committee." *Journal of Law and Politics* 7 (1990–91): 353–77.

Neel, R. F., Jr. "Campaign Hyperbole: The Advisability of Legislating False Statements out of Politics." *Journal of Law and Politics* 2 (1985): 405–24.

Winbro, J. "Misrepresentation in Political Advertising: The Role of Legal Sanctions." *Emory Law Journal* 36 (1987): 853–916.

Wright, J. S. "Money and the Pollution of Politics: Is the First Amendment an Obstacle to Equality?" *Columbia Law Review* 82 (1982): 609–45.

Ronald
Garay

POLITICIANS AND
TELEVISION TIME

There are approximately 98 million television-owning households in the United States. In late 1998, persons in these households had access to roughly 3,650 television stations and 11,600 cable television systems. Moreover, approximately 12,276 radio stations reached a listening audience in millions of American homes and automobiles. Candidates running for public office during the 1998 fall elections were predicted to spend nearly a billion dollars buying time on these television and radio stations and cable systems in hopes of reaching their massive audience.

Only persons who have lived their lives in total isolation would fail to see the connections between politics and the electronic mass media. Members of the U.S. Congress, especially, have come to rely on television and radio and such emerging media as the Internet to communicate with the American public. Their message has been either an institutional one about the business of the U.S. Senate or House of Representatives or a personal one about a position on legislative matters or a campaign statement. And only when airtime has been purchased can a congressman's message go unedited. Otherwise, that message is subject to the filtering influence of such "gatekeepers" as news reporters, editors, and producers.

KEEPING IN TOUCH: THE INSTITUTION

Radio first became a means for Congress to speak directly to the American public in 1922. Radio broadcasting was not yet widespread (America's first radio station, KDKA in Pittsburgh, had begun operations only in 1920), but several congressmen nonetheless introduced legislation aimed at broadcasting House and Senate floor proceedings to listeners nationwide. The effort failed, primarily because of technical barriers and cost, and little serious attention was given to the matter for the next quarter-century. During that period, however, the two major radio networks, NBC and CBS, maintained standing policies of allowing free airtime upon request to members of Congress.

Attention returned to congressional broadcasting in the post–World War II years when television became a mass medium. Congress's more relaxed view toward electronic coverage coupled with the television industry's eagerness to experiment with programming ideas meant that the time was ripe for Americans to have their first electronic peek at legislative business. That peek finally came in the late 1940s when Congress opened not its floor proceedings but rather its committee proceedings to television. Senate Crime Committee hearings in 1951 caused a sensation when committee chairman Estes Kefauver opened them to television cameras. Equally sensational were telecasts of the Army-McCarthy hearings in 1954. Besides giving such hearings far greater exposure than they likely would have received otherwise, television also boosted the celebrity of hearing participants. Estes Kefauver, for instance, rose from committee chair to presidential contender in 1952.

As successful as committee hearings were in publicizing specific issues, Congress began to fall behind the president during the 1960s and 1970s in using television to address the public on important issues. Presidents Kennedy, Johnson, and Nixon were particularly astute at using television to speak directly to the American people.

Congress responded to this institutional imbalance in 1973 by establishing the Joint Committee on Congressional Operations that, among other things, began serious investigation of implementing televised coverage of House and Senate chamber proceedings. The committee found little reason to continue barring television cameras from congressional chambers, and as a result the U.S. House voted in 1977 to allow such access. Not until March 1979, however, would live televised coverage begin.

The U.S. Senate was not as quick as the House to televise its floor debate. One reason was a feeling shared by several Senate veterans that their chamber's procedural rules might create a negative public image of the body. For instance, senators are free to speak as long as they desire on whatever topic they choose. And senators engaged in the traditional filibuster as a means of blocking legislation have been known to read entire books aloud to avoid relinquishing the floor to their opponents.

Senators Howard Baker and Robert Byrd argued that despite procedural issues, the Senate stood to gain far more than it would lose by televising its proceedings. The arguments proved convincing, and Senate sessions began to be televised in 1986. Television feeds from both the Senate and House were made available to any television station or network wishing to carry them. In addition, the cable television industry created a unique program service called the Cable-Satellite Public Affairs Network (C-SPAN) to carry live congressional debates to households receiving cable television.

KEEPING IN TOUCH: THE INDIVIDUAL

One reason Congress agreed to televise coverage of its proceedings was to improve its public image. That has yet to happen, though, as opinion polls consistently place the institutional popularity of Congress below that of the president. Even in late 1998, when the U.S. House prepared to conduct impeachment hearings against President Bill Clinton, a Gallup Poll showed that the president's 60+ percent approval rating was nearly 20 percentage points above that of Congress.

A phenomenon of opinion polling is that the public traditionally thinks more highly of individual members of Congress than of the collective Congress. Part of the reason for this is that members of Congress begin from their first arrival in Washington to establish themselves as independent voices. And television has assisted their efforts. Congressional hearings were for many years the foremost means by which U.S. senators and representatives brought attention to themselves. Reporters have noted that committee members' attendance at hearings often coincided with the presence of television cameras.

Perhaps remembering the free time that radio networks afforded members of Congress in earlier years, Senator William Fulbright introduced legislation in the late 1960s that would mandate television networks to provide free time periodically to congressional spokespersons to present House and Senate views on important public issues. The Fulbright measure met opposition from persons who believed it was futile to suppose that one or only a few persons could represent the collective views of Congress. More important, though, the powerful National Association of Broadcasters, representing television and radio station owners on whom members of Congress relied for support, regarded the Fulbright proposal as an intrusion on the First Amendment and an unnecessary invasion of broadcasters' programming prerogatives. The troublesome measure never moved beyond committee, and nothing similar has emerged from Congress since.

Failure to legislate a congressional "right of access" to television did not mean that U.S. senators and representatives lacked the resources or the creativity to achieve some access to radio, television, and cable. There are at least three means at their disposal for getting their voices and images to the public and, most important, to constituents.

The first of these for U.S. House members comes courtesy of the short speeches made from the House floor either before or immediately following each day's legislative business. Called "one-minute speeches" at the beginning of the day or "special order speeches" at day's end, these brief statements allow House members to address colleagues on topics ranging from the mundane to the significant. Such comments make perfect soundbytes that radio or television stations may record for later airing. Special order speeches have become particularly partisan in recent years, and House members who have used them effectively, such as Representative Newt Gingrich, have risen from obscurity to prominence.

Many U.S. radio and television stations may send their own reporters to Washington or rely on "stringers" for news about Congress, and all major networks have at least one congressional correspondent. These reporters have access to U.S. senators and representatives in their offices and in small House and Senate radio and television gallery studios. In 1994, radio talk show hosts were even provided facilities in the Capitol basement from which to originate their programs.

The U.S. House and Senate both maintain well-appointed recording studios for their respective members to record programs and interviews that may then be provided to radio and television stations in their home districts. The studios also may link members of Congress to local stations via satellite for live interviews. Both the Republican and Democratic Parties now maintain their own recording facilities in Washington complete with satellite uplinks.

REACHING THE VOTER

Members of Congress make few radio and television "performance-of-duty" appearances that are not infused with some degree of self-aggrandizement, for elected officials nearly always are looking to the next election. And now more than ever, a candidate's success is measured by how effectively he or she uses radio and television. "You cannot run for major office nowadays," according to writer Max Frankel, "without spending millions for television commercials that spread your fame, shout your slogans, denounce your opponents and counteract television attacks." Indeed, the sums of money required to finance a political campaign have become so great in recent years that illegal or simply questionable activities associated with fund-raising have become more prevalent. And since so much campaign money is earmarked for the electronic media, reformers have begun searching for ways to reduce that expense and, thus, the fund-raising burden.

One obvious way of relieving that burden is for radio and television stations and cable television systems to provide candidates for federal elective office free airtime. The major television networks provided limited free time for major party presidential candidates during the 1996 election. Free time for congressional candidates, however, is rare because it must come from local broadcasters and cablecasters who generally are unwilling to give away time that could otherwise generate advertising revenue.

Efforts to mandate free airtime for congressional candidates seemed promising in 1997, when a campaign finance reform bill sponsored by Senators John McCain (R-Arizona) and Russell Feingold (D-Wisconsin) included a provision that would have provided free airtime for candidates who agreed to observe certain campaign spending limits. The provision was dropped, however, after broadcasters complained that it violated the First Amendment.

Current legal responsibilities and parameters for using radio, television, and cable television facilities for political campaign announcements and programs are embedded in Sections 312 and 315 of the Communications Act of 1934. The Communications Act, despite several major revisions through the years, remains the foundation law for regulating the electronic media in the United States. Section 312 of the act requires that legally qualified candidates for federal elective office be provided reasonable access to station and cable facilities, and Section 315 requires that legally qualified opponents of these candidates be afforded equal opportunities to use such facilities. The Federal Communications Commission has defined "legally qualified candidate" as any person who "has publicly announced his or her intention to run for nomination or office" and "is qualified under the applicable local, State or Federal law to hold the office for which he or she is a candidate."

Broadcasters and cablecasters also are prohibited from censoring any comments aired under Section 315's authority. Moreover, a candidate's appearance in a bona fide newscast, news interview, news documentary, or on-the-spot coverage of a bona fide news event exempts broad-casters and cablecasters from equal opportunity requirements. Most important monetarily is the Section 315 requirement that candidates be charged the lowest unit rate for time purchased.

Candidates are also turning to newer forms of electronic mass media such as the Internet to counteract the impact of issue ads. Internet campaign items can be more lengthy than paid campaign commercials or free campaign coverage by the news media, and Internet-based content is not subjected to any news media gatekeeping control. In fact, a 1998 *Campaigns & Elections* survey indicated that a growing number of candidates are using the Internet not only to distribute campaign information but also to communicate directly with voters via electronic mail. The survey found that roughly 71 percent of those running for congressional offices in 1998 had their own World Wide Web site.

Reference to the Internet's use in political campaigns brings this chapter full circle, for the Internet is beginning to revolutionize the performance-of-duty communication routines of U.S. House and Senate members. In 1995, the U.S. House inaugurated a system enabling House documents to be accessed via the Internet. That system has since progressed to the THOMAS Web site that makes a wide variety of congressional documents from both the Senate and House available to Internet users.

Can electronic mass media technologies and delivery systems that range from the Internet to C-SPAN make Congress more effective and more responsive to the needs of U.S. citizens? This and similar questions were pondered during a 1996 House hearing titled *21st Century Congress.* Hearing participants were less than optimistic about congressional use of electronic mass media in the next century. Problems foreseen were not ones of ineffectiveness, as might be expected, but rather ones of overabundance. Simply put, the electronic mass media are evolving in such ways that their use, unless carefully and thoughtfully planned and managed, could well transform the U.S. Capitol of the twenty-first century into a modern-day Tower of Babel.

SUGGESTED READINGS

Frantzick, Stephen E. *The C-SPAN Revolution.* Norman: University of Oklahoma Press, 1996.

Garay, Ronald. "Broadcasting of Congressional Proceedings." In Donald C. Bacon et al., eds., *The Encyclopedia of the United States Congress*, Vol. 1. New York: Simon & Schuster, 1995.

———. *Congressional Television: A Legislative History*. Westport, Conn.: Greenwood Press, 1984.

Hess, Stephen. *Live from Capitol Hill!: Studies of Congress and the Media*. Washington, D.C.: The Brookings Institution, 1991.

National Association of Broadcasters. *Political Broadcast Catechism*. 14th ed. Washington, D.C.: National Association of Broadcasters, 1996.

Edward Zuckerman

PACs AND CAMPAIGN FINANCE

During the 1997–98 election cycle, candidates for the U.S. House and Senate collectively spent over $650 million. Only about $100 million of these funds were supplied or borrowed by the candidate or his or her campaign. The rest of the money was donated by political parties and a mind-boggling array of more than four thousand federally registered political action committees (PACs) which pursue legislative and ideological goals of every imaginable stripe.

This system is a novelty: until only recently, political money flowed from a relatively small circle of wealthy benefactors whose secret payments were used by political parties to meet election day voter turnout expenses. Today, the circle of donors has been greatly expanded (even laborers, bartenders, and merchant seamen use their collective power to make contributions that can match those made by captains of industry) and the fund-raising franchise has spread to every candidate's own campaign committee.

Probably more surprising to the average voter is the relatively recent affirmation that raising and giving money to a political candidate is constitutionally protected. When it concluded in its 1976 *Buckley v. Valeo* opinion that the First Amendment cannot tolerate a limit on how much money a person or group could spend to influence an election, the U.S. Supreme Court argued:

> A restriction on the amount of money a person or group can spend on political communication during a campaign necessarily reduces the quantity of expression by restricting the number of issues discussed, the depth of their exploration, and the size of the audience reached. This is because virtually every means of communicating ideas in today's mass society requires the expenditure of money. The distribution of the humblest handbill or leaflet entails printing, paper and circulation costs. Speeches and rallies generally necessitate hiring a hall and publicizing the event. The electorate's increasing dependence on television, radio and other mass media for news and information has made these expensive modes of communication indispensable instruments of effective political speech.

To drive home the point, the Court added in an oft-quoted footnote: "Being free to engage in unlimited political expression subject to a ceiling on expenditures is like being free to drive an automobile as far and as often as one desires on a single tank of gasoline."

Nevertheless, the majority of Americans agree that the present system is unfair and imbalanced. To the questions, "Do we need campaign finance reform?" and "Is there too much special interest money spent on politics?" Americans will answer a resounding "yes." Such poll results, however, need to be interpreted with care. "Special interests" turn out to be anybody *except* the industry, union, or issue that the respondent is a member of or gives money to. In addition, most polls produce majorities who support "public funds" but oppose "taxpayer funds" for financing election campaigns. Usually, those who favor public funds change their minds when informed that it is a euphemism for "taxpayer funds." The clearest indication for lack of public support for taxpayer-funded elections is the declining number of taxpayers who designate $3 of their taxes to help finance elections. Such numbers indicate a disconnect on the issue. Understanding the actual rather than the mythic nature of campaign finance and PACs thus becomes crucial to any rational discussion of the merits and failings of the current—or any possible future—system of politics and money in America.

REFORM AND COUNTERREFORM

The first effort by Congress to impose a restriction on how its elections could be financed, the 1907 Tillman Act prohibiting corporations from making contributions or expenditures in federal elections, was approved with seemingly little resistance. But its enactment by voice vote after a perfunctory debate in the House, and by unanimous consent in the Senate, belies its origins in the Progressive reform movement, which were aptly described by one historian as "a struggle between the robbers and the robbed."

Impetus for the 1907 law's enactment—apart from a political climate that also produced major reform laws such as those dealing with child labor, antitrust, and meat inspection—sprang from several sources. Key among them were a series of articles titled "Treason in the Senate" revealing corruption and perfidy to the mass circulation readership of William Randolph Hearst's *Cosmopolitan* magazine in 1906 and the previous year's investigation by the New York legislature that exposed insurance company payments to the state political parties. The 1907 Tillman Act remains in force today, as a section of the Federal Election Campaign Act along with other congressional enactments, particularly the 1943 War Disputes Act (Smith-Connally) and the 1947 Labor-Management Relations Act (Taft-Hartley), which temporarily and later permanently extended the corporate prohibition to labor unions.

The ban on labor union contributions was meant to deny a source of financial support for President Franklin D. Roosevelt's unprecedented 1944 reelection to a fourth term. But John L. Lewis, then president of both the Congress of Industrial Organizations and the United Mine Workers of America, dodged the ban against using union treasury funds by establishing the National Coalminer's Political Action Committee to raise voluntary contributions for Roosevelt's campaign. The U.S. Supreme Court upheld the collection of voluntarily contributed political funds as protected by the First Amendment.

In 1971, following years of debate, Congress enacted the Federal Election Campaign Act to require candidates and political committees to make public disclosure of their receipts and expenditures, as well as to identify donors and vendors who gave or were paid more than $200. The law took effect on April 7, 1972, provoking a last-minute rush by candidates to raise money that would not be subject to public disclosure.

Reacting to abuses that were exposed during the Watergate scandal, Congress rewrote the 1971 law by setting limits on contributions and expenditures. Soon after its enactment, a group of opponents led by Senator James Buckley (R-New York) challenged the law's constitutionality (Francis X. Valeo, the suit's first-named defendant, was the secretary of the Senate). The result was the landmark opinion cited above.

The Court, however, drew a distinction between a candidate's expenditures and a supporter's contributions and determined that large contributions could be subject to reasonable limits to help eliminate actual or perceived corruption. Congress repaired the law's constitutional infirmities by deleting the spending limit provisions and repassing it in time for the 1976 elections.

Because of the *Buckley* decision and Congress's quick-fix response, the last quarter-century's elections have been regulated by a disproportionate campaign finance system that was originally envisioned by its designers to strike a balance between political contributions and expenditures.

Yet campaign finance statistics collected since the 1971 law's enactment show quite impressively that most elections are won by candidates who outspent their opponents. Still, there have been many candidates who were defeated by lesser-funded opponents who nevertheless raised enough money to communicate their views and qualifications to voters. It cannot be said that having a lot of money guarantees victory, but it can be said that having no money guarantees defeat.

Regardless, the data collected from the last dozen elections provide inescapable evidence of unfairness. The political finance system has evolved into one that rewards those candidates who can raise small contributions from a large number of donors. With rare exceptions, the system benefits incumbent lawmakers who can draw contributions from a national donor network and, conversely, penalizes challengers who usually draw the bulk of their campaign funds from highly localized donor pools. This institutionalized fund-raising imbalance between incumbents and challengers is often cited among reasons why 95 percent or more of all incumbents succeed in their reelection campaigns. It is also a main complaint of advocates for campaign finance reform who claim new legislation is needed to "level the playing field" and enable challengers to wage competitive campaigns.

CURRENT REGULATIONS

Today, whether gathered by passing a hat in a union meeting hall or selling $1,000 tickets to a reception in a corporate boardroom, all money that is raised and spent in connection with federal elections must comply with stringent government regulations. These "birth-to-death" rules, which are administered and enforced by the Federal Election Commission (FEC), cover every conceivable aspect of soliciting, collecting, depositing, and spending money by candidates, political parties, and PACs. The law and the FEC's implementing regulations require that every dollar be contributed by an individual who is a U.S. citizen and that all receipts and expenditures be fully disclosed in a timely manner.

Under the laws and regulations in effect for the last twenty-five years, no person can contribute more than $1,000 to a federal candidate's election, more than $20,000 during a calendar year to a political party committee, or more than $5,000 during a calendar year to a PAC. The law further imposes a $25,000 overall limit on contributions that individuals can make during a calendar year to candidates, parties, and PACs.

A $5,000-per-election contribution limit applies to "qualified" PACs—those that have been in existence at least six months, have made contributions to at least five federal candidates, and have received contributions from at least fifty donors—with no overall limit on their contributions.

This would appear to be a fairly straightforward regulatory regime. But because the law must be "narrowly tailored" to achieve objectives that might otherwise be forbidden by the First Amendment, the Federal Election Campaign Act (FECA) is teeming with exceptions, exemptions, and intricacies (some call them "loopholes") that permit money to flow more generously and imaginatively than a fair reading of its provisions might suggest. Some examples follow.

Per-election donations. Because the law's limits are set on a "per election" basis (and the FEC's regulations define them as separate events), the amounts that individuals and PACs can contribute to candidates is effectively doubled to $2,000 and $10,000, respectively, for all candidates who run in primary and general elections and tripled for some candidates who must also compete in runoff elections. Once an election is concluded, candidates may no longer receive contributions unless they have remaining debts. Nevertheless, candidates have been known to devise creative bookkeeping strategies to maintain debts from their primary elections so they can accommodate late-arriving contributions.

Employee and member contributions. Although laws dating as far back as 1907 in the case of corporations and 1943 in the case of labor unions have made it unlawful for them to use treasury funds for any federal election–related contribution or expenditure, the 1974 law's definitions of "contribution" and "expenditure" specifically exempt any payments for "the establishment, administration and solicitation of contributions to a separate segregated fund." (A separate segregated fund, or SSF, is the law's terminology for what has become more popularly known as a political action committee, or PAC.) Stated differently, the law enables corporations and labor unions to use money collected from their executives or members for political interests they cannot advance with their own money.

Political party expenditures. Under the terms of the U.S. Supreme Court's *Buckley* decision, the federal government cannot limit the amount of money that any individual citizen or organized group can spend to promote a candidate's election or defeat, provided there is no consultation or coordination with the candidate who benefits from such "independent expenditures." More recently, in a case involving expenditures by the Colorado Republican Party, the high Court concluded that political parties have the right to engage in independent expenditure activities under the same rules that apply to individuals and groups, although it is hard to imagine how a political party might make such expenditures without prior consultation or coordination with its candidates.

Soft money and issue advocacy. The 1976 *Buckley* decision flatly declares that the law's prohibitions, limitations, and disclosure obligations apply only to public communications that "expressly advocate" the election or defeat of a clearly identified candidate for federal office. A new campaign finance regime now flourishes on the obverse side of the Court's opinion. In this world of legalized opposites, "soft money" refers to contributions made for purposes not related to federal elections (drawing its label because it is the opposite of "hard money," so named because it must be raised and spent under complex regulations). "Issue advocacy" refers to public communications that do not exhort voters to elect or defeat any particular candidate. Thus both find shelter from government regulation between the lines of the *Buckley* opinion.

THE PROBLEM OF REFORM

The recent explosion of soft money contributions and issue advocacy expenditures has so alarmed advocates of campaign finance reform that they have abandoned their earlier proposals to concentrate on them. Past versions of legislation, such as measures supported in the Senate by John McCain and Russell Feingold and in the House by Christopher Shays (R-Connecticut) and Martin Meehan (D-Massachusetts), sought to abolish PAC contributions and expenditures in federal elections and provide rewards such as free or reduced-price television commercials and postage to candidates who voluntarily agreed to limit their campaign expenditures. The revised McCain-Feingold and Shays-Meehan measures have a different goal: namely, to abolish soft money contributions and to impose the FECA's fund-raising regulations for issue advocacy expenditures that contain reference to a federal candidate within ninety days of a federal election. In other words, the main legislative proposals for campaign finance reform have undergone an amazing transformation from banning PAC participation altogether in federal elections to a requirement that only PACs can make election-related statements (along with candidates and political parties) during a federal election campaign.

This suggests that the problem may be a misunderstanding of the nature of political economics. The response by campaign reform advocates, when confronted by new forms of political spending, is to seek enactment of further restrictions that are meant to choke the supply of money flowing in and around federal elections. These solutions, however, ignore that these seepages and evasions are evidence that money behaves in the political world much the same way that water does in the natural world. Money, like water, is fungible. Just as water can be pushed through a tube without losing its volume, money can be transferred from one pocket or bank account to another without losing its value. Furthermore, no matter what regulations might be devised to dam its flow, the tiniest fracture that allows a small amount of money to trickle into the political finance system will eventually grow into a torrent of monumental and potentially destructive proportions, particularly if there is no relief valve to dampen the pressure.

Nonetheless, proposals to restrict hard money and outlaw soft money as well as expand the definition of "express advocacy" to engulf "issue advocacy" enjoy unflinching support from "good government" groups such as Common Cause and the League of Women Voters and the editorial pages of such influential publications as the *New York Times* and the *Washington Post*.

These proposals fail to recognize that the spending activities they seek to restrict or prohibit are merely symptoms of pressure that has intensified behind an inflexible regulatory dam. The "dam" is the FECA's contribution limits, which have remained unchanged since their enactment twenty-five years ago. The "pressure" has been created by a quarter-century's worth of inflation that has reduced the value of a contribution to barely one-quarter of its original value, while costs have risen steadily through inflation in the marketplace where campaigns are waged.

In practical terms, this means that candidates seeking election to federal office in today's economic climate must raise $4,000 to purchase the same goods and services that cost $1,000 when the law was enacted. It also means that candidates must collect money from four times as many donors in order to achieve parity, something which incumbents can accomplish more readily than challengers, and explaining why congressional refusal to increase the law's contribution limits can be viewed as a protection device for incumbents.

But as the recent inventions of soft money contributions and issue advocacy expenditures demonstrate, there is no limit to the imagination of American people who desire to engage in First Amendment–protected speech and association. Government regulations designed to prohibit or restrict their activities will eventually be swept aside by Supreme Court decisions, which have consistently held that, of all forms of speech and association, political expression deserves the highest degree of constitutional protection.

REAL REFORM

The best prescription for reform is one that seeks to enhance the ability of all Americans to exert their First Amendment rights of political speech and association with minimal government intrusion and to remove regulations and restrictions that have the effect of providing advantages to one set of candidates over another.

One solution, admittedly not likely to appeal to either side, would be to repeal contribution limits altogether. This would assure that all credible candidates could raise enough money to wage competitive campaigns, while also making soft money contributions and issue advocacy expenditures less attractive methods for evading government restrictions on political funds.

Failing total repeal of contribution limits, a special high limit of $10,000 or more should be established for individuals who contribute to the campaigns of candidates in whose elections they are eligible to cast a vote. This would allow challengers, who draw most of their campaign funds from local donors, to raise money at a rate that would enable them to be competitive. It would also encourage incumbents to redirect their fund-raising efforts to constituent donors and possibly focus less attention on PAC fund-raising activity.

Additionally, the $100 tax credit should be restored for political contributions. Unlike the one that Congress repealed, the new one should be available for contributions made to the general election campaigns of candidates for whom taxpayers are eligible to cast a ballot. By its wording, such a tax credit would prevent premature general election fund-raising by making it available only to candidates who have won their primary elections. Also, unlike the previous tax credit, which could be claimed without proof, candidates would be required to provide dated receipts that donors would attach to their tax returns to authenticate the validity of their claims.

During the final ninety days preceding a federal election, all candidates, political parties, and PACs should be required to make daily electronic disclosure of all receipts and expenditures to the FEC, which would set up software for this purpose. Within twenty-four hours after receipt of the information, the FEC should display the data, including aggregate totals, on its Internet Web site. Also, the FEC's electronic disclosure system should devote the same degree of categorization and analysis to expenditures as the present system now provides to contributions.

Finally, candidates should not be allowed to transfer unspent campaign funds from the last election to the next one. When the 1998 congressional elections were concluded, the 402 incumbents who were reelected carried more than $100 million into their year 2000 reelection campaigns. When the 106th Congress convened, 167 of its members already had $200,000 or more banked for the next election, and 102 more had at least $100,000. Each election cycle should begin with all candidates on an equal footing—with empty war chests!

With such a system in place, the flow of money into politics would complete its historical evolution to becoming utterly without secrecy or subterfuge; that may be the only reform we can enforce or maintain.

SUGGESTED READINGS

Buckley v. Valeo, 424 U.S. 1 [http://supct.law.cornell.edu/supct/cases/name.htm]

Thayer, George. *Who Shakes the Money Tree?* New York: Simon & Schuster, 1973.

Weinberg, Arthur, and Lila Weinberg, eds., *The Muckrakers*. New York: Simon & Schuster, 1961.

TECHNIQUES AND TYPES

Bill
Hamilton
and Dave
Beattie

MODERN CAMPAIGN
POLLING

THE DEVELOPMENT OF POLLING

In the first half of the century, political campaign strategy translated to using a political party's organization to turn out partisans on election day. Over the past three decades, however, party identification and organization have withered. Voters today seek a unique rationale for their political choices—and they expect individual political candidates, not parties, to deliver them that rationale. The increasing cost of communicating with voters through paid media has forced campaigns to search for ways to target the campaign's "best" (or least worst) message to the most persuadable voters.

The emergence of polling as a central element in political campaigns has evolved through three historic eras. In the pioneer era, from the 1930s through 1967, pollsters, led by George Gallup, searched for and developed techniques to forecast public opinion and project the outcome of political races. Polling remained peripheral to most political campaigns into the 1950s, although some larger campaigns occasionally called on a pollster to "see how things were going." Late in this period, in the mid-1960s, the present-day polling firms arose as partisan resources serving one of the two major parties. In the ensuing technician era (1967–78), pollsters began developing increasingly sophisticated methods of tracking opinion, but the slow process—much interviewing was conducted door-to-door—did not allow campaigns fully to exploit polling as part of strategy. Nevertheless, the pressure to provide current information increased as the pace and volume of communication accelerated.

The present strategic era began with the successful use of telephone interviewing in the 1978 presidential election. Some of the six or eight national polling firms responsible for the majority of political polling formed their own phone banks by the early 1980s. Several independent, centralized phone facilities also formed during this time. As telephone interviewing became widespread, new ways to construct questionnaires were developed to account for the limited time respondents were willing to stay on the telephone and respond to questions without the use of visual aids. New sampling techniques to take advantage of the widespread penetration of telephones were developed as the 1980s progressed.

The number of pollsters ballooned in the 1980s. Independent phone banks and personal computers allowed younger analysts, with experience gained at the national firms, to hang out their own shingles. Little up-front investment was necessary for these new pollsters; minimal experience in research design and questionnaire construction allowed them to purchase a sample from a vendor, hire an independent phone bank and data entry services, and inexpensively produce reports on their personal computers.

The lower cost of polling, coupled with the changing nature of news coverage, also led to a proliferation of media polls during this time. Polls became accepted in political news stories, and polling became expected, even demanded, by more candidates and consultants.

Other research tools were added to the strategic analysis arsenal in the mid-1980s as candidates relied more on the insight of pollsters. Focus groups were borrowed from market research to give a "touchy-feely," qualitative aspect to analysis. How voters felt about an issue could be explored through focus groups before surveys were used to quantify how many voters felt that way. Focus groups also became a tool for testing and improving media before resources were poured into mailing or airing a potentially flawed message.

The increasingly rapid turnaround of surveys and the depth of analysis allowed strategic decisions based on current information to be used at every step in the campaign. With new techniques, pollsters earned their seat at the strategic table by constantly providing a finger on the pulse of public opinion translated into real-world, real-time actions.

HIRING AND USING A POLLSTER

Most campaigns today hire a pollster to provide reconnaissance of the political environment. There are several general rules to follow to ensure that a pollster is the "right fit" for a campaign. First, hire a pollster early. Don't conduct a poll before you are ready, but build a relationship with your pollster as soon as you consider running. Allow your pollster to work with your campaign team during the early planning process. Second, don't spend too much money on research. A campaign should spend about 5 to 10 percent of its budget on opinion research to hone its message and provide reality checks. A campaign that spends much more on researching and perfecting a message is eating into its ability to communicate with voters. Campaigns that spend much less than 5 percent could be in danger of communicating a flawed message.

- *Be wary of a pollster who wants you to sign a contract that specifies a certain number of studies but that does not indicate the cost.*

The following are five crucial criteria for selecting a pollster:

Personality. Candidates and campaign personnel must be comfortable with the personality of the pollster and the numbers he or she delivers. A good pollster will be flexible enough to work with a campaign team and help them maximize their strengths. As the core message development strategist and reality check of the campaign, your pollster should work closely with the communication team to make full use of his insight and analysis.

Experience. Polling is a science that takes time, training, and experience to master. A pollster with successful experience in similar campaigns will understand the best research tools for your campaign and will be a resource before research begins.

Innovation. Political survey research is constantly changing. You want to work with a pollster who approaches each project willing to maximize new questionnaire construction and data-collection techniques to your advantage.

Availability. Tension between a pollster and a campaign often arises when the campaign feels ignored by the pollster: the campaign team thought they hired one member of a firm but are serviced by another. You should know who will be working on your campaign. If a firm is using a research team with a primary consultant and a junior analyst or assistant as the first line of contact, you should know that up front. Many firms use a research team to provide campaigns greater accessibility, but a few take on too many clients and stretch the senior partner too thin.

Referrals. There is no better way to check on a pollster's personality, experience, innovation, and availability than talking with former clients. Ask what former clients liked or disliked about the pollster. Was the strategy on target? Were the numbers accurate? Would they hire the pollster again? Was the pollster available to the campaign near election day or did he or she virtually disappear in September and October? Talk with at least one *losing* client and find out their impressions.

THE RESEARCH ARSENAL

Over the past fifteen years three general types of polls have been conducted during campaigns: the benchmark, the trend or "brushfire," and some type of endgame tracking. Focus groups are also used to help develop and test possible themes and messages.

THE BENCHMARK SURVEY

These basic surveys are the most extensive piece of research conducted by campaigns. They have a larger sample (from about five hundred for a congressional district to eight hundred or more for a statewide race) and are generally longer (twenty or more minutes and seventy-five to eighty questions) than other surveys. Before the benchmark is conducted, however, candidates should answer several questions about both themselves and the opposition:

1. Why is the sponsor/opposition running?
2. Why is the sponsor/opposition the "right choice" for voters?
3. What does the sponsor/opposition want to accomplish?
4. What has the sponsor/opposition done wrong in the past?

A campaign team must honestly assess *both* their own answers and how they believe the opposition would answer the same questions before a pollster can develop an effective questionnaire tailored to a specific campaign.

- *Be wary of a pollster who writes a complete benchmark questionnaire with little or no input from the campaign. A cookie-cutter approach to your central strategic tool is not in your best interest.*

There are five key elements of a benchmark study:

1. The political mood: Political mood deals with broad concepts such as evaluations of the economy, the direction of the state or district, and assessments of key political institutions. The political mood frequently includes a generic measure of the saliency of several important issues (e.g., health care, crime, education). Voters may assign dif-

ferent "important" issues to different offices; for example, the most important issue for a county executive may be traffic congestion, but the voters may say their congressperson should concentrate mainly on Social Security. The mood can be a driving factor in an election. In 1994, there was an antiestablishment discontentment in the electorate and voters punished those they viewed as insiders. By contrast, 1998 was a status quo election with voters avoiding dramatic change and rewarding experience in government. Without testing the "political winds," a candidate is in jeopardy of stressing the wrong tone in his or her electoral story.

2. Views on important issues: Issue positions can convey a candidate's values and view of government's role to the voters. Candidates often have many sets of issues they care about; identifying the issues on which both sides in a political contest have distinct differences can provide a contrasting choice to voters. It is the pollster's job to focus the resources of a campaign on the issues and messages that contrast favorably—and make a difference in voters' electoral choices.

3. Personalities: Politics today is about personality. A pollster can help determine how voters perceive candidates and what attributes they assign to the candidates (who they trust, who is "better" at handling issues, who is most "like themselves," and so on). For example, in 1987, pollsters for Vice-President George Bush discovered that voters viewed him as "weak." To address this problem, Bush's team in the 1988 presidential campaign stressed his military and athletic achievements.

4. Sponsor roadblocks: Whether a first-time candidate or a long-term public servant, every candidate has voted for, said, implied, or done something that will upset some group. No candidate can win votes from everyone. By testing the impact of potential weaknesses the campaign can prepare to respond to attacks (from the opposition or the media).

5. Opposition contrasts: How voters react to negative information about a candidate changes each cycle, and what worked in the past may not work today. Researching the arguments against the opposition helps determine what voters see as "fair" and what they feel is out of bounds, what they see as critical to that office or extraneous.

- *Voters are becoming more distrustful of information taken out of context by political campaigns. Easily explainable, current, and verifiable information about policy positions or opponent attacks is the most believable to voters.*

An example of typical congressional benchmark questions is displayed in Figure 2. The elements flow together to develop a story of how the candidate's and opposition's issue positions and personalities fit the district. Strengths to highlight and weaknesses to address should be spelled out in the final poll analysis.

There is no concrete time line for when a benchmark survey should be completed, but generally it should be conducted before communication with voters begins. Because some high-level races start a year and a half before election day, some pollsters advocate a small in-depth initial survey, saving the main strategic research until about six to nine months before communication with average voters begins. To help campaigns with research in the months before election, our firm has experimented with initially conducting "qualitative" phone interviews combining a series of open-ended questions with the "hard numbers" of a few standard survey questions. By using a random sample we avoid some of the response bias and the small number of respondents of focus groups while providing strategic direction early in the election cycle.

Telephone surveys are conducted using either listed or Random Digit Dialed (RDD) samples. Listed samples come from lists, such as voter registration files, with phone numbers matched to them. Listed samples tend to be the choice in smaller legislative districts where phone exchanges overlap into neighboring districts. Primary elections, in which only a portion of the electorate is eligible to vote, are also appropriate for using listed samples. But listed samples have inherent problems: people move, new voters register, and lists become dated. Some states have poor phone match rates caused by low-income, rural or transitory populations. Lists in other states provide little information about voters (demographic information, vote history, party registration). Larger states, where survey research of all kinds is conducted more frequently, tend to have the most complete and current lists. Lists continue to improve overall.

RDD samples are computer generated and are frequently "cleaned" to remove business phone numbers. They are often the choice of pollsters in presidential years when turnout is highest. They help alleviate the problems of unlisted numbers and people moving or changing phone numbers. But in lower-level races and primaries, it is necessary

1. Do you think this area is moving in the right direction, or do you think that things are off track and moving in the wrong direction?

2. In the next 3-4 years, do you think the economy in this area will improve, get worse or stay about the same?

3. Now I'd like to ask you your impressions of some people in public life. As I read each one, just tell me whether you have a very favorable opinion of that person, a somewhat favorable opinion, a somewhat unfavorable opinion, or a very unfavorable opinion. If you don't recognize them, just say so. Here's the first one.... **(REPEAT RESPONSES)**

   a) Joe Sponsor, b) Bill Clinton, c) Amy Opponent

4. Which one of the following issues do you feel is the most important for you and your family?

	1st MENT	2nd MENT
Improving the quality of education -1		-1
Reforming health care -2		-2
Protecting the environment and managing growth -3		-3
Strengthening crime fighting -4		-4
Protecting Social Security and Medicare -5		-5
Protecting a woman's right to choose -6		-6
Don't know -7		-7

(A R O — ARROW)

4a. Of the other issues I just mentioned, what would you say would be the <u>next</u> most important?

5. Suppose the candidates for the US Congress were Joe Sponsor, the Democrat, Amy Opponent, the Republican, and others — who do you think you would support? (<u>IF UNDECIDED</u>) Well, which one do you lean toward at this time?

(IF "VOTE FOR" OR "LEAN TO" ABOVE IN Q. 5)

5a.	How sure are you that you'll actually end up voting for (<u>CHOICE</u>) – are you very sure, somewhat sure, or not too sure about your choice?

ASK OF ONE-HALF SAMPLE

5b.	What is the main reason you support (<u>CHOICE</u>) over (<u>NOT CHOICE</u>)? What else?

6. Now I'd like to read you a few statements about some of the candidates for Congress and have you tell me whether you agree or not with each statement. Here's the first one – do you strongly agree, somewhat agree, somewhat disagree, or strongly disagree?

   A a. Joe Sponsor understands the problems of people like me.

   R b. I think less of "Amy Opponent" because she has supported extreme proposals of the gun lobby, the religious right and pro-life groups.

   O c. I am less likely to support Joe Sponsor because he voted against impeachment of President Clinton in the US House.

RETURN TO DEMOGRAPHICS ON FRONT PAGE.

Figure 2. Sample benchmark questions

Courtesy Hamilton Beattie & Staff

to have several screening questions to ensure that likely voters, not adults who won't turn out, constitute the sample.

TREND/BRUSHFIRE SURVEYS

These smaller surveys are conducted during the "midgame" of a campaign. Trend studies are shorter (six to twelve minutes with twenty-five to fifty questions) but usually have the same sample size as the benchmark survey. These studies should be conducted when a strategic decision needs to be made. A pollster who has been part of the campaign can quickly develop a questionnaire based on prior research and intimate knowledge of all aspects of the campaign. Frequently these studies are conducted to look closely at a new issue or to explore responses to an attack.

TRACKING/QUICKIES

These quick studies can be powerful tools at the endgame to detect the impact of campaign communication such as a new television ad. By conducting several small studies in the last weeks of a campaign or by using rolling average tracking, a campaign can get an up-to-date read on the electorate. Tracking studies tend to be about four to seven minutes (sixteen to thirty questions) in length and usually focus on the impact of campaign communication rather than exploring new concepts.

Larger campaigns may use rolling average tracking, with one hundred or more interviews conducted each night. The rolling average refreshes the sample after each wave of tracking; the wave may last one, two, or three nights. This process adds the most recent interviews to the growing database while dropping the oldest interviews. This research technique provides the campaign with the most stable and accurate measure of a trend line and the basis for timely strategic decision making.

FOCUS GROUPS

Focus groups consist of ten to twelve participants whom the pollster selects and meets with for up to two hours. The pollster/moderator

THE COST OF RESEARCH

	(Open) Statewide (N = 700)[a]	(Competitive) Congressional District (N = 400)
Benchmark survey	$20,000–28,000 (2)[b]	$12,000–16,000 (1)
Trend/brushfire survey	$12,000–15,000 (2–4)	$7,000–9,000 (1–2)
Tracking (rolling average)	$8,000–11,000/wk	$5,000–7,000/wk
	(4–5 weeks)	(3–4 weeks)
	$95,000–170,000[c]	$35,000–65,000

[a]Number of interviews for a medium-sized state. A large state might use a sample size of a thousand. The cost would be about $75,000 more.
[b]Cost per survey and number of surveys conducted during the campaigns.
[c]This wide range can occur in the same state and the same race. One candidate can be significantly better funded or use more research and intelligence than the other.

uses a general question guide to cover broad study objectives, but the key is allowing participants to discuss politics freely in their own words. Generally a minimum of two focus groups are conducted together before a report on the findings is written. It is important for consumers of research to understand that focus groups are powerful tools to assist in exploring and developing concepts but are weak for generalizing about the total electorate. Each focus group usually costs $4,000–$6,000.

Some campaigns conduct focus groups initially to search for unanticipated perceptions of candidates or issues before conducting the benchmark survey. Focus groups help explore voters' perceptions and can strengthen the benchmark survey questionnaire.

Focus groups can also be used to test media. Voters are shown advertising pieces and then discuss their merits. In larger campaigns some pollsters use "dial groups," gathering up to one hundred people in an auditorium to view advertising and constantly rating what they are viewing with a hand-held monitor. The sum of all the participants' reactions provides a rating of the ad. Generally these large groups are followed by several small focus groups to discuss the ads in more depth.

Our firm has also used mall-intercept interviews to test ads, bringing 150 or more likely voters into research facilities to view several commercials and provide individual ratings of each ad. The respondents are also asked several open-ended questions to help evaluate the ads. This process provides overall impressions of ads rather than the second-by-second rating of the dial groups.

OUTPUT FROM THE POLL

A good pollster identifies and focuses on the key strategic elements facing a campaign, helping members of the campaign team use the research rather than leaving them to wade through the voluminous data individually. Following any research study the pollster should have a story to tell about where the campaign stands with the electorate and where to move for success. A pollster frequently uses charts and tables to pull together and highlight the key aspects of the research, making it quickly accessible for the whole campaign team. Following benchmark and trend surveys, a pollster generally provides a strategic memo laying out and explaining the campaign's "story" and the strategic steps necessary for victory.

Tracking studies require the pollster to report data in the most understandable and expeditious manner. After each wave, results are usually e-mailed or faxed to the campaign team. Then, the client, consultants, and pollster analyze the impact of the results, by phone, before noon on the morning after interviewing ends. Regardless of the type of poll, a campaign should always receive a tabular report of survey questions and responses by key subgroups. A good pollster will provide the subgroups of strategic importance to that campaign, not just every conceivable subgroup. A sample tabular report and some key analysis elements are displayed in Figure 3.

- *Be wary of a pollster who does not display the size of subgroups (either as a percentage or raw number). A campaign team must know the sample size of groups they are relying on to make strategic decisions.*

Throughout the campaign the pollster must remain an interactive resource. The pollster should be constantly available to answer questions based on his or her research to date. Because surveys conducted for a campaign are interactive, the pollster can regroup the data to improve targeting and message development as the campaign progresses. Regular access to the pollster—not just after a study is conducted—is imperative for a campaign to use his or her strategic insight fully.

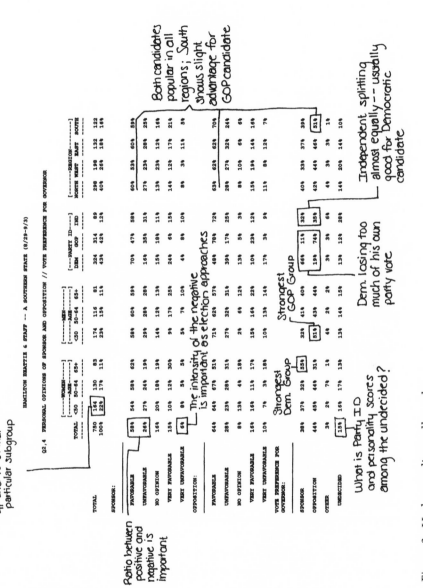

Figure 3. Understanding poll results

Courtesy Hamilton Beattie & Staff

Campaign polling and opinion research have become vital intelligence tools in modern political campaigns. The speed, accuracy, and sophistication of polling have changed over the past thirty-five to forty years as rapid communication led to the need for constant information. Now at the center of the strategic process, polling has made this seemingly chaotic process of electoral politics more rational.

John Bovée | OPPOSITION RESEARCH

For any serious campaign for public office, opposition research is one of the cornerstones of success. The basic task is to examine the character and policy leanings of a political candidate's opponent _and_ those of the candidate. The actual work is conducted in front of computer terminals or in the bowels of government archives buildings, scouring everything from newspaper articles to civil and criminal court records. The following questions need to be addressed: Where has the opponent stood on the major issues of the day? Does he enjoy the perks and privileges of public office or decline them? Does he pay his taxes? Does he exercise his right to vote?

In its finest form, top-flight opposition research turns the answers to these queries—the raw data—into _actionable intelligence_ that aids in developing a campaign's message. Ideally conducted early in the campaign cycle, opposition research will reveal the strengths and weaknesses of the candidate and the opponent. These findings can then be incorporated into a benchmark survey to determine what the voters perceive as each side's vulnerabilities and strengths. This information can be used to develop a strategic plan that best exploits the opponent's weaknesses, minimizes or obscures a candidate's weak points, and capitalizes on his or her strengths.

THE MYTHS OF OPPOSITION RESEARCH

As with most aspects of the political consulting business, opposition research has more than its fair share of associated misconceptions.

1. _"I don't have anything that can be used against me."_

This is the biggest myth in the political research field. When a consultant first meets with a client to review his or her personal and professional histories, probing questions can elicit pertinent information, as the client recalls episodes in the past that had been forgotten or deemed irrelevant.

> At our first meeting, a Republican candidate started out with the familiar, _"I don't have anything that can be used against me." After ninety minutes,_

107

he remembered having worked at a phone bank for California Democrat Jerry Brown, that his wife had volunteered at Planned Parenthood, and that an attempted adoption of a relative's child became disputed and mean-spirited.

2. *"I cast the votes, I know how I voted."*

For anyone serving in public office, opposition research on oneself is crucial. Incumbent officeholders cast hundreds to thousands of votes every year. Over a four-year period in the California legislature, more than twenty thousand pieces of legislation are introduced. No matter how sure one's memory is, it is impossible to remember the votes on every bill.

3. *"Why search beyond anything other than voting records? Isn't everything else just dirt?"*

In American politics, voters still care about, as Martin Luther King, Jr., described it, "the content of one's character." While obviously some matters are personal and not political, others are fair game for open scrutiny. A conviction for child molestation, a string of drunk driving arrests, or lying about a military service record have legitimate relevance to judging someone's suitability for public office.

COMPILATION

Research can be broken down into two parts: compilation and analysis. The first step concerns what to look for and where to look for it. While, like snowflakes, no two opposition research projects will ever be alike, there are some standard starting points.

1. *Incumbent Legislative Voting Record, Candidate Personal Voting Record and Registration*

Incumbents' voting records are, according to polling data, of great interest to—and can influence the preferences of—the public. How many votes did the incumbent fail to cast? How many times did he flip-flop on an issue? If she said she was going to be tough on crime, did she live up to that campaign pledge? How did he vote on controversial issues? What type of legislation did the incumbent author? Did any of that legislation pass?

Many state legislative voting records are fully online and accessible to the general public. In other states, private companies maintain these legislative vote files, and they can be accessed for a fee. The congressional legislative record is also online and available for inspection.

Most local municipalities are not yet online; thus voting records in these localities must still be examined by hand.

The voting record also refers to voting in elections as a citizen. After all, who wants to vote for someone who didn't bother to participate in the democratic process? In addition to tracking how many elections a candidate may have missed voting in, an opposition researcher looks for switching of political parties or the falsifying of voter registration when examining voting history. This information is relatively easy to gather: most states provide public access to voter history at the county registrar of voters.

2. *Property Records*

A search here can uncover tax liens (a judgment of unpaid taxes), mechanics liens (disputes with a vendor who did work on the home), or false homeowners' exemptions (taking a homeowner's exemption even though the home is not the principal place of residence). Occasionally these records can be found on the Internet, but more likely are found at the county assessor's office.

3. *Court Records*

Civil and criminal court records include divorce court, small claims court, and bankruptcy court. search for what type if any litigation the subject has been involved in. Did he win or lose the case? Was he the plaintiff or the defendant?

Many national and state court records are available online, but they usually provide only the briefest of summaries of the cases. For the most part, these online court filings can be used only to point to the proper direction for further research. It is often necessary to pursue the case in the courthouse files by hand.

> One search uncovered that a candidate had sued his own father on the father's deathbed. After the father died, the candidate continued the lawsuit against the widow, the subject's stepmother.

4. *Interest Group Ratings*

Many special interest groups, including agricultural interests, teachers, Chamber of Commerce, Sierra Club, and the National Rifle Association keep "score cards" detailing how incumbent officeholders have voted on issues of concern to them. Many of these ratings can be reviewed online or provided by the group upon request.

5. *Résumé Verification*

In every campaign, the opponent's (and the client's) résumé should be verified. More often than we might like to think, an office-seeker has embellished his or her life or work history. Obtaining a subject's résumé is usually as simple as logging onto his or her Web page or picking one up at campaign headquarters. An opposition researcher might also call the various schools, employers, and affiliations the candidate lists on the résumé to verify the information.

> *A young man running for the state legislature listed a variety of periodicals to which he was a frequent contributor. A periodical search and a call to the various publications indicated no articles or contributions listed under his name.*

6. *Newspaper Search*

One of the least costly and often most productive searches is the local newspapers, which can now be accessed online by simply keywording in the candidate's name. The rest of the newspaper search, however, relies on human judgment: sifting for controversial quotes, arrogant statements, conflicts of interest, broken campaign promises, and scandals. In cases involving rural or smaller papers, or researching years that have not been entered into online archives, old-fashioned page flipping and microfiche scanning are still the only available methods of analysis.

7. *Government Budget Analysis*

Taxpayer-financed junkets, lavish personal perks, and office remodeling projects are some of the items that might be found in an incumbent's record in the annual government budget. In addition, an analysis of the government budget may yield evidence of inadequate levels of public safety staffing, cuts in vital programs, or wasteful government spending.

Most government budgets will be found at the site of the government entity being researched or even at the local library. Unless one is familiar with the intricacies of government finance, analyzing a government budget can be complex and sometimes convoluted. Nevertheless, it can yield very substantial results for the researcher.

> *A local city council had contracted with a management firm to run a city golf course. A clause in the golf course contract allowed each member of the council a free round of golf once a week.*

8. *Statements of Economic Interest*

Most state and local municipalities require their elected officials and candidates to fill out statements of economic interest or conflict of interest. Federal officeholders must fill out similar statements. These statements contain lists of items owned, such as stocks, bonds, and rental property. They also indicate sources of income and gifts received over the past year.

When examining these records, a researcher should look for controversial investments, potential conflicts of interest with votes cast, filing inconsistencies, and gifts received. These documents are usually obtained in hard copy from the state or local elections division of the office the candidate is seeking.

9. *Campaign Finance Disclosure Statements*

Candidates are required to fill out statements detailing sources and amounts of campaign contributions. Questions to ask: Did anyone controversial donate to the campaign? Can any contributions be tied to legislation on which the incumbent voted around the time the campaign contribution was received? Finally, what did the candidate spend the money on?

Longtime officeholders sometimes forget that there are legal and ethical restraints on how campaign funds can be spent. Spanish lessons, new suits, and luxury hotel getaways are just some politicians' expenditures that have had serious repercussions when revealed to the voting public.

Many states now have campaign contributions online for everyone to examine; some are paid services, others free. Congressional campaign contributions are online as well. A hard copy of campaign finance reports can generally be picked up at the local elections division.

ANALYSIS

Raw data are useless unless converted into actionable intelligence. Unfortunately, research does not come neatly packaged with an outline, flow chart, and table of contents. In today's world, raw research data are voluminous, mostly irrelevant, and sometimes flat-out wrong. A researcher must separate the wheat from the chaff, make the sometimes seemingly disparate connections, and develop an overall theme on the subject in question.

The first step in analysis is to read *all* the data that have been gathered on the subject. Absorbing the big picture and the smallest details, the researcher begins to make connections and identify patterns. Malfeasance, it often turns out, is rarely isolated. For example, someone who continually fails to pay his taxes probably also has mechanics liens filed against him and perhaps a trail of litigation. Someone who flip-flops on one major issue has probably done it a dozen times over his career.

All the material should be scanned once without making any judgments as to its usefulness. By the end of this first run-through, the researcher should have a feel for the individual in question: who he is (liberal/conservative), how he acts (honest/upright, shifty/underhanded), and what motivates him (power, money, fame, family). At this point, several disparate facts may have been noted that, when linked together, may prove useful for the campaign.

After the initial reading of the raw data, it is imperative to go back and read the material again and start to write the report with categories that fit the data that have been collected. This second reading and writing of the report usually produces more connections and also leads to the discarding of irrelevant facts.

After the first draft of the report is written, a dozen or more questions usually arise related to the initial findings. For example, incumbents usually miss voting on hundreds of bills during their term in office. The researcher now may want to find out if any of those bills were relevant to the candidate's district or related to major issues or concerns in the upcoming campaign.

While writing the first draft of a report, one must go back and double-check and then triple-check the facts.

• Did the subject really fail to pay her property taxes two years ago? Or did the tax office misfile the payment?

• Was the subject really convicted of contributing to the delinquency of a minor or only charged with that crime but later found innocent in the trial?

Since opposition research is frequently converted into campaign messages, errors often prove fatal to the candidate.

A northern California legislative race was lost on election day because of poorly executed opposition research. In the last week of the campaign, a candidate put out a mailer accusing his opponent of not paying her taxes. The charge was false. The media made a big story out of it, and on election day, despite carrying the absentee vote, which largely was cast before the mailer was sent out, the candidate who sent the erroneous hit piece lost by 5 percentage points.

ORGANIZE IT!

After the dozens of loose ends are tracked down, verified, or discarded, it is time to put the finishing touches on the product and deliver it to the client. This is also the time to organize the hard copy materials into an easy-to-retrieve formatted loose-leaf binder. Any research used in the report will require the hard copy backup for use in direct mail, television, or radio. In addition, the press may want to see the hard copy documentation of any charges.

Surprisingly, collating the material may be even more difficult and time-consuming than the research itself. Over the years our firm has delivered projects that require up to twenty-one five-inch-thick binders of hard copy. For a project to be complete, any individual not familiar with the project should be able to flip through the summary and go to the exact place where the hard copy backup data can be found.

But even after the presentation of the findings, the job is not finished. A good campaign research director is on call throughout the campaign to answer questions, track down and verify additional leads, and serve as a fact checker when ad copy is produced. Inevitably, the better the research, the more likely a client's opponent is to denounce it as a bald-faced lie. If the job was done right, however, the campaign will have all the documentation to back up every fact and charge.

Joseph A.
Glick

FOCUS GROUPS IN
POLITICAL CAMPAIGNS

The focus group is a discussion among six to twelve people and a moderator lasting approximately two hours, centered on some topic of interest to those commissioning the group. Political campaigns use focus groups to formulate strategy, to test strategic moves before communicating with the general public, and as feedback and fine-tuning to maximize the effectiveness of a strategic plan. People are chosen to participate in these groups on the basis of criteria relating to the campaign's focus or potential focus. For example, a campaign trying to design ads that attract the favor of rural, female, senior Americans might gather several groups of people fitting these demographics to discuss the issues of concern to them. Alternately, a group may be gathered to focus on the image of a particular candidate, as in "Let's talk about the governor." The group might also be asked to react to a media message: "Let's take a look at some ads that Senator Smith is thinking about running. I want to hear what you think of them." In practical terms, then, a focus group is an opportunity to hear real people express their thoughts to a campaign's representatives.

POLLS AND FOCUS GROUPS

Focus groups are only part of a campaign's public opinion–related research activities. They are generally used in conjunction with their "big brother," public opinion polling, to try to answer the basic questions facing every campaign: Who to talk to? about what? and in what way? The poll and the focus group, however, differ from each other profoundly. The poll asks preformulated questions and codifies the answers in preestablished categories. The poll is generally conducted by phone with a large enough sample to give a statistically reliable estimate of general population trends. Polls attempt to uncover strategic directions from a quantitative analysis that links variations in opinion with one another or by segmenting variations in opinion by demographic groupings. In this sense the poll simulates an election and is, in the media, often treated as a preelection election. Leaking or concealing poll results then becomes part of a campaign's strategy to influence news media commentary and public opinion.

The focus group, in contrast, makes no pretense of representing general election trends. Instead it offers in-depth focus by using face-to-face contact for a long enough time to probe into people's ways of thinking about things. It attempts to uncover strategic directions by different, more qualitative, means.

Opinions and Frameworks for Thinking

From the perspective of the focus group, while people have opinions that may be mined and counted by a poll, these opinions generally rest on a framework of thinking about the world and its problems. The framework, as opposed to the opinion, is an underlying "master story" about what the world is like, what is important in it, and where we stand within that landscape. Since we have all lived in complicated times with historically layered experiences, many frameworks are generally available to us, which come variably, but predictably, into play. To some extent, opinions change more slowly than their underlying frameworks. Campaigns struggle, often against great odds, to "control the dialogue" and to "position" the election—tactics directed more toward the framework than toward people's opinions. Focus groups can be used to identify these frameworks for thinking and the core issues to be packaged in them.

For example, almost no one has an opinion *against* education, and people, regardless of gender, race, ethnicity, religion, income, level of education, party affiliation, or even ideology, generally place "improving education" high on a list of opinion-related priorities. Knowing this helps the campaign very little; somehow education will have to be addressed, but without understanding the framework within which education-related opinions are held, the campaign team won't really know what to say about education. Do people think about the issue in terms of "more dollars" for education, or in terms of "increased parental responsibility" for children's educational achievement, or in terms of "stricter standards" to be applied to students, or teachers, or administrators? Or do they mean that education seems like a long-term solution which is easier to talk about than addressing more immediate and inherently more perplexing problems—for example, long-term educational planning is the answer to economic insecurity today? Without knowing *how* education-related opinions fit within the larger frameworks of people's lives, a campaign will not know how well an education-related message will hold up and what forms it will take when it is embedded within a larger dialogue about taxes, race relations, religion, economic insecurity, or the role of government.

Every campaign must make a decision about "what this election is about" and must focus its communications on that issue while resisting the temptation to talk about all those things that come along about which people seem to have opinions. The campaign, again, is really a struggle for control of the framework, much more than addressing public opinions. "It's the economy, stupid," made famous in the 1992 election, is an example of the centrality of strategic focus and the importance of framework. That the slogan had to be posted all over campaign offices testifies to the difficulties of holding to focus.

Powerful Images and Thinking

The focus group methodology is inherently a "dialogic" mode of encounter in which ideas are not only expressed but also defended in relation to other ideas. For example, in one group, the discussion turned to a local real estate boom and its impact on the job rating of the mayor and people's sense of well-being. One respondent focused on the increase in property values: "We're all a lot better off now; our houses are worth so much." Another respondent countered, "But there are yuppies coming in, and they will push us out. We are people who have families and they are people who have dogs. They even complained at a recent community policing meeting about the noise from our church bells." As the discussion developed, it became clear that though things were getting much better and people noticed many neighborhood improvements and positive changes in their quality of life, the underlying issue facing all was the basic question, "Who is all of this for?"

As opposed to a poll, in which opinions may be identified by answers to questions, the focus group places people in the position of talking with each other, of convincing or disagreeing with each other. In that sort of encounter, people tend to use their most powerful frameworks to do the convincing. In the course of doing that, the larger frameworks for thinking tend to surface—as the substrate, or grounds, for opinions.

Doing a focus group well involves listening intensely for the argument (framework) beneath the opinions expressed and leaving just enough room in a discussion for some degree of confrontation and probing to bring that substrate into clearer focus. Too many focus groups are treated as mini-polls that seek the points of agreement about issues. The focus group, instead, should strive to identify—and provoke—disagreement to allow the frameworks for thinking to emerge more clearly in people's attempts to interact with and convince one another.

When nonconsensus and disagreement are encouraged, two things generally emerge in group discussions: opinions become nuanced in ways that begin to reveal underlying thought frameworks, and people often invoke powerful images which to them make the point about why their opinion and way of thinking is correct. Opinions and frameworks for thinking do not exist only in some conversational space— they exist in relation to some world, real or imagined, that they address. Who can forget Ronald Reagan's invocation of the image of the food stamp recipient "welfare queen" in the Cadillac as a way of making a point about the misuse of government benefits—and as a way of undoing the Great Society commitment to perfecting government as a vehicle for delivering benefits? Images such as these underlie, and help to frame, public thought processes. Good campaigns, and good focus groups, help to identify these powerful images and underlying patterns of thought.

For example, in one Senate campaign in a southern state several years ago, the sitting governor, a centrist and progressive Democrat, was running against a very conservative Republican senator who had developed a staunchly obstructionist reputation. In initial focus groups, it became clear that, although it seemed that these men represented opposite ends of the political spectrum, people wanted both to win. What emerged in discussion, and later in the election, was the image that people had of each *office*. A governor is supposed to make things better for people—and in this case, the progressive governor was filling the bill. The image of senator, however, is framed more in moral terms, and efficiency and benefits delivered to constituents are less important than the ability to define a "moral" position and hold to it. The senator won the election, and the governor was reelected. People seemed to be happy with both.

FEEDBACK AND FEEDFORWARD

Electoral campaigns involve the expenditure of huge amounts of money and effort to "get the message out" in a usually very crowded communications environment. You may be talking, but not everybody may be listening. Since this is the case, it is economically rational to make sure that whatever message is communicated delivers the most "bang for the buck" and is most precisely attuned to the campaign's strategy.

Anyone contemplating using focus groups in a political campaign should be aware that they are relatively costly, yet powerful, tools. The costs of a focus group are driven by a number of factors: "screening" to get the desired demographic population; "respondents' fees" paid to people who participate; and the costs of rental of a facility and food for respondents and those observing. Prices will vary from area to area, but it is a safe bet to anticipate a cost range from $3,500 (a broad screen in which the bulk of the population will qualify and in areas where respondents' fees can be low) to $5,500 (in which screening criteria are more particular or respondents' fees, because of market conditions, must be higher).

The focus group (or related audience reaction techniques), when not used for strategic formation purposes, is an ideal vehicle for assessing the likely impact of media and for fine-tuning the execution of campaign communications. The focus group presents an artificial communications environment where, as opposed to real life, the message does get through. People paid to sit in a room for two hours can come into direct and focal contact with campaign communications (e.g., commercials, video clips of the candidate, or texts of speeches). The participants must pay attention in ways that they would probably not ordinarily do; you can't channel surf in a focus group, and you can't watch media in a poll.

People respond to campaign media not just with respect to its intended message (the verbal channel) but with visceral reactions to the multimedia details of its execution; we notice look and feel as much as message. Often we vote on that basis as well. When there is too much information out there to be processed, and when in a campaign different versions of reality are being pitted against one another, it is almost inevitable that people will fall back on information-processing strategies that will reduce the confusion. This leads to a cognitive strategy that might be described as "seeing through" the presented information and images so as to "look at" what is really going on.

These days, people have become media literate and politically skeptical. They know that they are being manipulated. Therefore, when people are presented with commercials, they are often as much primed to detect the manipulations as they are to listen to the messages. How do they do that? People actively look for details of media presentation that somehow "sneak in" unintentionally. This is akin to our people-reading activities, when we pay as much attention to body language or details of attire or personal grooming as we do to language. The way this works out in the medium of television is that we become inordinately sensitive to "inadvertent cues." When viewing televised debates we watch for these details more than we listen to what is said. Are the candidate's eyes shifty? Does his or her body give a lie away? Does this person look friendly and open or ominous and scary?

This phenomenon plays out in strange ways in testing commercials through focus groups. For example, in one election the candidate cut a commercial in which he delivered the message that he was "on the side of the ordinary working man and woman." Yet, when people in a focus group watched the commercial, it seemed that all they saw was this guy (a sitting governor) wearing a Rolex watch. That alone served to unhinge the message. Revealingly, none of the professionals running the campaign and producing the ad, from the candidate himself to the media consultant to the camera crew, perceived that the Rolex was the most important (and negatively suggestive) object in the visual frame to ordinary people. Only the focus group provided this necessary and subtle reality check from the lips of real potential voters.

THE KEY ROLE: THE MODERATOR

It is often said that a focus group is only as good as its moderator. One of the key elements that distinguishes the focus group methodology is that it must be prepared for surprises, less focused on people's opinions and more focused on people's ways of thinking. Three dangers loom here: that the moderator will end up driving people into giving responses that are unnatural, that is, what the moderator wants them to say rather than what they really think; that a lax moderator might let the conversation wander so that there is no focus from the group on the original issues they were brought together to discuss; and that there may be a joker in the deck, an extremely domineering and opinionated group member who drives others to agree with him (or her)—at least out loud—and thereby suppresses their actual opinions.

Keeping these threats in check—letting people talk naturally, not letting anyone dominate, and keeping everyone on subject—is an art and a science. The direction is set by the guidelines the moderator establishes. These tend to consist of a basic set of principles:

1. The discussion, after personal (first name only) introductions, is constructed using a concentric circle form—going from the most general, for example, "I'm a stranger, what's it like to live here?" "How are things going here?" "What are the major issues that folks are talking about?" to the more specific, for example, "and just what can and should be done about———?"

2. Open-ended questioning precedes more focused topic-oriented questioning. In this way people may provide you with new takes on issues that you wish to understand, which would not be revealed if you were only asking them to respond to your understanding of the situation.

3. The formalized and routinized part of the focus group should be the mere skeleton. The flesh is provided by "probe" questions—the answers to which are not predictable in advance—that follow a person's train of thought to deeper levels and invite group discussion.

4. Most important, the moderator should always be on the verge of tearing up the guidelines and constructing new ones on the fly as discussion develops and the group begins to venture to unanticipated places. These places are almost always more important than those to which the moderator might initially have wanted to go.

To follow these rules, the moderator must have a comprehensive understanding of history and campaign dynamics (both locally and nationally) so that the research process is flexible enough to have a sense of where the important pockets of unforeseen but eminently useful information may be found.

THE VALUE OF FOCUS GROUPS

The distinctive value of focus groups in political campaigns is that they treat people as conversationalists and institute a mode of contact that is artificially natural. At the strategic end of things, the focus group methodology treats people as if they exist in conversational, dialogic settings and are not merely repositories of opinions. More than having opinions, people are seen as telling stories that make sense of their world to themselves and to others.

At the execution end, the artificiality of the focus group guarantees that media messages will be attended to and that whatever messages they really give (as opposed to the messages they try to give) can be identified. Again, there is a view embedded here that people are not just message processors but also active "bullshit detectors," scanning the broadcast or spoken message for inadvertent and uncontrollable clues that indicate whether someone is saying what he or she knows you want to hear or is telling the truth as he sees it. Sincerity is almost always recognized and ultimately rewarded.

The strength of the focus group is that it allows people to be people. This in turn puts extraordinary demands on the quality and sensitivity of the moderator—to sense, to hear, and to open up discussion to reveal deeper levels of conversation that go considerably beyond the mere registering of opinions. In the focus group method, then, there is an appreciation of the interest and value of entering into people's lives and in trying to understand their reality from the inside; campaigns can learn not just about the ammunition for strategic decisions but about the hopes and fears of real people.

Jon M.
Hutchens

POLITICAL MEDIA BUYING

Imagine a scenario in which the CEO of Coca-Cola arrives at a March corporate planning meeting and makes the following statement: "Eight months from today, on November 3, this company must achieve a 51 percent market share of all soft drink consumers. If this goal is not reached, on November 4 this company will be disbanded, and all of you will be without jobs." Such a statement would surely concentrate the thinking of the attending executives. The CFO would sell off assets and borrow money to finance a massive advertising blitz, and the VP for advertising would create ad strategies about how Pepsi is made from poison.

Yet this same victory-or-death scenario faces every political campaign. To be successful, a political campaign must capture one out of every two voters during an extremely short time frame that ends on a very specific date. This goal inherently makes political campaigns *market-share* advertisers and not *unit-sales* advertisers.

Companies with market-share goals like McDonald's, Nike, and Coca-Cola, and even local companies like supermarkets and car dealers, employ mass marketing strategies to expose as many people as possible to their brand image. These companies must not only convert new customers to expand their market share but also must reinforce existing customers to prevent any defections from their market share.

ACHIEVING A POLITICAL CAMPAIGN'S GOAL

Political campaigns face the same task as any company that is market-share driven. To capture 51 percent of the market, a campaign must provide an opportunity for as many voters as possible to receive its message to capture new supporters, while preventing existing supporters from defecting. An apt analogy would be the process of weaving a net to catch voters. The tighter a campaign weaves its communication net, the less likely a voter can pass through without being touched in some manner by a campaign message.

Voter targeting plays an important role in designing a campaign's advertising strategy. Sophisticated survey research and analysis of past election results isolate which voters will be most receptive to a campaign's message and which will be most strategically important in winning an election. Targeting, however, will not reduce the need for campaigns to communicate to as many voters as possible. Rather, targeting helps campaigns decide which voters need to be communicated to more frequently (i.e., prospective new converts, voters with issue or partisan cross-pressures) as opposed to those voters who may not require as much communication (i.e., strong partisans and committed supporters).

MEDIA BUYING TERMINOLOGY

Listed below are relevant terms and concepts used when evaluating the types of media that might be most effective in developing advertising recommendations.

Media Markets

Media markets are the geographic definition of the combined viewership for an area's TV stations and the combined listenership for an area's radio stations. A media market's geography is defined at the county level, and a county's membership in a particular media market is determined by which area's TV or radio stations receive a majority of combined viewership and listenership from each county's residents.

The cost of advertising in a specific media market is largely determined by the population size of a given media market. Shown below are examples of weekly costs for a moderate-level TV buy in various markets.

The different fund-raising pressures on campaigns can be significant based on the cost of media markets. For example, an Arkansas U.S.

Market	National Market Rank	Cost
New York City, N.Y.	1	$530,400
Phoenix, Ariz.	17	$117,600
Kansas City, Mo.	32	$70,800
Baton Rouge, La.	98	$20,400
Rapid City, S.D.	172	$12,000

Senate candidate in 1998 was on the air for ten weeks and spent about $750,000, while an Ohio gubernatorial candidate was also on the air for ten weeks but spent more than $5 million.

For political advertisers, the relationship between media market geography and the campaign's geographic election area (congressional district, statewide, and so on) is key in determining how a campaign should budget its advertising resources. A state senate candidate whose district falls inside the Chicago media market would find TV and radio to be highly inefficient because the state senate district is only a small portion of the Chicago market. In contrast, TV and radio advertising could be highly efficient for a statewide candidate in Texas because very little of the media markets covering Texas spill out of state.

GRPs

GRPs (gross rating points) quantify how many people are reached by a given television or radio program. A highly watched prime-time program like *ER* will typically receive close to a 15 rating, which means that an advertisement during this program would reach 15 percent of the total television audience.

GRPs also quantify the amount of advertising a campaign has purchased or needs to purchase. If the rating points for all the programs in which a campaign has purchased advertisements total 100 GRPs, in theory the campaign has reached 100 percent of the total audience one time. If the rating points total 500 GRPs, theoretically the campaign will have reached 100 percent of the total audience five times.

Reach

Reach is a definition of the type of audience delivered by a particular program or schedule of programs. Highly rated programs like *ER* and *60 Minutes* have a broad reach not only because they are watched by a large audience but also because they are watched by a relatively diversified audience. Shows like *Xena, Warrior Princess*, on the other hand, have a narrow reach not just because ratings are low but also because the audience is more homogeneous—mostly downscale lower-income white males under the age of thirty.

Reach can be an important strategic characteristic in a campaign's media buy. In most campaigns, with the burden of reaching 51 percent, an advertising plan with a broad reach is essential to ensure that the campaign's message reaches as many voters as possible. In a tight campaign close to the election, with fewer undecided voters, however, campaigns will narrow the reach of their advertising to focus on the type of voters who could put the campaign over the top.

Frequency

Frequency is simply the number of times a voter is exposed to a campaign advertisement. Commercial advertisers have found that maintaining market share and brand awareness requires three to four ad exposures weekly. For political advertisers in a relatively uncluttered ad environment (usually earlier in a campaign), six to seven ad exposures weekly are required to ensure that a campaign's messages are being retained. In a cluttered and competitive environment (usually later in a campaign), ten to twelve ad exposures weekly are required to ensure that the message punches through. These exposures, however, must be continual and uninterrupted; on-again, off-again ad campaigns don't stick in the public memory.

Intrusiveness

In politics, only a small proportion of voters will seek out campaign information voluntarily. For most voters, campaign messages must *intrude* into their daily lives and consciousness for the messages to be retained. The quality of intrusiveness relates both to the type of medium used to communicate and to the nature of the message communicated. For example, a passive or complicated advertisement may require more frequency before it is retained than a more dramatic or simplistic advertisement.

TYPES OF MEDIA

Campaigns typically select one medium as the dominant method to communicate with voters and then use other supportive media as the campaign budget allows. The choice of a dominant medium is usually determined based on which medium will most efficiently communicate with the largest possible audience.

Television

Television is the preferred medium for most campaigns for several reasons. First, television is highly efficient in delivering a message to a broad audience, which is a key characteristic given the market-share nature of politics. In commercial advertising, market-share-driven companies usually spend between 80 and 95 percent of their total communications budget on television advertising. If a campaign has a goal of reaching as many voters as possible in a given media market, on a cost-per-contact basis television tends to be much less expensive than any other medium.

Second, television's intrusiveness is unmatched. The audience is semipassive, either watching *and* listening to TV or, if engaged in another activity, at least listening to the soundtrack. Advertising messages can easily flood into the viewer's brain with little resistance, and the viewer takes no action to receive the message. Also, the dual audio and visual capabilities of television are effective at creating emotional and nonlinear messages, which can be quite powerful in political communications.

Third, television viewership is a highly time-dominant activity. A television is on an average of seven hours a day in a typical household. Television viewership has continued to grow since television was invented; however, *how* we watch television has changed, with much lower shares for broadcast networks and greater viewership of independent stations and cable networks.

Fourth, television viewership is probably the most researched behavior on the planet; consequently, an incredible wealth of ratings data is available to fine-tune a television buy into a targeted communications vehicle. These data, covering all aspects of audience segmentation, including detailed demographics, lifestyles, psychographics, and consumer preferences, will only become more valuable as television viewership continues to fragment to many different viewership options. Television becomes a bad choice for most campaigns only when its strong reach characteristics are inefficient for a campaign's needs, such as when the media market geography does not efficiently correlate to a campaign's political geography.

Finally, when campaign staffers talk about using "TV" what they almost always mean are ads on broadcast channels (although these are likely received into the home through cable). However, campaigns do have the option to place ads on cable-only channels. Cable itself is inherently a targeting and frequency medium, so it is somewhat unfair to compare costs with broadcast television. Broadcast will always have a lower cost-per-contact than any other medium when attempting to reach a large audience. For example, buying 100 GRPs on all the cable systems in the Denver, Colorado media market would cost $38,500, while buying 100 GRPs on Denver broadcast stations would cost $16,500. However, to buy 100 cable GRPs in Boulder (a smaller city covered by the Denver media market), the cost would be $4,100.

Radio

Radio's communications characteristics are unlike those of television, which leads it to be used differently in most campaigns. Radio's listenership tends to be highly fragmented because of the unique format of most stations, with each format designed to appeal to a specific audience demographic. In addition, most people listen to the radio for fewer hours during the week than they watch television. Finally, radio tends to be a background medium, with most listeners engaged in other activities while they are listening (driving, exercising, cooking, and the like), which makes it a less intrusive medium than television.

Because of its limited reach characteristics, radio is seldom used as the dominant method of communicating in most campaigns. Radio's excellent audience segmentation capabilities, however, result in its frequent use in campaigns in a supportive role to build message frequency among specific target audiences.

Direct Mail

Direct mail is often thought of as a targeting mechanism in most campaigns because messages can be delivered to a precise set of households with little chance of nontargeted households also receiving the message. Like radio, direct mail is mostly used in a supportive role in most campaigns to deliver specific messages to a highly targeted audience on a frequent basis.

In certain circumstances, however, where television is too inefficient to reach a specific election region with accuracy, direct mail will serve as a campaign's dominant method of communication. Direct mail lacks the intrusive quality of TV and radio because it requires the participation and willingness of the mail recipient to read the mail piece. Creative mail designs help overcome direct mail's intrusiveness limitations and will increase readership and message retention.

Newspaper

High-circulation daily newspapers are seldom used in campaigns as the dominant method of communication. Advertisements must be large (half a page or larger) to ensure readership, and this is often very expensive. This medium also depends on the readers making a conscious decision to read the ad; therefore, it lacks intrusiveness. In addition, it is difficult to target newspaper ads to specific demographic groups.

Newspaper ads can provide more time and space to communicate than do TV or radio ads. Newspaper can be effective in certain situations when a complicated issue needs explaining, such as in initiative and referendum campaigns. Newspaper can also be effective for short-term purposes, such as inviting people to a campaign event or to build interest in a televised debate.

Internet

Internet advertising costing is difficult, because there has not yet been a universal standard developed that accurately measures usage and viewership. All other forms of advertising use audience size and quality (for example, income and age) as the basis for the costing of advertising. More sophisticated Internet content providers like America On-line (AOL) can be more precise on their costing and audience size since they have a very detailed database on individual users. AOL can cost their advertising on a per thousand basis, since they know exactly how many AOL users they will be sending ads to when the users log on to the service. As of this writing (spring 1999), AOL prices their ads at $30 per thousand, which is roughly comparable in cost to direct mail. Other, less sophisticated, content providers try to determine their ad value based on the number of hits their Web site may receive, but this does not tell you anything about the characteristics of their site's audience. As an example of costs, the *Dallas Morning News* charges $10,000 for a month's run of a rotating banner ad on their Web site.

A MEDIA BUYER'S CAMPAIGN ROLE

A campaign media buyer has two key responsibilities: one as an analyst helping to develop communication strategy, and the other as an implementer of the communications strategy. The table below details the various components of these two key responsibilities.

ROLE OF CAMPAIGN MEDIA BUYER

Develop Communications Strategy	*Implement Communications Strategy*
Evaluate efficiencies of available media options	Develop specific media schedules based on the planning budget
Incorporate targeting and polling recommendations	Place and negotiate schedules with media outlets
Assess fund-raising goals and limitations	Coordinate trafficking of commercials at media outlets
Develop detailed media planning budget on costs, timing, and weight of various media options	Manage and reconcile campaign's media funds
	Track media expenditures of campaign's opponent

THE FUTURE OF POLITICAL MEDIA BUYING

A political media buyer must stay in tune with the changing nature of voters' communications habits. Over the past decade, cable television played a key role in fragmenting television viewership behavior, which now mandates that cable be as important to a media schedule as would a broadcast network affiliate. The Internet also shows promise as a crucial reach vehicle, particularly if it can live up to the hype of becoming a dominant information and entertainment hybrid. Currently, the Internet seems to be used more as a tool to help build organizational and fund-raising networks for campaigns as opposed to being used as an intrusive communications vehicle directed toward unconnected voters. Campaigns now have the ability to place banner ads on content providers like AOL and the MSN Network, or search engines like Yahoo, and use these ads as magnetic gateways to direct voters to a campaign's Web site where a pitch can be made for organizational and fund-raising help. On AOL, campaigns can even target their banner ads to appear only for specified AOL users to help improve the efficiency of their fund-raising and organizational appeals using a significant array of demographic, geographic, and attitudinal targeting characteristics culled from AOL's proprietary user database.

Regardless of how voters' communications habits may evolve in the future, unless our country's political structure and culture changes radically the nature of political advertising strategy probably will not alter significantly. Political advertisers will still need to be market-share advertisers, with the goal of trying to reach as many voters as possible in an intrusive manner. At present, Internet usage and online advertising techniques have yet to mature to the point where this medium can be feasible as a broadcast advertising vehicle. However, as voters' communications options continue to fragment, it is likely that political advertisers will be forced to rely on a wider range of communication vehicles to ensure they are reaching a large audience of voters. Currently, most campaigns can usually rely on television (and cable) exclusively to provide a broad reach among voters. In the future, campaigns may find the need for a second or third reach vehicle to fill the gap that increased Internet usage (or some other cool thing we don't know about yet) will create.

Gerald S.
Tyson

GOTV: GET OUT THE VOTE

Voting involves two decisions on the part of a registered voter. Although those decisions may be made in reverse order, they typically are, first, that the voter favors a particular candidate or cause, and second, that he or she will actually cast a ballot in support of that decision. While most forms of political communication are geared toward *persuading* voters what or whom to support, it is largely the direct voter contact aspects of the campaign that have the most impact on voters' decisions to complete the process and actually *cast their ballots*. To use an analogy, although print, electronic, and direct mail advertising may persuade a customer to buy a Buick, it takes a dealership's sales representative to close the sale and put him or her in a new car. Similarly, a campaign's get-out-the-vote (GOTV) efforts "close the sale" with voters and put them in the voting booth.

ENHANCING VOTER TURNOUT

Get-out-the-vote techniques can generally be divided into three categories of direct voter contacts: telephone, direct mail, and face-to-face. That order is also reflective of the relative frequency with which most campaigns employ each type of contact, despite significant differences in their effects.

The proliferation of voting by mail and preelection day, in-person voting throughout the country has made consultants and candidates extremely inventive in finding ways to urge people to vote. Whereas a mail/phone/door-knock scheme deployed just before E-Day once was the norm, the opportunity to vote as early as forty-five days before the election now means that some campaigns have a GOTV period stretching over several weeks. This gives political parties and candidates a significantly enhanced opportunity to "bank" votes early, before late-appearing negative advertising can suppress favorable turnout.

In states where voting by mail (VBM) is available, a candidate's (or party's) reliable supporters are frequently subjected to several rounds of mail, phone, and door-to-door visits to induce voters to sign and submit a VBM application and, subsequently, to fill out and mail the ballot.

Some states permit the use of informal VBM applications in lieu of official ones, giving campaigns an opportunity to simplify the application instrument and send it to voters along with persuasive materials and messages. Other states impose varying restrictions, in some cases requiring that voters use only those applications provided by and mailed from the local elections board. In addition, some states require either notarization or witnessing of VBM applications or mail ballots.

Where it is believed that broad dissemination of information about mail balloting is beneficial, campaigns will use electronic and display advertising to remind voters of such opportunities. If one believes, for example, that Republican voters are generally more knowledgeable about such opportunities, Democratic candidates—with everything to be gained from increased awareness on the part of Democratic voters—may want to ensure that all appeals for support include mention of mail balloting.

Early, in-person voting is another increasingly popular method of extending the voting franchise. As in the case of voting by mail, campaigns go to great lengths to ensure that their supporters are fully informed of such opportunities, issuing myriad communications to urge voters to cast their ballots in this manner. Direct mail is an especially valuable tool in jurisdictions where multiple early-voting sites exist and where evening and weekend voting is offered. Providing such instruction to voters can increase the numbers that avail themselves of such opportunities. Using phone calls to call attention to these mailings is also helpful.

Rallies held near early-voting locations can enhance the use of this method. In the 1989 special election to fill the seat he had vacated, U.S. House Speaker Jim Wright spoke to a gathering of union workers near the General Dynamics aircraft plant in Fort Worth and then led them down the street to cast their ballots at a nearby voting station. In the same election, phone banks were used to set appointments for early voting over a sixteen-day period. Vehicles picked up voters at their scheduled times, drove them to early-voting locations, and delivered them home again.

Still, most voters tend to vote on election day, whether because of a respect for tradition, a desire to act on last-minute information about candidates, or mere procrastination. Thus campaigns must continue to conduct eleventh-hour GOTV activities among a vast majority of voter households; the result is a flood of telephone, mail, and face-to-face communications with voters over a five-day period ending on election day.

Sometimes, multimodal communications conflate astoundingly. In an effort to elevate turnout in a Houston mayoral race some years ago, one campaign used volunteer block captains to maximize the number of voters who would be contacted face-to-face just before the election, providing a valuable supplement to its phone and mail communications. One voter, answering a phone call placed by the candidate himself, was quoted as saying, "Yes, I was just reading this telegram from the mayor. Oh, just a minute! Someone [the block captain, it turned out] is at the door." This was but one of many instances in which phone, mail, and door-to-door contacts jointly focused the attention of voters.

TARGETING GOTV ACTIVITIES

Voters selected for GOTV treatment must be carefully chosen, a process known as targeting. While it is sometimes possible to win an election simply by elevating turnout among broad demographic groups or within definable geographic areas, today's political landscape usually calls for a combination of approaches to find, persuade, and deliver the various segments of a minimum essential coalition of voters necessary to assure victory.

Typically, the tools used to define and target the voter subgroups required to build a winning margin are polling, precinct analysis, and assessment of voters' histories and other attributes available on the subject jurisdiction's voter registration file. Armed with such knowledge, a campaign strategist can piece together a potentially successful targeting scheme. Such a strategy usually includes attempts to elevate gross turnout within certain definable groups where the candidate has overwhelming strength and measures to identify and selectively increase participation among voter subgroups where strength exists but is not dominant. In the latter case, voter subgroups are prioritized on the basis of their potential "yield," and phone canvassing is used to identify supporters in these groups. In the end, *presumed* supporters (from "gross" turnout groups) and *identified* supporters (from "selective" turnout groups) are subjected to personal contact designed to maximize their vote.

STRENGTHS AND WEAKNESSES OF GOTV METHODS

Each of the three methods of personal contact—phone, mail, and face-to-face—has its advantages and constraints.

Telephone

Telephone contact is limited in its reach, especially among voters with high mobility (who, not incidentally, also have the lowest rates of voting participation). But this method is also the easiest and quickest way to communicate an urgent message. For this reason, telephone contact enjoys the widest use among the three personal contact methods. In addition, phone contacts are interactive and can be used to respond to voters' questions about how, where, and when to vote.

Added to the multitude of "live" calls in recent cycles are calls disseminating recorded messages from a variety of messengers. Such "robo-calls," which were especially abundant in the 1998 campaign, can be effective when employed judiciously. Used to convey an urgent message from a popular figure to an audience of high affinity, for example, such calls can affect voter participation. In addition, although somewhat less effective, they can be used to alert targeted voters to the impending arrival of critical mailings (e.g., VBM applications) or to warn voters that VBM ballots must be mailed soon. In the last weeks of the 1998 campaign, however, the proportion of fully delivered robo-call messages diminished over time, while the proportion of terminations increased, a sure sign that the novelty (and efficacy) of the method was short-lived. Nonetheless, the demand for this tactic can be expected to remain high in the next cycle or two; to maximize the effect of this innovation, candidates and campaigns must carefully match their messages, messengers and audiences.

Direct Mail

One of the most important uses of direct mail in enhancing turnout is to help infrequent voters gain information sufficient to overcome their uncertainty about voting. Because infrequent voters often lack not only a rationale for voting but also knowledge of the process itself, direct mail messages may convey a reason to vote as well as instructions on how to vote. Habitual voters tend to overlook the potential intimidation factors associated with voting, not the least of which is knowing where and when to vote. By sending voters simple instructions about the process—including the address of their polling place and the hours during which they may vote—a campaign can help overcome fundamental uncertainties and enhance participation.

Like telephone contact, however, direct-mail contact is limited by deliverability. Despite the efforts of election boards and voter file vendors to maximize the accuracy of addresses on voter registration files, a substantial number of voters cannot be reached at addresses of record. This problem is mitigated when get-out-the-vote mail is aimed at entire precincts and is directed to "addressee or current resident."

Face-to-Face

Although phone and mail contacts are the most frequently used methods of enhancing voter turnout, face-to-face contact arguably has far more impact in elevating turnout. This is in part because, unlike the other two methods, door-to-door sweeps potentially have universal reach. More important is the comparative impact generated by the face-to-face contact between a voter and a candidate or surrogate. Various studies have found that such contact has as much as *three times* the turnout elevation effect that phone contact has.

There are problems associated with face-to-face contact, however. Most obvious are the logistical difficulty and tremendous cost in resources of deploying a program of door-to-door visits. In addition, such contact frequently has little or no effect on candidate preference—no persuasive or conversion effect on behalf of the candidate making the contact—except in elections in which that contact is the only source of information received by the voter. Therefore, a campaign attempting significant face-to-face contact with voters must make certain of its targets, visiting only the homes of voters who are highly likely to support that candidate.

COATTAILS AND DOWN-BALLOT RACES

A lot of attention is given to the concept of the "coattails" effect of up-ballot (higher statewide or federal) candidates on down-ballot (local city or county) races, and there is little question but that high-visibility races affect overall turnout. But a down-ballot candidate cannot depend on such effects to create turnout in his or her race, for even in states where straight-ticket voting is permitted, down-ballot falloff in the number of votes cast is significant. In the 1992 presidential election, for example, the falloff from the presidential race to the congressional race in competitive districts (where the winner received less than 70 percent) was 5.5 percent, or about ten thousand votes per district, clearly enough to make a difference in close races. Although the falloff further down the ballot was not measured, it is safe to assume that voter interest and participation continued to decline, with fewer votes cast in many legislative and local races. For these short-term (election day) reasons—and in the interests of building voter allegiance over the longer term—it is important for down-ballot candidates to undertake their own programs of personal contact to increase voter participation.

Furthermore, there are those who believe that voter participation at the top of the ticket can be supported from the bottom up—the "reverse coattails" effect. Voters attracted to candidates in down-ballot races can be expected to vote up and down the ballot, so it behooves up-ballot candidates to make certain that attractive candidates in local and legislative races have sufficient resources to promulgate their messages and to enhance turnout among their supporters.

Everyone on the ballot has an interest in GOTV.

Walter D. Clinton and Anne E. Clinton

TELEPHONE AND DIRECT MAIL

The political campaign should be a dialogue between the candidate and the voter. Of the five methods of political communication—expensive mass media tools like television, radio, newspaper advertisements, and billboards; the Internet; less expensive grassroots methods like the home visit; the telephone; and direct mail—the telephone is the most essential mechanism to facilitate the conversation between office-seeker and potential supporter. No other medium has the capability to engage the voter in a live, two-way dialogue, thereby actively involving the voter in the campaign process as well as generating valuable response information. Put another way, when you talk to voters, they talk back. Moreover, no other political communication vehicle can be as precisely targeted; the telephone allows for the development of specific messages to persuade specific populations. Finally, the telephone is a highly personal form of political communication. With a telephone call, the candidate's representative has the voter's complete, if momentary, attention, and it is up to the skill of that representative to be effective in using and extending that period of total focus.

Moreover, the telephone, when properly integrated into the total campaign effort, can be an extremely effective and persuasive medium. While many people recognize the value of the telephone for get-out-the-vote efforts, a successful telephone-based communications program begins early in the campaign and is properly coordinated with the total campaign communication effort. The telephone is an invaluable tool for building name recognition, creating campaign activity, recruiting volunteers, raising funds, developing lists, identifying voters' attitudes, inoculating voters against future opponent attacks, and motivating voters to go to the polls.

LISTS AND MESSAGE DEVELOPMENT

The fundamental tool of the political telecommunicator is the voter registration list. This list should be enhanced with geodemographic data gathered from census information (income, education, profession, type of housing) as well as with lifestyle indexes gathered from commercial marketing data (magazine subscriptions and credit card information). Message development and refinement is a continuous process of matching the research with campaign needs so as to categorize the electorate into smaller groups. The political telecommunicator then develops specific persuasive messages to be delivered to these electorate subgroups to motivate them to vote for a particular candidate or issue. It is critical for the telecommunicator to be involved with and have access to all of the campaign's attitudinal research data, both qualitative (focus groups) and quantitative (surveys), to ensure the quality of message development and the coordination of campaign goals.

The skilled political telemarketer is familiar with research processes and can develop as many specific messages for each wave of telephoning as required. This provides for maximum effectiveness because the telephone interviewer is prepared with a persuasive message specific to the voter's individual profile. Careful attention to information gathering also generates valuable information for future communication phases.

Message development is a continuous process that occurs throughout the campaign. In each communication phase, the campaign-to-voter dialogue is analyzed and refined. Initially, the enhanced voter registration list serves as the basis for the development of messages targeted at different categories of voters. For example, in a recent governor's race our firm worked in, "preserving Social Security" was determined to be the most important issue from the polling and focus group research for voters aged sixty-five and over. In contrast, women aged thirty to forty-five ranked as most important issues pertaining to secondary education, child care, and health care.

Messages for the initial stage of voter contact are structured differently from introduction to conclusion according to various factors: party identification, level of voter activism, race/ethnicity, age, gender, region or geography, and family status. This broad voter categorization is then attached to the individual voter file and is continually revisited and refined as the campaign-voter conversation continues. Throughout the process, a record of this dialogue is kept in the voter file. That way, the campaign can maintain a journal noting which issues are or are not salient to a particular voter and which messages are or are not persuasive. The telephone thus becomes a highly precise campaign communication tool. Moreover, in an atmosphere of increasingly negative campaigns, the telephone provides an effective means of protection against opponent attacks. For example, in the governor's campaign, the history of voter contact attached to the voter profile allowed the campaign to determine which voters were most susceptible to the negative campaign strategies of the opposition, which voters could be inoculated against the attacks, and which messages would be most effective in responding to those attacks. Using the data generated by the telephone campaign, the candidate was able to concentrate his resources and win the election.

TELEPHONE TECHNOLOGY

Modern technology allows the political telecommunicator to engage voters in a highly personalized dialogue while simultaneously maintaining cost and time efficacy. An example involves the simple act of dialing a number to reach someone. In the "dark ages" of telemarketing—until about ten years ago—the caller punched numbers on an actual phone, listened to ringing, and hoped the gentleman or lady of the house was in. Today this process is enhanced by a predictive dialer—an electronic system whereby a computer dials the loaded telephone numbers and sorts the busy signals, answering machines, wrong numbers, and no-answers to deliver a live voice to the telephone operator. The pertinent voter information as well as the corresponding targeted message (in script form) appear on the operator's computer screen.

Not only does the predictive dialer increase the number of human-to-human connections and allow for highly specialized messages for various voter profiles, it also increases the speed at which information gathered during a conversation can be returned to the campaign. This translates into greater efficiency and success for the campaign effort, since mailers can immediately be sent, messages can be quickly refined, and the electorate's pulse can be constantly read.

Another important technological tool for the political campaign is inbound/outbound calls. These, commonly known as "800" numbers, can be used in conjunction with mass communication vehicles like television, radio, and print advertisements to cultivate the development of an interactive campaign, as well as to raise funds and recruit volunteers.

```
Campaign # 19B6     OP_COM:                                    FDISP : FD

Contact Info
Contact Name  :  Mrs. Holly F. Woodruff        DOB     :    02/10/36
Address       :  9847 North Division, Apt. #5  Age     :    63
City          :  Horse Cave                    Sex     :    F
State         :  Kentucky                      Race    :    W
ZipCode       :  48956                         Party   :    D
Phone         :  504-896-2509                  Vote History:  GE: 2/3    LE: 3/3

Voter Contact Journal:
9/16/99    s/t    no answer
9/17/99    s/t  s/m  issue: social security
10/20/99   I/t  I/m  ID: Somewhat Favorable  issues: social security, education, crime
10/29      p/t  p/t  issues: social security, taxes
11/3       gotv m
11/4       gotv t  no answer
11/5       gotv t  favorable

Hello Ms. Woodruff, this is Edgar McGee calling on behalf of Fran Smith.  I am calling to remind
you that your vote can make a difference in today's election. Please help Fran Smith preserve our
Social Security benefits by voting today.  Can we count on you to go to the polls and vote for Mrs.
Smith? (wait for response)

Don't forget, the polls close at 8PM.  Mrs. Smith is counting on your support.

Thank you and have a nice day.

*Q1  _____

          Deliver Message

          Did Not Deliver Message

          STALINE
```

Figure 4. Phone script

Courtesy The Clinton Group

THE ROLE OF DIRECT MAIL

The combination of a telephone dialogue with a coordinated mailer has proven highly successful in educating, activating, persuading, and motivating voters. Mail is an especially valuable tool in expressing complicated issues because it uses both written and graphic language: the political communicator can "show and tell" the likely voter. As with the telephone, direct mail allows for a targeted persuasive message on issues identified by the research and therefore a more personalized contact with the campaign. Moreover, a carefully coordinated direct mail/telephone campaign continues and reinforces the dialogue between the candidate and the voter.

THE FOUR PHASES OF A TELEPHONE/DIRECT MAIL CAMPAIGN

The success of the grassroots effort depends on the frequency and quality of contact between the campaign and the voter. The prototypical telephone/direct mail campaign has four basic phases.

Sensitizing

There are many variations used in this first phase, but the basic method is a short and simple telephone call alerting the voter to the existence and goal of the candidate or issue. The sensitizing call also establishes the campaign-to-voter-to-campaign dialogue by eliciting a small but affirmative commitment to the campaign: a promise from the voter to read a piece of mail about the candidate or issue: "I know the election is still two months away, but we are going to send you an information packet in the mail explaining our candidate's qualifications. You will take the time to look it over, won't you, Mr./Mrs. Voter?"

After the telephone call, each voter receives a substantive piece of mail from the campaign addressing an issue generated by the initial research. In the governor's race, people over the age of sixty-five received a mail piece discussing the candidate's position on preserving Social Security. Middle-aged women were sent a packet highlighting the candidate's past achievements in increasing the quality and decreasing the price of the state's child care facilities.

Sample Four-Phase Voter Contact Program

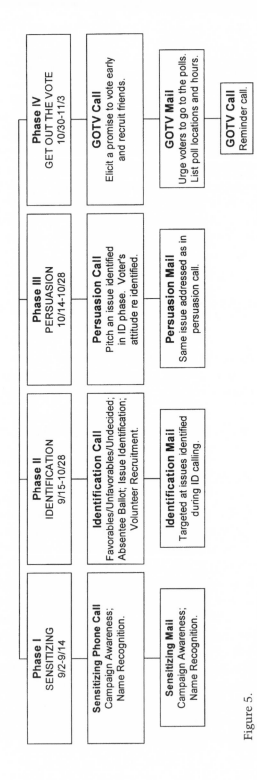

Figure 5.

Courtesy The Clinton Group

The sensitizing phase generally occurs two months before election day. All voters in a targeted universe receive this first contact. Since calls are billed according to length, the sensitizing call, at forty to fifty-five seconds each, is moderately priced.

Identification

Four to six weeks before election day, another telephone call identifies the individual voter's attitude about the candidate and the issue of greatest concern. Telemarketers use a multiquestion format to preserve the complexity of opinions; a single question ("How do you feel about Candidate X?") yields inadequate information to continue a high-quality dialogue. This phase separates supporters from opponents and establishes the strength of the voter's commitment to the candidate. Solidly favorable voters are encouraged to participate in the campaign through fund-raising or volunteer efforts or marked to be called back near election day. Unalterably opposed voters are eliminated from the list and are not contacted again.

Most important, this phase identifies the group of persuadable voters and determines which issues will be used to convince them to vote for the candidate. Issues theoretically determined to be salient to a certain voter are tested and the results analyzed and recorded for future message refinement. This last voter group is crucial because it is generally the "undecided, open to persuasion" population that determines elections. In the case of the gubernatorial race, many of the undecided voters were middle-aged women whose research-generated concerns included health care, education, and day care. At this stage of the telephone campaign, however, it was determined that for most women in this category, secondary and postsecondary educational issues were the most important.

All voters except those unalterably opposed will also receive targeted personalized mail usually addressing the issue of greatest concern to the individual voter. People who are truly undecided receive a specialized mail communication from the campaign. Strong "favorables" will be asked to volunteer, while "persuadables" will be asked to examine the candidate's stance on a certain issue. This piece is designed to make the voter think, "This candidate seems to know what I'm most worried about and knows how I feel about the important things."

Telephone calls in the sensitizing and identification phases average

Defining the Contact Universe

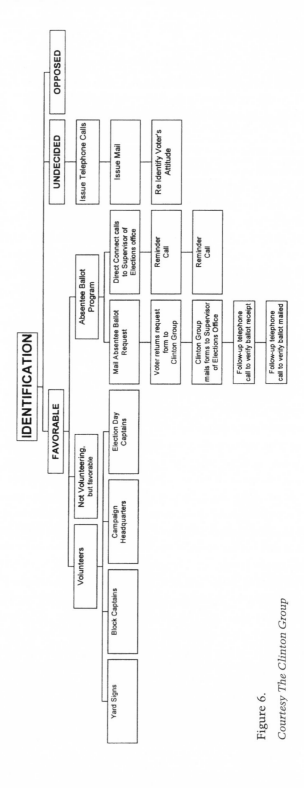

Figure 6.
Courtesy The Clinton Group

forty-five to sixty seconds. They are moderate to costly calls to make because higher-quality, multiquestion calls take more time.

Persuasion

This phase of the telephone/direct mail campaign is targeted at all voters identified as persuadable: somewhat favorable, slightly favorable, undecided, slightly unfavorable, or somewhat unfavorable. Each voter is given a strong pitch on the candidate's stand on the issue defined during the identification telephone call, and the voter's attitude is subsequently reidentified once again. This persuasive contact allows the candidate to convey his or her message and demonstrates to the voter that the candidate is receptive. One to two days later, the voter receives a piece of follow-up persuasion mail, addressing the same issue as the telephone call.

The persuasion phase is where the telephone's capability for precision shines. Many elections are won or lost in this phase, especially as the importance of party affiliation wanes and voters increasingly split tickets or vote for different parties on one ballot. In the governor's race the "undecided, open to persuasion" category included a broad range of voter profiles. Mass media political communication tools were too blunt to sway a patchwork quilt of voters that ranged from rural professionals to retired African Americans to single mothers. By using the campaign's attitudinal research in combination with the enhanced voter registration list and the attached record of voter contact, tailored messages were created to fit each very narrowly defined voter profile. For example, there were different messages for rural white women professionals, retired urban African Americans, single suburban professional women, and retired suburban white voters. The telephone provided an accurate and precise medium to persuade and motivate individual voters and consequently helped to win the election.

The persuasion phase occurs approximately one week or ten days before election day. These calls last forty-five seconds or more, depending on the issues and audience.

Get Out the Vote (GOTV)

Just as the entire campaign is focused on motivating supporters to get to the polls and vote, the goal of the preceding three phases is to generate a list of favorable voters for the GOTV campaign. This phase consists of a minimum of two telephone calls to each identified favorable. A few days before election day, these self-expressed, likely supporters receive a call urging them to go to the polls. The voters are also requested to vote before a certain time and asked if they need assistance in getting to the polls. Recruiting volunteers for help during the GOTV drive can also occur at this point. Using volunteers to make phone calls, hand out literature at the polls, and provide rides to the polls is an effective way of activating supporters and controlling costs. A second phone call comes either the day before or the day of the election. Each GOTV call lasts fifteen to twenty-five seconds.

Shortly before the election, all identified favorable voters are also sent a mailer—listing poll locations and hours—urging them to the polls. Often, specific issues are used as persuasion in this last personalized campaign contact.

In choosing a telecommunications vendor for your campaign, be sure to select a company with *political* telemarketing experience. Political telemarketers are specifically oriented toward quality of contact, not quantity of contact—a big difference from commercial telemarketers who are driven by quota expectations and do not understand the subtle nuances of political communication. In contrast, the political telemarketer's goal is a two-way conversation with a potential supporter to persuade and motivate and to gather data to be appended to the voter files and returned to the campaign for analysis. Commercial telemarketers are interested in finding the sale, not identifying the undecideds. For the political telemarketer, however, the undecideds often make the difference between winning and losing.

Ann E. W. Stone

STEALTH CAMPAIGNING

WINNING "UNDER THE RADAR"

When Ronald Reagan won the presidential election of 1980, the media were taken by surprise. Newspaper and magazine articles appeared in December 1980 and January 1981 asking, "How could this have happened?" and "Who are all those people and organizations that helped elect him?"

Reagan, contrary to the media spin, was not the boardroom candidate in that year; John Connally and George Bush were the favored candidates of the fat cats. Ronald Reagan's campaign funding, for the most part, came in $15, $25, and $35 checks, from hundreds of thousands of people across the country. These people had been giving to Reagan or, more correctly, to direct mail solicitations sent out under his signature, for a wide range of conservative and Republican fund-raising organizations nationwide. Years before he ever announced his candidacy, Reagan had begun to build a direct mail army of supporters, donors, and volunteers all across the country. Thus by the time he declared he would run for the office of president, Reagan's campaign was able to tap a huge network of small-walleted sympathizers.

Further, the organizations that came forward to support Reagan had also been built largely through the power of direct mail fund-raising. Groups like the Heritage Foundation, the National Conservative Political Action Committee, the Fund for a Conservative Majority, and the American Conservative Union, now widely familiar, were unknown to the general public back then. These groups had been building their membership, credibility, and influence behind the scenes for years, under the media's radar screen.

In some ways, it was no surprise the media were so astonished at the power of all these groups and the ability of Ronald Reagan to overcome the odds and be elected president of the United States. The media did not understand that the Republican Party, and specifically the conservative movement, had created a direct marketing machine that would sustain them and put them ahead in fund-raising ability for decades to come, even to this day. More important, targeted solicitations did not seem as newsworthy as television ads and televised debates—"junk mail" rarely merits a headline.

Most of the public would still be surprised to learn that, even in the last (1998) election cycle, the majority of donors to the Republican Party had a *lower* average contribution than those who gave to the Democrats. In fact, the average contribution to the GOP until it took control of Congress was in the $25 to $35 range, while the average donation to the Democrats was $250. That situation should be, and is, changing, since large contributions from the special interest groups always follow the power; the GOP will now get a bigger share of the larger-dollar gifts.

But money is not the only advantage direct mail provided Ronald Reagan. Direct mail was used to generate and motivate volunteers and to hold "house parties" for Reagan to help with grassroots organizing. Mailers were sent to alert grassroots groups on how to counter the media bias against Reagan and to generate letters to the editor campaigns and op-ed pieces and, ultimately, for get-out-the-vote efforts.

Those who worked for Reagan's election would attest that direct mail was the great equalizer in that campaign. The media and the pundits did not take the Republican candidate seriously. They also opposed most of what he stood for, so even when they would cover him, they were less than kind. Direct mail enabled Reagan to get his message out unfiltered by the media. He put millions of packets of information in the hands of his dedicated followers for them to pass on to friends and neighbors.

LESSONS LEARNED

Reagan's example was repeated in many federal and local elections. Yet these days many general political consultants seem to dismiss the use of mail or slough it off on volunteers or anyone who thinks he or she can write a letter. This prejudice is owed partly to "TV-hypnosis": we've heard so often that television ads make or break campaigns that we begin to believe it. To the contrary, one of the reasons the Democrats caught the Republicans by surprise in the 1998 elections was that the Democrats' allies—the unions, environmental groups, and others—who had spent millions on splashy television ads in 1996 got smart and took their campaigns underground. They spent more of their money on direct mail and grassroots and less on the TV networks.

Direct mail was also the covert weapon used by the unions to counter Proposition 226 in California in the 1998 election cycle. This proposition, dubbed the Paycheck Protection initiative by the Republicans, would have mandated that unions obtain the permission of their members before using any of their dues for political purposes. This would have hamstrung the unions, possibly ending their effectiveness as a political force. At the outset, this proposition looked like a sure thing for the Republicans. Even among union members, it was showing up in surveys as wildly popular.

So what happened? According to the AFL-CIO's own poll conducted by Peter Hart, union members reported that direct mail was the number one reason they voted against the measure. In fact, it was cited at almost a two-to-one ratio—more than any radio or TV ads that had been run.

This success has been repeated not only in campaign elections but also in lobbying campaigns by many other special interest groups. Associations like the Credit Union National Association (CUNA) effectively used direct mail and other covert direct-response tools to generate grassroots support, largely unnoticed by the media. CUNA was able to pass the Credit Union Membership Act, which allowed credit unions to expand membership eligibility.

COVERTNESS AND EFFECTIVENESS

Why is stealth campaigning (through direct mail) so effective? Its success may largely be owing to the covert nature of this campaign tool. Think about it. If you mail a letter to someone, who else knows what is inside the envelope? Only you and the recipient. And the recipient will never know just how many other people you have written to or just exactly what you have said.

Direct mail allows you to target your message to your audience, provide them with facts and information in black and white, all the while out of the sight of your opponent and the media. Compare this to the use of high-visibility television ad campaigns. If your opponent's campaign is competent, they can find out how much media you are buying and where. By watching the different channels and observing the message you are putting out, they will see your strategy. Further, by taking note of when and where you change your commercials, they will know what your polling is telling you and therefore how your strategy is changing. It is completely overt.

An example occurred in the 1998 campaign, with fatal results for the

Republican Party's hopes of expanding its majority in the House and Senate. In the last weeks before election day, Republican Party leaders decided *selectively* to "go Lewinsky," that is, in certain targeted rural, conservative districts to run TV ads suggesting that the vote was a referendum on President Clinton's (im)moral leadership. The problem with trying to be selective in a mass-mediated age, however, is that ads themselves become news if they are sufficiently controversial. Often this is a good thing—free publicity through earned media time and space. But when the message is aimed at one constituency, it can backfire if it is replayed in news and critiqued by press pundits in the view of other groups of voters. The press picked up on the anti-Clinton ads, making it sound as if "GOP attacks Clinton personally" was the general Republican message of 1998 for the entire nation. What was a local injection became a national broadcast—and this hurt Republicans in districts where voters were weary of messages condemning the president's private behavior and ready to vote against the messenger.

As a result, the best campaigns in the future may more fully use the old-fashioned, more subdued media tactics, eschewing those that have absorbed most of the campaign dollars in recent elections. Astute Republicans will return to the proven direct-response tools that laid the foundation for their successes in the 1980s and 1990s.

Direct-response marketing through print media such as direct mail or through telemarketing is a tough proposition to sell in some quarters; candidates and organizations generally prefer high-visibility media like TV or radio. The candidates and their families like seeing themselves on television or hearing themselves on radio; it's an ego rush. A direct mail package, in contrast, is not as exciting, nor do the consultants make as much money on that service.

Nevertheless, even radio and television budgets should have a direct-response component. Although those media do not have the covert advantage of other forms of direct response, DRTV (direct-response TV) and radio ads can provide a toll-free number so that viewers or listeners may call in for more information, to volunteer, or to send money. This is a great way to generate extra cash, volunteers, and votes and actually measure the success of the ad. Of course, one reason that many media consultants do not use direct response is because their efforts *can* be measured. Imagine the reaction of a candidate who has a direct-response ad on TV listing a phone number for voters to call in on, and no one calls in! That would be one very unhappy client.

I do not mean to recommend that campaigns never use radio or television, but rather that consultants realize that they need to look at direct-response covert tools first, adding TV and radio to help give credibility and raise name identification, if needed. That formula may not be as sexy or flashy, but history tells us it gets the job done—and done well.

Sean Reilly | OUTDOOR ADVERTISING

In his 1983 rematch with incumbent governor Dave Treen, former governor Edwin Edwards set the tone early. Though he was personally popular and respected, Dave Treen's administration was laboring under a sputtering economy. There was a sense among the electorate that times weren't as good as when the "crafty Cajun" Edwards occupied the governor's mansion. So, a year before election day, billboards went up all over the state saying simply, "Hang on Louisiana, Edwin's coming!"

This short and pointed message was executed in the familiar blue and yellow graphics of the Edwards campaign and hit every motorist in the state right through the windshield for six months. Down the stretch, these boards would reinforce television delivering the same message, as Edwards's thirty-second spots—which carried the same tagline—depicted the Louisiana ship of state as the *Titanic* going down.

This creative use of outdoor advertising to establish a campaign theme *early on* represented the use of billboards at their best. The graphics were simple and the copy was short. But most important, the content had wit and bite. Such qualities projected a message that could be instantly understood by an audience driving by at high speed. In addition, as with other well-executed political billboards, the "Hang On" campaign caught the eye of other media, garnering extensive free coverage by television and newspapers.

Another example of effective outdoor advertising from Louisiana political lore is the independent expenditure that erected a billboard for Edwards's fourth race for governor, that against former Ku Klux Klansman David Duke in 1991. Here the graphics were stark and insistent. The billboard simply spelled out "DUKE" followed by a huge swastika with a superimposed slashed red circle. This message was certainly not subtle, but it was effective. Pictures of that billboard showed up in television newscasts and newspaper layouts across the state. Indeed, in this instance news coverage extended nationwide as wire services from across the country picked up the story.

GETTING THE NAME OUT

Outdoor advertising has long been used to build candidate name recognition; this remains the primary reason candidates buy outdoor media early on in a campaign cycle. Also, outdoor advertising can be more cost effective than other media because of its relatively low cost per thousand impressions and the opportunity it provides a candidate to target his or her message to specific voters in the district.

In statewide races, outdoor advertising's cost effectiveness allows a candidate to save much-needed resources for the home stretch. The cost per thousand impressions is typically one-third that of radio expenditures and one-tenth that of television. This means the budget will not be blown too early on the simple function of name identification. There is added value in getting the candidate's graphics, name, and picture across the state a year to nine months before an election. This makes the candidate a "player" in the eyes of the voters, so that as the campaign unfolds other media appearances and speeches resonate to a greater degree. This is the "name in lights" effect: from our filmgoing experience, we think of people whose names are biggest as the "stars."

In nonstatewide elections where the district consists of a portion of a major media market, billboards can be targeted at voters in certain neighborhoods in the district. The use of costly television and newspaper for the simple function of introducing the candidate to the voters in a small district race would be an imprudent use of funds. Outdoor media, in contrast, can be highly targeted so that advertising dollars aren't spent on those who don't live in the district.

THE RULES OF OUTDOOR ADVERTISING

Production for a name recognition message has simple ground rules. The technology of digital printing on vinyl has made it possible to create outstanding, magazine-quality graphics, so a flattering photograph of the candidate works best. The graphics and colors should be clean and simple, the copy short and uncluttered.

Whether the message is name recognition or something with a little more substance, there are some standard guidelines to follow:

First, type and lettering should be clear and easy to read. Words made up entirely of capital letters are usually not as legible as words in both upper and lower cases. Care should be take with spacing between letters and words. Letters with too little spacing tend to merge when viewed from a distance. Avoid overly bold or thin lettering. Heavy typefaces tend to blur at long distances while fine typefaces tend to fade or break up visually. Simple, sans serif typefaces work best in outdoor advertising, but ornate serif do not. Typefaces with excessive contrast between thick and thin elements greatly reduce legibility.

Second, when choosing colors for outdoor executions, the designer should use those with high contrast in both hue and value: hue is the identity of the color, such as red, green, or yellow; value is a measure of the color's lightness or darkness. Contrasting colors work best when viewed from a distance. Colors without contrast blend together and obscure the message. Hence reversing white out of any dark value color enhances visibility by providing a strong and effective contrast.

THE PRACTICE

A testimonial for getting out a tough political message with outdoor advertising was given by Gerry Nicholls, communications director for Ontarians for Responsible Government. His group deployed an outdoor campaign in downtown Ontario aimed at incumbent premier Bob Rae, whose economic and tax policies lent themselves to satiric attack. One billboard ad featured a series of three photos: a mousetrap subtitled "Mouse Killer," a fly swatter subtitled "Bug Killer," and a photo of Bob Rae subtitled "Job Killer."

Over the course of the campaign cycle this billboard generated controversy and attracted much attention. Later in the campaign, the billboard depicted Bob Rae smiling, with copy to the right asking, "How do you like socialism so far?" Toward the end of the campaign, as polls showed Bob Rae's popularity falling, this copy was changed to read, "Bye Bye Bob! Socialism didn't work." Media coverage of this campaign was extensive as newspaper editors sent photographers to snap pictures that appeared in local papers. Wire services picked up those pictures, which ended up in every newspaper across the country. In this instance, the billboard became the media celebrity, and in this race Bob Rae was voted out of office in a landslide. As proof of the devastating impact of the attention-grabbing outdoor campaign, Rae referred to this billboard in his memoirs.

Ontarians for Responsible Government were so happy with the results of their anti-Rae efforts that they retained this billboard for other campaigns. Gerry Nicholls cites several reasons for its success. First, the message was creative, eye-catching, and concise. Second, the copy was seven words or less. And finally, photographic or graphic material clearly supported the content.

In summary, the same elements that work for Madison Avenue when convincing people what to buy also work in elections when convincing people how to vote. Keep the message simple, keep the graphics interesting, and keep the copy short. If the goal is to attract the attention of other media, produce an ad whose overall tone is witty or even a bit controversial. If executed early and well, a billboard can become a political landmark.

Thomas N. Edmonds | **PRINT ADS**

The vast majority of political advertising dollars are spent on television and, to a lesser extent, radio—the two most glamorous media. Broadcasting is favored because it allows the advertiser to reach a wider audience and to use moving images and sound to convey a clear message and leave a lasting impression. Moreover, broadcast is a "quick change" medium, that is, it allows the advertiser to alter an existing ad or replace it altogether with just a few hours' notice should circumstances warrant such a change. Print, however, has been neglected by many political media professionals. This is in large part because of its long-standing, and to a degree deserved, reputation as a less-than-adaptable medium for political purposes. But many newspapers and magazines have in recent years gone to great lengths to attract political advertisers, and today they offer many distinct benefits for candidates and their campaigns.

NEWSPAPERS

Before radio and television, newspapers were virtually the only medium capable of reaching diverse, mass audiences across a city, county, or even state. With no competition, newspapers set the rules for political advertising—rules that were not accommodating to the needs of campaigns. The landscape began to change in the 1930s, when Franklin Roosevelt effectively used radio to break the newspapers' monopoly on mass communication. Despite the competition from radio, however, the print medium steadfastly adhered to its old ways. Even the arrival of television could not prod newspapers into reexamining their policies on political advertising, and the old power players quickly became nothing more than an afterthought for many major campaigns.

The common criticisms of newspapers in the political community were many:

- *Newspapers cost too much.*
- *Their salespeople aren't receptive to our needs.*

- *Newspapers turn down ads that conflict with their endorsements.*
- *Their extensive campaign coverage means readers get the message without anyone having to buy space.*
- *Newspapers can't respond quickly enough in the heat of the campaign.*
- *Newspapers lack the impact of television and radio messages.*
- *Newspapers can't be targeted to specific voters.*

Increasingly, however, newspapers have developed programs and services to address these concerns. Many have lowered price rates for political ads, loosened standards on advertising, established shorter placement deadlines during the election season, trained their staffs to work with political campaigns, embraced new production technologies, and offered new products and services. In areas where such changes were implemented, political advertising in newspapers has increased, and many consultants are discovering the distinct advantages newspapers offer and the benefits of using print in addition to television and radio.

ADVANTAGES OF NEWSPAPER

Newspapers offer political advertisers several benefits that other media cannot.

Newspapers are the original news medium. Of the major media, newspapers are the only true news medium. People who seek out in-depth, detailed political information read a newspaper; for that reason alone it makes sense for candidates to provide their information in print right next to the coverage of the campaign. Conversely, television and radio are for the most part entertainment media. Or, put another way, nobody reads a paper to "zonk" or "veg" or escape from reality, while this is often the case with the viewers of and listeners to radio and television. The newspaper thus is the medium best suited to supply the facts to back up the positions taken by candidates. Moreover, by simply appearing in the "News," "Metro," or "Views and Opinions" section, a campaign ad takes on an aspect of soberness, respectability, and credibility—perhaps more so in our modern era of "infotainment" television news.

Newspapers reach high-turnout voters. Newspaper readers vote;

television watchers may or may not. Research indicates that the citizens who are most likely to vote and participate in political campaigns are better educated and have higher incomes than those who do not—and are typically the most faithful newspaper readers, which makes newspapers the best medium for reaching them. Newspapers are also well suited to reach primary voters, those who vote for down-ballot (nonfederal, nonstatewide) offices in off-year elections, and those who vote in special elections.

Interestingly, newspapers are particularly useful in reaching the all-important ticket-splitters (people who divide their votes across party lines). Research shows that some 65 percent of ticket-splitters read the political coverage in their newspaper every day or almost every day. By contrast, television is the medium that reaches the largest number of nonvoters.

Newspapers reach a local audience. As Tip O'Neill said, "All politics is local." In many rural areas, weekly newspapers have never lost their predominance. Campaigns cannot afford to ignore this universal, cover-to-cover readership. In metropolitan areas, most newspapers have established sections based on geographic zones and can also target a preprinted flyer or brochure for delivery in specific zip codes. Many can target delivery down to the block or census tract level. Newspaper databases of subscribers and nonsubscribers are increasingly coded with PRIZM data, which is a common demographic targeting system, and other useful information.

Newspapers can target specific types of voters. Newspapers are offering readers an increasing number of sections and features tailored to their individual interests or lifestyles. Candidates can place their advertisements where they will have the highest likelihood of reaching their targeted audience.

THE CONTENTS OF NEWSPAPER ADS

Because of the amount of text that can be included, newspaper advertisements are ideally suited for longer-format, informational pieces. For instance, a newspaper ad is the perfect place to list endorsements garnered by the candidate or to highlight notable supporters. Newspaper ads also allow candidates to explain in detail their support or opposition of a particular issue, which can be used to reinforce radio or television ads on the same subject or to rebut an opponent's attack.

Newspapers also lend themselves well to point-by-point comparisons between candidates and to contrasts between the candidates' experience or the number of endorsements they have. In each case, it is not necessary for the voter to read the *entire* copy—the sheer copiousness of information in the print format may suggest to a potential voter that there is substance in the candidate's positions.

Newspaper ads can also, like direct mail, appeal for contributions and volunteer support. The copy and graphics tell voters why they should support a particular candidate and what they can do to help elect him or her. Tear-off coupons serve as a response device to get the reader involved. It is also useful to include an Internet Web site address for the campaign in print advertisements because it is easier for the reader to remember (and find again) an address printed in a newspaper than one that is flashed on a television screen for just a few seconds.

BUYING AND PLACING NEWSPAPER ADS

One way newspapers have become more accommodating to ad agencies is through the emergence of companies such as Adnet America that understand political print advertising and the needs of consultants. With one phone call to Adnet, agencies can obtain key information on almost any newspaper in the country, including many local, regional, and weekly papers. Information such as circulation, deadlines, and cost can usually be faxed within minutes. Another advantage to using companies such as Adnet is that it allows the agencies to write one insertion order and thus one check no matter how many newspapers are bought. It is also convenient to deal with one individual instead of multiple salespersons all across the country.

An additional development by the newspaper industry to help political ad-makers is allowing companies to send their artwork electronically. By not having to produce mechanical artwork and "pull film" (find, print, and send the photos), agencies save an enormous amount of time. Agencies also like this system because sending the artwork electronically decreases the cost of producing traditional artwork.

Finally, one of the newest innovations offered by newspapers, which is being used successfully by campaigns all across the country, is pre-printed poly-bags, which are the plastic bags in which newspapers are delivered to their subscribers. Campaigns are always looking for new ways to catch voters' attention; poly-bags allow the campaign to deliver a bold message in color that is hard to ignore. Many newspapers offer geographic targeting for poly-bag advertisers. The most obvious timing for a campaign "bagvertisement" is election day delivery—reminding voters in favorable districts to vote and providing maps to their precinct polling stations.

COST

Just as with television and radio, the rates charged by newspapers vary widely depending on the market and the audience size. For instance, a full-page advertisement in the Sunday edition of a large-city paper can cost close to $100,000, while the same ad in a smaller, local paper may cost less than $3,000. Compare the differences between the rates charged by three Illinois newspapers:

	Circulation	Full-page Ad Cost
Chicago Tribune		
Daily	747,654	$61,740
Sunday	1,131,226	$86,688
Joliet Herald News		
Daily	43,112	$2,443
Sunday	45,296	$2,565
Havana Mason County Democrat		
Weekly (Wednesday)	3,546	$1,122

Keep in mind that many newspapers can target an insert for delivery in specific zip codes, which may reduce the rate charged.

MAGAZINES

In today's world, the selection of magazines available to advertisers is almost endless. From *Macramé Today* to *Civil War Digest* to *Newsweek*, there are magazines covering virtually every profession, interest, and hobby. Most metropolitan areas have one or more glossy monthlies. Magazines have been all but ignored by political advertisers, however, and for good reasons, not the least of which are the long lead times between the placement of an ad and its actual publication, sometimes two or three months later. Furthermore, magazine ads could not be selectively targeted to reach only a portion of the general audience. Also, the cost of an ad in a national magazine was prohibitive for a political campaign. Just as with newspapers, however, significant improvements have been made in recent years that make magazines a more attractive and viable option for political advertisers.

TARGETING MAGAZINE ADS GEOGRAPHICALLY

Studies show that magazine subscribers are generally more affluent than the general population, and national magazines offer credibility and prestige to the advertiser's message. Still, it wouldn't make much sense for a congressional candidate to buy an ad in a magazine that would run nationwide. But political advertisers can take advantage of the benefits offered by magazines like *Time, Newsweek*, and *U.S. News* by targeting their ads to appear only in certain metropolitan areas through the use of Media Networks, Inc. (MNI). By offering coverage on a market-by-market basis, MNI makes magazine advertising far more affordable for political customers.

MNI targeting is available in 150 metropolitan areas and in some areas on a county-by-county basis. MNI also offers various packages of magazines depending on the target audience. For instance, to reach men, MNI offers a package that includes *Sports Illustrated, Sport, Road & Track*, and *Field & Stream.*

Even on a regional basis, magazine advertising remains expensive. For some campaigns, however, it may make sense to employ magazine advertising. The following are examples of pricing for a full-page, color advertisement in MNI's news magazine package (*Time, Newsweek, U.S. News*) in various metropolitan areas:

	Circulation	Cost
Atlanta, Ga.	116,920	$17,415
Des Moines, Ia.	40,030	$7,640
Los Angeles, Calif.	70,900	$10,050

MAKING PRINT ADS WORK

Advertising is a complex mix of science and art, with many different schools of thought on what works and what doesn't. Nevertheless, there are some tried and true rules that should always be observed when creating a print ad, whether it be for a newspaper or a magazine.

Get the reader's attention with short, punchy headlines. Your ad is competing with hundreds of others. The headline and any graphics must catch the reader's attention. Use the headline to appeal to his needs or offer a direct benefit. Expand on these points in the copy.

Keep the ad simple. One of print's biggest benefits is the amount of information that can be conveyed in a single ad. But don't overdo it. Leave plenty of room for art and white space, which will make the add more attractive and enhance readability.

Use multiple (complementary) ads. A large single ad followed by a series of smaller ads scattered throughout the same edition builds a candidate's image, reminds readers of the main message, and reinforces a sense of urgency.

Above all, it is important for campaigns to understand that print ads are not typically the vanguard of a political strategy. In numerous races where the margin of victory is only a couple of percentage points, however, newspapers and magazines offer candidates revitalized communications media that can help them reach the winner's circle.

RESOURCES

Newspaper Association of America
6 South 230 Concord Road
Naperville, IL 60540
630/428-0794

Media Networks, Inc.
7600-B Leesburg Pike
Suite 340
Falls Church, VA 22043
703/749-6236

Adnet America
11006 Lakeridge Parkway
Ashland, VA 23005
804/550-2361

It just makes sense...

...to protect our way of life.

It's no secret that millions of working Americans are also gun owners and hunters. And that's why millions of people have joined the National Rifle Association — to help protect the Second Amendment.

We're a "special interest group," and proud of it. No other organization is more effective in defending our "special interest" — the rights guaranteed by the Second Amendment that belong to all of us, including the fundamental right of self-defense, as well as our heritage of hunting and wildlife conservation.

These issues are the measure — the only measure — by which we judge our elected representatives and candidates for office.

Politicians take stands on lots of other issues — that's their job. But we don't.

Democrat or Republican, liberal or conservative — labels matter to some. But not us.

Other groups are involved in other issues — that's their job. But we're not.

For 125 years, this has been our mission. And so it is in Election Year 1996.

The bottom line is that it just makes sense to support the organizations that protect your way of life.

Don't let someone else make the decision for you. It's up to you to get involved, register to vote, and stay informed about the issues that matter to you. Most importantly, on Election Day, support the candidates who will defend the most *special* interests of all: *your* interests.

For more information, call our toll-free Grassroots Hotline: **1-800-392-8683**

This ad will appear in the July, 1996 Issue of *Trade Union Courier*.

Figure 7. NRA print ad

Courtesy Edmonds Associates

Bill Fletcher | **RADIO ADS**

Television is the dominant medium in America, and that includes politics at virtually every level. But in spite of the power, growth, and reach of television, radio remains a dynamic medium for modern politics. On radio democracy and commerce collide. It offers politicians and political groups a relatively captive audience twice each day, on the morning drive to work and the afternoon return home. Radio is also the most imaginative medium: one can suggest in a few reasonably priced words and sound effects what would take millions of dollars to visualize on a television screen.

Because radio deals in sounds and impressions, it is a much less forgiving medium than film or television. If you throw enough money at any film script it can look slick and almost obscure poor plotting, ridiculous situations, and inane dialogue. But you can't hide bad writing in a radio commercial. A poorly conceived and scripted spot will sound rough even if it is created in a room full of computerized equipment and voiced by a Broadway actor hired through a New York agency. Alternately, one can make a great radio commercial at a small radio station where the owner voices the spot and then edits it with a razor blade and tape.

For this reason, the technology should always be secondary to the talent—and that talent is expressed in the voices, the script (the writing, plot, and ideas), direction (managing voice, words, and action), and, equally important, the media buying (when and where to place the spot).

VOICE

The voice is the heart and soul of a good radio commercial. That is why political professionals use *voice actors*, not radio personalities. Most radio announcers are ill suited to voice a political commercial. They usually have one gear for their voice, and they stay in it all the time. A great voice actor can shift tone and diction with ease so as to connect with the listener at an emotional level.

Political professionals often develop creative partnerships with voice actors. Often when I'm writing for television or radio, I will hear the voice of the actor I plan to use in my head as I write the spot. These professional relationships are a "value added" that political professionals bring to the table. We know the voice actors who have the range and acting ability to pull off a soft biographical spot, a hard sell, an attack, or an explanation.

SCRIPT

The most common error in radio scripting is overlong or overripe writing. Freed from the limitation of thirty-second television spots, many consultants try to jam too many ideas, words, and concepts into a sixty-second radio commercial. Then they compound the error by forcing the voice actor to rip through the spot, rushing past the natural breaks, until the entire commercial takes on the semblance of a legal disclaimer for a car dealer.

The best way to make sure you haven't tried to cram too much into a radio spot is to read it aloud and time yourself. Be careful to enunciate each word clearly so as not to cheat the time. Most political radio commercials are sixty seconds in length. (Radio stations often discourage thirty-second commercials in favor of sixty-second spots. A station that charges $100 for a sixty-second spot might charge $75 for a thirty-second commercial.) With the legally required disclaimer detailing who paid for and authorized the ad, this leaves about fifty-five seconds. Allowing for time to establish music and for any sound effects, the voice actor's script should be between fifty and fifty-three seconds long.

The first sentence of a radio commercial is the most crucial. In most cases, it should be simple, declarative, and designed to invite the listener to tarry for a moment. The opening of a radio spot is also a good place to trot out those quotes and other bon mots you've been saving in your filing system since college.

Below are some examples of good opening lines for a radio spot:

"Once in a very great while . . . someone moves us, changes us, gives us hope. This year that extraordinary person is congressional candidate Jane Doe."

"You can tell a lot about a man by what he does when he thinks no one is watching."

"There once was a man who took from the poor and gave to the rich. His name is John Smith, the Reverse Robin Hood." [Delivered in a Monty Python-like British accent.]

"The year was 1985, and somewhere, a child was crying. And not just one child . . . hundreds. John Smith heard the children and became their champion."

"They're counting on you. In the corridors of political power . . . they are counting on you . . . not to vote."

"Everybody knows a man like John Smith . . . up with the sun, loving his family, working on his farm, serving his community."

By design, none of these openings sound particularly political. The only way to hold the modern, cynical audience and to communicate a political message is to begin with an emotional connection or an intellectual challenge.

Following are a few bad ways to start a political radio commercial:

"This is State Representative Bubba Gump and I want to ask for your vote."

"John Smith is a liar and I'm here to set the record straight."

"The election is just a few days away. . . ."

Start a radio commercial like that and the next sound you will hear is hundreds of thousands of people changing the radio station to try to find a traffic report.

The basic point is to make every word count because in good writing of any kind it must. In *A Moveable Feast*, Ernest Hemingway spoke of a technique he used in his short stories. He wrote in the cafés of Paris and then set his work aside for a few days or weeks. When he returned to his manuscript, he would read it until he found the first "true" thought; then he would discard everything else and begin again from that point.

The brevity and emotional understatement present in Hemingway's work is a great tutorial for radio writers. Write down your thoughts, then comb through them looking for the truth—the essence of what you're trying to communicate. Then jettison the chaff and commence with that thought.

DIRECTION

Even the best voice actor needs direction when voicing a political commercial. They need to know the tone of the commercial and the context of the spot in the overall campaign. Voice actors with whom I've worked for years have often complained to me about producers and directors who simply don't know what they want.

When directing a radio commercial, it's not enough to tell the actor, "Just read it." For example, let's assume you are producing a political commercial for a congressional candidate. The first third of the spot is biographical, the middle third touches on the major issues of the campaign, and the final third is an appeal for support and votes. You might say something like this to the voice actor:

"Perform the first two paragraphs in a soft, languid, nostalgic style. Then shift to a tougher, faster, news read and punch the first two words as you come to each major issue such as Social Security, the Environment, Health Care. Then, for the close, shift back to the original tone and tempo but read with great authority and confidence."

Typically, the voice actor will make notes and marks on the script to indicate your direction. After the first read, offer comment and criticism and let the actor read the script again. Usually, you will get the read you're looking for in five or six attempts. If you get the first half of the spot down just the way you want it, don't make the actor read that part over and over again. Spend your time on getting the second half right and let your audio engineer edit the reads together.

BUYING RADIO TIME

Radio is a tough medium to buy for political campaigns. Stations are constantly changing formats, which means the station that was rock and roll last week might be gospel today. Also, there is a widely held misconception that radio is cheap. The only cheap radio is on small stations with tiny audiences. Commercials on large, major market stations are often nearly as expensive as television commercials in some markets.

The campaign should employ the services of a professional media buyer who is either familiar with the market or who can research the market and identify where the voters congregate.

In general, people listen consistently to one format: country music, talk shows, oldies, urban contemporary, light rock, or (unfortunately for media buyers) public radio. Alternative and modern rock stations usually don't have significant numbers of voters. There are exceptions in every market, of course, which is why a professional media buyer is critical.

Radio listeners also divide themselves along race, sex, age, and other demographic lines. Women, Latinos, African Americans, angry white men, conservatives, Christians, and many other subsets of the general electorate congregate at stations that cater to their music, culture, and ideas.

One efficient way to buy radio time is through radio news service networks, typically organized by state. They gather groups of stations together and make it relatively easy to buy time on dozens of radio stations using one central contact.

The various ratings services offer valuable information to media buyers on the demographics and listening habits of radio audiences. Keep in mind that these ratings measure listenership every quarter-hour: this short span is necessary because people tend to jump from one radio station to another as they drive. Most political buys are placed on the top four to seven radio stations in a market to make sure to reach all the voters as they jump from station to station. Your best political buys are during the morning and evening commuting times on weekdays.

THE END OF POLITICAL RADIO ADVERTISING?

One major reform is desperately needed in American politics as it relates to radio. Even while newspapers and commentators decry the dwindling participation of the American electorate, many radio stations have begun to limit political advertising. State and local campaigns in particular are increasingly shut out at the larger radio stations because current law allows them to refuse *all* state and local political advertising. Federal candidates, under rules and regulations established by the Federal Election Commission and the Federal Communications Commission, can usually gain access to any radio station for advertising purposes in a "window" that opens a few weeks before each election.

The federal government, or state governments, should extend those rights to every state and local campaign. Candidates have a basic right to communicate, and voters should have access to the ideas of all campaigns, not just those at the top of the ticket. This basic reform would increase voter participation and awareness and make electronic adver-

tising available even to small campaigns. By allowing down-ballot rac-
ers and smaller political groups to reach out to the mind of the public
through radio, we better uphold the free flow of ideas—which since
before the time of radio was identified as the basis of a functioning
democracy.

Sample Script: "History Train"
:60 Radio—McKinney for Congress
Fletcher and Rowley, Inc.

DISCLAIMER (SFX = Sound effect)
VOICE-OVER
(SFX—TRAIN SOUNDS FROM A DISTANCE)
Listen. The train called History is coming.
And when we stand and deliver for Cynthia McKinney on Tuesday—
each one of us will be a part of that history.
(SFX—TRAIN ROARS BY)
   Cynthia McKinney—she's the first African American woman from
Georgia to serve in Congress.
   Cynthia McKinney—she voted for the crime bill, for an increase in
the minimum wage, and stood up to the extremists who tried to cut
health care for the elderly to give a tax break to the rich.
(SFX—TRAIN SOUNDS FROM A DISTANCE)
   Listen. Every generation gets a chance to ride the train called His-
tory. Some marched with Dr. King. Others faced the Klan with Andrew
Young and John Lewis—and now, we have the opportunity to vote for
Cynthia McKinney for Congress.
   Call 404–YYY–5574 to get a ride to the polls.
   Take your family. Take a friend. Don't sit on the sidelines. Vote for
Cynthia McKinney and ride the train called History.
(SFX—TRAIN ROARS BY)
   The Pride of Georgia. Cynthia McKinney. Congress.

Notes on "History Train"

This spot was written collaboratively by Bill Fletcher and John Rowley,
partners in Fletcher and Rowley, Inc. From a production standpoint,
the spot is powerful and emotional. We made liberal use of the sound
of a rushing freight train throughout the commercial for emphasis and
dramatic effect.

The main purpose of the commercial is simple: to deliver a phone number to those who need a ride to the polls. But the spot contains powerful images that advance Cynthia McKinney's campaign message on a variety of levels. The spot mentions that she is "the first African American woman from Georgia to serve in Congress" and provides information about her votes in Congress.

But the heart and soul of the spot is the invocation of images and names from the civil rights movement and the invitation to listeners to "ride the train called History."

We played the commercial the first time for Cynthia and her supporters over the phone at a campaign meeting just a few days before the election. It served to focus her workers on the historic importance of their tasks. On election night, with hundreds of supporters gathered and the national and local media represented by a dozen video cameras, Cynthia McKinney began her victory speech by quieting the raucous crowd and saying, "Listen . . . the train called History is coming."

Sheldon
Smith

VOICE-OVERS

The voice-over is an ancient concept. Technically, God, in his many vocal (but not corporeal) appearances in the Bible—such as in the Burning Bush—was the first voice-over artist. The analogy is not much strained because in modern tele-democracy, voice-overs tell people how to vote and thus decide the future of the country, although, as too in ancient times, there is no guarantee that the audience will take heed. Unlike God, however, who always spoke as himself, voice artists are appropriately anonymous. They are playing a role within the story space of an ad, either as a character or as a narrator, offering information and instruction. Indeed, most people who do voices in ads like to think of themselves as actors rather than speakers. While they are limited in the range of roles—some voices are better for some characters—they try to think and act their way through the persona of a part as much as any stage or screen actor.

This kind of acting involves an ability to interpret copy and convey the emotion of the words for the purpose of making clear the message and communicating that message to the listener or viewer. The reason for this is simple: the voice-over must be credible to the audience. If the performance sounds too much like a staging, it distracts people from the message. All the thought and effort put into making ads that include off-camera voices or voice-overs is—or should be—directed toward building that trust.

For the voice artist, the process starts with a phone call. In my case, the consultant calls up and asks if I'm "available" in a certain state or congressional district; in other words, am I already doing something in the area? Generally, when I'm working for a consultant in one state I don't work for a second consultant in the same state, even if there's no competition between the races, without consulting with the first client. For the audience to hear me too often—to note the familiarity of my voice, and the ubiquity of my endorsements, rather than concentrate on the message—is counterproductive. For the same reason, "available" also means there must be no media market overlap. For example, a governor's election campaign in Missouri and a Senate cam-

171

paign in Illinois will both hit television in St. Louis; in such cases, one must avoid overlap regardless of race or party.

After we agree that I'm available, we schedule studio time. The date might be weeks or hours in advance—I get calls up to the night before election day. At that point, the consultant has prepared the script or has a general idea of what the script is going to be. He may or may not have shot video if it is a television commercial. Some consultants prefer to record the script first and then put video to it, while others prefer to shoot video first and then insert the narration. Then I go to the studio and record the spot under the consultant's personal direction. Alternately, with modern ISDN phone connections, I can record in a studio while the consultant listens in another city. Or we can do a "phone patch," where I narrate over digital phone lines with no loss of audio quality, and the narration is recorded at a distant location.

In creating the voice-over, there are basically two issues to consider: time and character. The first challenge is to fit into the time frame. Commercials usually run either thirty or sixty seconds, although some ten- and fifteen-second commercials are now being produced. Because of this tiny window, scripts almost always run a bit long when actually voiced out, so cutting is necessary. Timing is simply a matter of speeding up or slowing down the narration, but if done poorly it can undermine the credibility of the message.

Character is more complicated. Scripts do not arrive complete with elaborate instructions for speed, tone, or emphasis. Such direction comes from the consultant or someone from his firm, in the studio or on the phone. What is most effective for me, and I think for most professional voice-over performers, is for people to tell us what *emotion* they want to convey with the spot and then let us interpret that emotion. Often, a beginning director, not even necessarily in a political spot but any commercial, will instruct, "read it slower," "faster," "louder," or "softer," but it is much more effective if the director says, "you're feeling disappointed" or "you're offended"; that tells me the way to interpret the copy and is effective direction. It is important to know the purpose of the commercial. What's the motivation? What does the campaign hope to accomplish?

Both time and character are affected by the professionalism of all those involved in the production of the ad, including the voice-over artist. Voice-overs are sometimes done by a candidate's relative, a local theater actor, or a church acquaintance with a pleasant voice, and the results may be acceptable. But studio time is expensive. In a postproduction facility for TV commercials, the rate is several hundred dollars an hour just to be there. Professional actors are hired for this work because it is time-saving (in the studio), and therefore cost-effective, because professionals know what to do immediately. Even if a first read is not perfect, at least upon direction it will quickly be done right. Voice artists can "make the audience hear it," and that's what is necessary to get the message across.

In addition, political ads are run next to professional, expensively produced commercial product ads—such as those for Acura and Budweiser, whose budgets may be up to a million dollars. Political campaign ads are usually produced on a budget of $2,500 to $5,000. The total media budget of a campaign, in fact, may not even run to $25,000. Thus, although one pays much more for a professional voice actor, the commercial will at least *sound* competitive with professionally produced ads.

The actual cost structure of the voice-over process varies considerably. Most of this work is unionized through either the Screen Actor's Guild or the American Federation of Television Artists. The union establishes minimum rates for everything. There is a preset minimum for a commercial, regardless of how much of it is actually read by a voice actor. So there is a flat fee: radio commercials—just for the voice-over for one spot—begin at $200 and go up; TV begins at $350 and goes up. Rates for performers on camera are higher yet. The rates also reflect where the commercial will be run. New York City, for example, will be well over $1,000; this is true for California, Texas, Chicago, and other heavily populated areas. Of course, this is relatively inexpensive when compared to commercial advertising, where the voice-over for one commercial—run nationally on a thirteen-week cycle on network television throughout the broadcast day—would probably be well over $20,000.

A potential downside of hiring a professional is that, because we become professionals by working often, we thus are heard by audiences all over the country over and over for many years. I worry about my own voice being used too frequently for one particular type of advertisement in one media market. This is why I do candidates from only one party and not more than one candidate in a given area. Other voice actors may feel differently. Most voice actors do ads for candidates of both parties; very few limit themselves to just one, which is all right if there is no overlap in campaigns (for example, congressional races in Delaware and Nevada). Some markets, however (like Pennsylvania), cross over and are heard in several other states. Also, campaigns tend to rerun all their advertising on the last few days of the race; the likelihood of overconcentration of voice then is obviously greater. Professional voice actors should tell consultants up front if they expect exclusivity, that is, if they prefer not to be overexposed in any given market.

There are two schools of thought on whether a voice should be identifiable. Much national product advertising today is being done by Hollywood stars (e.g., Kelsey Grammer for MCI, Gene Hackman for United Airlines and Oppenheimer Group, Jack Lemmon for Honda) although scale performers like me do this as well. Some producers in product advertising feel there is a cachet in having a celebrity do the voice-over. The downside is that the star is never identified; listeners often don't know who it is—so why pay a higher fee for them? These acting professionals are also able to interpret copy, but ad-makers should consider the images a famous voice conjures up, regardless of the skill of its use. For example, the fine actor and stentorian-voiced James Earl Jones did some political advertising a few years ago, but his voice was so well known that it overpowered the candidate: it was as if Darth Vader was doing the commercial, not a very positive endorsement!

Being a professional does not, of course, mean you shut off your brain or your heart. Voice-over artists who specialize in political work are unlike regular commercial actors in a significant way—we care about the products we endorse. I have never done an ad I *knew* to be untrue. I won't do an ad, for example, that implies I'm a Democrat rather than a Republican. But much of the copy refers to items whose truth value I can't know so I must rely on the credibility of the consultants for whom I work. In one case, although the script may not have been untrue, the approach was "ham-handed"; I compromised by using a voice unrecognizable as mine. I was already doing several ads in that media market for other candidates, and I felt it was important to keep a separation from that particular ad.

There are candidates I would choose not to work for (for example, former Klansman David Duke) and spots I've chosen not to read. I'd have reservations about attack or comparison ads that went too far or were too personal. But a good media consultant knows he can't go over the line there, so by the time the script gets to me it does not contain wild, unprovable accusations. I'm the last person in the ad production process to see the script; before me there is the media consultant, the pollster, the candidate, the campaign staff and manager, sometimes even the finance staff. Any outrageous items will have been deleted from the script by other professionals before I see it. At that point, if a message is not credible to me, it probably won't be to the public either.

Raymond D.	PREPARING CANDIDATES
Strother	FOR TELEVISION

In the simplest definition, a political campaign is nothing more than a vehicle for the delivery of a message. The job of a media consultant is to find efficient and creative surrogate messengers to replace a tightly stretched candidate. Television, radio, direct mail, telephoning, and nonbroadcast video all have their strengths depending on the race, time, audience, and budget. But to argue about whether a biographical mailer is more effective than a negative radio spot in the Cleveland market with two weeks left of an open-seat congressional race misses a bigger point. Everyone working in politics should have a sign in big letters over their desk reminding them that *the most important political medium is the candidate.* If people don't "buy" him, don't trust him to fulfill his promises, don't believe his image, they won't vote for him—no matter how snazzy his ad graphics or snappy his slogans.

Every electronic and print medium is a poor substitute for a candidate personally looking a voter in the eye and explaining why he or she should be emperor, president, or even mayor. The problem is that, unless one is running for sheriff of Mayberry, pressing the flesh of and chatting with all the voters are no longer cost-efficient or even achievable goals. Only television—through campaign ads, news and coverage of debates, appearances, and press conferences—allows masses of potential voters to see and feel that this is a woman or man worth trusting with their pocketbook and liberty. It follows that, if a candidate is the primary medium, media consultants for a campaign must ensure that the candidate is shown on television in the most favorable way.

STYLING THE CANDIDATE

You cannot spend too much time getting a candidate ready for a television appearance. The first step in this preparation is assessing the material—and this is why outside consultants are often better judges than loved ones and friends of the office-seeker. Some people are blessed by God with features made for TV. Lucille Ball had such perfect skin hue that cinematographers called her "Technicolor Tessie." Yet most ordinary humans rarely look good on camera unless they are made to do so. (For that matter, have you leafed through the *National Enquirer* photo spreads where they catch the glamorous and beautiful stars taking their garbage out without makeup and mood lighting?)

Every political media consultant and television director has a long list of styling techniques, based on general research on how the camera communicates and contextual research on what situations the candidate faces in the race. If a candidate is short, cast short people to be standing around him in the ads or have him stand on a riser (apple box) out of the lighting truck. (Seated candidates seldom display strength or energy.) If a candidate is fat, shoot him with Rembrandt lighting and put him in darker colors. If he looks too old, diffusion filters or even a nylon stocking over the lens will help makeup dissolve years.

This is not untruth-telling: it's translating the candidate into the language of television. For example, in filming Mississippi senator John Stennis in his last campaign before retirement, our firm faced several challenges. Stennis was an elderly man, in good health, but on camera he looked somewhat wan and frail. He also had ears that stuck out. In person, these traits would be overcome by the vigor of his manner and voice, the clarity of his gaze, and the personableness of his greeting. On television, with its laboratory microscope focus, the physical traits were distracting and damaging: he looked old and funny. So my cameraman constantly wore knee pads so he could shoot Stennis from a low angle to reinforce the senator's authority and power. In the final piece we edited together snips of film showing him moving, gesturing, walking fast, shaking hands, and waving to give a sense of vitality. Because he needed makeup and it is difficult to convince older candidates to submit to powder and paint, I hired an older makeup artist to enhance his comfort. Lillian Brown made up the senator and even pinned his ears back. It took twenty years off Stennis on camera. And it was not distortion, as in the case of Boris Yeltsin's videographers using selective cutting to make a sick, listless man into a model of vigor. We showed the voters the essential truth of John Stennis. And this was "on message" because in the campaign there were few ideological differences between Stennis and his Republican opponent. Age was virtually the only issue.

Every aspect of a commercial deserves attention, including the predominant color scheme. The color used can communicate a message about the candidate. There has been a great deal of research on the subconscious impression of color. For example, if the political climate dictates a desire for action and change, a response is to paint scenes with hot and bold colors. Splashes of red or yellow suggest excitement. Blues are calming and would be good for a candidate about whom voters express concerns that he is too "hotheaded" or "angry." Greens always work for personalities that tend to be elitist; a green image can be achieved by moving the candidate next to a tree or near a hillside.

Lighting is another important element in constructing a scene. Good scripts, exhaustive rehearsal, and artful makeup are not enough to make a television spot effective. A competent political producer will also understand the basics of photography (which means, after all, "writing with light"). Yet people trained in television news lighting have distorted the perception and understanding of lighting. Two hot lights arranged so that they form a triangle with the candidate or a blazing hand-held light near the camera are common television news techniques that result in plastic and unattractive images. For political ads, despite the limited budget, such low aesthetic standards would be disastrous.

Different lighting techniques can alter appearances and convey many moods. A main light positioned so that one side of the face and the other eye are illuminated can slim a candidate. A high light that creates a short shadow directly under the nose is usually flattering for a woman. Strong back lighting separates the subject from the background. Rembrandt lighting patterned after the Dutch master who used shadows to direct attention to his centers of interest is a technique for delivery of a serious message, although candidates are often leery of the severe effect. Children must be flooded with light and slightly underexposed. Eye shadows or cross lighting can make children look sad. Of course, colors matter: colored gels put over lights can change the visual message of a spot.

Best of all, though, are the dust-infused, red-hued natural tones of morning and evening—the magic hours. Our "gaffers" (lighting technicians) say that the "big gaffer in the sky" does this light. Even here, though, reflectors must usually be used to make the subject pop away from the background. Bright sun in the middle of the day, on the other hand, is generally a disaster—unless, of course, we want to convey a "wasteland" look in a negative scene such as a factory shut down by an opponent's legislative incompetence. In general, though, we attempt to shoot our outdoor scenes in the morning and evening and our studio spots in the heat of midday. Lighting, in short—like all television production techniques—must enhance the message, not obscure or distract from it.

Lighting is not independent of the selection and arrangement of scenery, other people, and props—what filmmakers call the mise-en-scène. The presence of persons and objects within the frame of the image can project symbolic ideas, themes, or emotions onto candidates. Suppose, for example, we want to tell the voters visually that the candidate is a family man. At times it is enough to have a framed photo of the candidate's spouse, kids, and collie on a desk or table. In other instances, the family needs to be marched out in starch and smiles. Simple and subtle supporting persons and objects abound: the American flag (patriotism), a factory production line (jobs), computers (high-tech), schoolchildren (education), and so on.

Of course, such associations should not strain the credulity of the audience. Remember that some bright campaign person assumed that the juxtaposition of Michael Dukakis with an M1A1 Abrams tank would negate the perception that the candidate was soft on defense. The pairing of person and tank did indeed turn out to be effective—as a weapon of ridicule in the hands of the opposition.

Figure 8. Stennis for U.S. Senate video still

Courtesy Strother Duffy Strother

But the methods of enhancing a candidate can be even more basic. Let's take the example of a particular concern of mine when faced with a middle-aged, male office-seeker. *How does he look in a suit?* It's a touchy issue, worth bringing up early in the campaign before it's too late: most middle-aged candidates could stand a few weeks in a gym to lose camera ballast. Then, despite the "rubber chicken" rigors of the campaign, you have to keep the candidate at this same fighting weight; five pounds up or down ruins how a suit hangs. It would not be helpful for him to change body shape from one commercial to another, especially since at the end of the campaign you often run many of the commercials you've made throughout its length.

That the candidate buy a new suit is one of my most important pieces of advice. Very few people on the street wear clothing that fits perfectly. I help the client select three tailor-made suits that could be used in filming for the entire campaign. The suits should be dark and of a conventional cut, with a classic, simple look and without faddish nuances. The suit must enhance, not distract. Willingness to buy the suits is also a good test of how serious a candidate is about running for office. A campaign that doesn't understand the principle of looking good and isn't willing to spend $3,000 on new suits is likely to be amateurishly run; they might not be willing later to invest money on some other important part of the process.

REHEARSING THE PERFORMANCE

Some people are born performers. When the red light went on, John F. Kennedy was as charming and witty on the small screen as he was among starlets and ambassadors at a state dinner. Many politicians are naturally eloquent and have instinctive stage presence—but even those prime players cannot just walk through a television commercial without extensive preparation. For this reason, I fight for my rehearsal time. Script approval must be given at least two days before we start shooting a television ad. Of the many turf disputes fought and bluffed between a campaign's staff and the outside media consultant, this can be the most tedious. Few people claim to be able to conduct statistical analysis of poll numbers, but it seems that everyone in any political campaign is a frustrated (and opinionated) screenwriter. (I usually don't fill in the visual side of the script form so that they can't get involved in the picture.) The campaign manager and the staff—and usually the chauffeur—all have bright ideas for adding and deleting words and concepts.

This is where the reputation of the consultant becomes crucial. Novices with no track record get pushed around; old bulls just dig in. Victory is walking away with your main objectives unedited and uncut; too many losses can jeopardize the campaign and may even force you to consider resigning because of your loss of authority. When the husband or the wife of the candidate gets involved, there is usually another long discussion. This is particularly true of inexperienced candidates who come out of a state legislature or congressional staff. Longtime politicians are more likely to trust the veteran consultants they hire. But the point is to work out all of the bugs at least a day before the actual filming so that conflict isn't reflected in the demeanor of the candidate.

I normally go onto location of a film shoot a day or two in advance and rehearse the candidate. I start slowly and begin talking about our objectives with the spot and explain how it grew out of research. Then I read the script as I would like to hear it on camera with gestures and pacing. This is an attempt to sell the script before the client decides to eviscerate it again. Few candidates can read a cold script and visualize it as a finished work. The consultant must paint mind pictures. Because teleprompters turn normal people into robots, I never use them for ads. Candidates memorize their lines the day before production so that on the shoot day we can work on walking, gestures, and pace. This is also the best time to find if a script is too long. I try to write thirty-second spots that are no more than seventy-six words. Only real-time rehearsal run-through can uncover a problem with length.

When the candidate is relaxed and confident I send him or her off to bed. I usually demand that the campaign's scheduler give me two uninterrupted days and nights. This allows the candidate to have a full night's sleep after an afternoon of rehearsals. A lack of sleep always shows, hurts concentration, and is reflected in the eyes. Also I ask the candidate not to drink alcohol the night before we shoot—that gets reflected in the eyes and makes the small red blood vessels more obvious in the face.

THE SHOOT

The actual camera shoot is the culmination of much activity. A typical case was a spot we made in the 1998 campaign for Roy Barnes's reelection to the Georgia governorship. We planned a "reforming HMOs" ad answering what our polls identified as a major concern of voters, especially older voters in the state—that many health plans didn't allow individuals to pick their own primary care physician. I arrived in Atlanta a day before the shoot and inspected the sound stage and set. My advance person, Kim Levine, had gone in a week earlier and made arrangements. The summer was hot, and to get the top performance out of the candidate I needed a cool, sound-proofed, and controlled location. Kim then drew maps to the location, found a place for the crew to eat lunch, and wrote detailed instructions to give to each crew member. You can never overexplain or overprepare.

The day before the filming I met Barnes and rehearsed the script. He was a quick study so the initial rehearsal did not last more than two hours. Then we selected his suits, shirts, and ties for the location. Earlier in the campaign Barnes, his wife, Marie, a clothing consultant, and I had gone with Roy to purchase suits appropriate for filming. The morning of the filming my crew arrived three hours ahead of the candidate to check lighting and plot out the spot. Using a stand-in, we adjusted lights, reduced unwanted reflections, and planned the camera moves. I sat down with the lighting director and my cameraman and did a cursory poll briefing so they would know what I wanted to accomplish—the big picture and the small details. I feel the important members of the crew must always know why I am making certain decisions; a short briefing allows them to contribute suggestions for the finished product. And again, it is imperative that all disputes with the crew be resolved before the candidate shows up. When we had settled on the look, sound checks were made and we were ready to turn on the camera when Barnes arrived.

When shooting begins I don't allow staff or family members on the set. I try to limit those present to the crew of about nine people and the candidate. I time production so that we do only one thirty-second spot before lunch and one in the afternoon. When the candidate arrives, I first take him or her aside and talk for a few minutes about the campaign, family matters, or anything that might be distracting. In Barnes's case, we knew each other well and this was not necessary. But in most instances I wait until the candidate and I sense we have reached a feeling of relaxed comradeship, then I have him read the first spot to me. Though Barnes was able to memorize the entire script quickly, there are times when I decide that the spot must be shot in nine- or ten-second segments because the candidate is not able to deliver the spot as a whole. If this is the case, in the course of a rehearsal—so that I don't destroy confidence—I explain that I want to shoot the spot in segments that can be cut together. When I am satisfied with the read but believe the candidate can deliver only in short takes, I leave him or her in the room alone to practice for about fifteen minutes and talk to my cameraman and lighting team about three different shooting angles that will allow edits. This usually means a slight adjustment in camera and lights between the segments. Often when I return to the candidate he or she has regained confidence and can recite the commercial in its entirety, but either way I am covered. Then I bring in the makeup artist to work magic, being careful to clear everyone else out of the makeup room. Most people are shy about being made up, so I give the candidate privacy.

I inspect the makeup and have the candidate go to his marks where my cameraman can also check through the lens so that other adjustments can be made. The most common problem is a cakelike appearance that does not show up in the makeup room lighting. Then we do a dry run of the language and actions of an actual shoot without burning film. While doing this the cameraman has time to practice and the lighting people have an opportunity to make the finite adjustments that hide neck rolls and protruding ears. I try to use boom mikes that hover just out of frame so the candidate does not feel nailed in place. Through these dress rehearsals, I help the candidate with pace and timing. We choreograph head moves, winks, smiles, and occasionally anger. Before shooting I position the camera and adjust the zoom to the framing I want. Then I look over the cameraman's shoulder to see as much as possible what he sees as we begin to roll. It always gives the candidate confidence if he thinks you are in complete command. When the candidate is close to peak performance I begin filming, knowing that we will waste a lot of Kodak's best before we finally get the perfect take.

Barnes's ad was not very complex: all he had to do was stand behind a desk surrounded by piles of Yellow Pages that represented most of the cities in Georgia. The opening line was, "There are fifteen thousand doctors listed in the Yellow Pages, but some managed health care company selects your doctor for you."

We did about fifteen rehearsals, making fine adjustments in delivery and tone as I listened through a headset with my back turned. It sounded a little rushed so I deleted four words. The spot opened wide

Figure 9. Barnes for Governor video still

Courtesy Strother Duffy Strother

so the viewer could see the office and the phone books and slowly moved in to focus on the candidate's face.

Barnes was wonderful. The second take was good, but one can't risk thousands of dollars in production on a single take. There could be a spot on the film, a hair in the camera, a scratch in processing. So I shot it four more times while Kim recorded times and took notes of my observations about each take. As added insurance, I shot the whole spot wide and then close. I figured that if all things failed, I could edit pieces together if we had different camera shots to cut to. After each take I conferred with the cameraman, sound person, and lighting director to check their impressions. Even with—or rather because of—all the careful work, we were finished in only two hours of the candidate's time and six hours of the crew's. More important for the candidate, we had a spot that—as later polling showed—helped to win the campaign.

The overall lesson is that good commercials take a lot of effort for all involved. To cut corners in time or film is foolish. Americans are expert at watching television. They spot your mistakes as quickly as you do. A twitch, a mouth movement, or a fly buzzing across the screen can ruin a spot and occasionally a campaign. If you agree that the candidate is the medium (and often the central message of a campaign), then political genius is always earned in the details of his or her presentation to the public on television. The candidate's confidence in the consultant, the technique, and the message is always reflected in the final impression that spills out of the television set.

| *Dane* | **TELEVISION ADS** |
| *Strother* | |

Television commercials are the B-52s of a political campaign. They can virtually carpet bomb a community or state; the political landscape is inexorably altered in their wake. Television has also changed political campaigns. At one time the national parties were the central medium of elections; rallying the faithful on the first Tuesday in November was their main function. Today the Democratic and Republican Parties are basically relegated to the role of raising money to buy more and more television time.

A television spot is usually produced either to create a problem for an opponent or to solve a problem for a client. Even seemingly innocuous spots lay a base for a future attack or response. But every spot is different, and each campaign requires a unique approach. Consultants who try to use cookie-cutter ads and simply plug one candidate into another candidate's spots will eventually fail. Candidates should be wary if a consultant assures him or her that "this script always works." For whom, where, how?

Yet, much as people may deny it in conversation, television ads can work—they can make a hero look like a villain, stir voter anger, seize hearts, and capture minds. Most of all they provide information about candidates and campaigns to the majority of Americans who read and research little about who or what they vote for. In all, today, politics is television and television is politics—second only to a candidate in importance to a campaign.

COSTS

Television, like any weapon of modern war, is tremendously expensive to create, deploy, and maintain. Most middle and down-ballot campaigns and even some congressional campaigns cannot afford the cost or can buy time only sporadically. This is especially true in big markets like New York, Los Angeles, and to a lesser degree Chicago, where it is unlikely that anything but a well-funded, statewide campaign can afford airtime.

Another problem with television is that its rates are volatile. Radio and television rates reflect the number of people who see or hear the spots; it is much less expensive to buy television in Des Moines than in New York. One buys television not by the number of spots but by the gross rating point (GRP). Arbitron, a rating service, determines how many people watch a certain show in a certain market. For example, we know that *Seinfeld* had a rating of 32 but no cable show enjoys a rating of even 1. A 32 means that 32 percent of viewers who are camped in front of a television while *Seinfeld* is airing are watching the show.

So buying an ad on *Seinfeld* would cost a great deal more than buying a show that had only, say, a 6 rating. Television time purchase rates are set at a cost per point. A purchase of 100 points yields enough spots for everyone in a market to have seen a commercial once. One thousand points of television ensures that the average person sees a spot ten times. The cost per point is set for each of the 211 markets in America, and every market has a slightly different cost. For example, the cost per point in Baton Rouge, Louisiana, is roughly $32; in Atlanta, with a population ten times higher, a point is roughly $300.

Buying television is a science. It is not enough simply to produce a spot and throw it on the air. The key is determining what shows a campaign's targets are watching and ensuring that the spots run during those shows. Saturday morning cartoons are out because children can't vote. But if the target audience for a campaign is working-class women over age fifty who have little education, then soap operas are prime buys.

Regardless of when it runs, no ad stands alone. The office-seekers of October have to compete not just with AT&T, Coors, and the local Buick dealer but also with hundreds of other candidates for all sorts of races. The explosion of advertising clutter means a spot must be hammered home over and over before the message is retained. Whereas a campaign might have once run a spot for 600 points, today 1,200 or 1,300 points are necessary. While we who make political ads try to distinguish ours from the pack, in the end it is understandable that voters might disconnect from so many similar messages, stagings, and plotlines. The result is increasing expenses to distribute less information with diminishing returns.

Accordingly, the goal for a political producer is to make a spot that has production values and a quality that stands up to the national ads that often bookend it on television *without* costing a fortune. Political producers are exceedingly adroit at making television spots quickly and cheaply.

A well-run campaign spends 75 percent of its war chest on television or mail. The idea is to keep overhead—salaries, candidate travel, and research costs—low so that the majority of resources are spent communicating with voters. In essence, a campaign is nothing more than a vehicle to deliver a message to voters; that message is a candidate's sales pitch. Giving voters a reason to support a candidacy is the only way to win a political campaign. And the more times voters hear the message—assuming it is a message they want to hear and that it is delivered well—the more likely those voters are going to remember the message.

Included in the 75 percent earmarked for communication is the cost of production. A rough guide is that production costs 10 percent of the actual time buy. This varies according to the producer's ego and ability to keep costs down. Political advertising differs greatly from commercial (products) advertising in the directness and cost of the production. Political producers are always looking for a way to keep production costs to a minimum. It is unusual for a political television commercial to cost more than $10,000, or about a tenth of what a consumer ad costs to make.

POSITIVE, CONTRASTIVE AND NEGATIVE ADS

There are basically three different types of political television commercials: positive, contrastive, and negative. The mix and use of these three genres seems to change virtually every election cycle: no "lessons" are permanent.

All three ad types are essentially used to *define both candidates*. The idea is to paint beautiful pictures of one's client and a less than appealing view of the opponent. Polls are used to determine what aspect of a candidate's life or views is best received by voters. For example, if the fact that a candidate is a self-made success moves undecided voters to him, then the television ad shows and tells that story: "John Doe is an up-by-the-bootstraps American success story. He's turned his life from challenge to fortune by believing he could, working hard, being honest, and standing up when tough times would knock most people down."

Positive ads seldom if ever mention the opponent. Rather, they may offer an introduction to a candidate and his family, testimonials from people he has helped, or an explanation of what he hopes to do if elected. Each firm has a different philosophy, but in the 1998 election cycle we used more positive ads, packed with more information, than we once did because they are more compelling and because we need to provide a lot of information in a short time.

Positive ads are the backbone of a good political campaign. But a good positive ad begins to set up a contrast with the opponent without it being obvious. In that sense, a positive ad can contain implied critiques of the opposition. This is because ultimately campaigns are about differences. Voters have to reach for one lever or another in the voting booth, and they usually know little more than they have gleaned from television ads or from neighbors or friends who got their information from television ads. A campaign must give voters a reason to support a certain candidate while at the same time providing a reason not to support the opponent.

Nevertheless, the rules of negativity are changing. In 1998, for the first time, political professionals began to see that harsh negative ads were backfiring. For a decade the pundits and national press corps had bemoaned that campaigns were little more than intellectual mud wrestling. Year after year, however, political professionals would use negative information about their opponent and see a positive effect: it seemed a textbook truism that "attacks work."

But a funny thing happened on the way to victory. Voters finally had enough of the malicious tactics; they seemed to be genuinely tiring of slashing, demeaning ads and reacted by tuning out the message and turning against the messenger. They are still receptive to information that is not complimentary to a candidate, but it must be delivered in a delicate manner: with a scalpel rather than a chainsaw. For example, in the 1998 Georgia governor's race, Guy Millner spent hundreds of thousands of dollars attacking his Democratic opponent, Roy Barnes, even before Barnes became the official nominee. Millner tried to make dozens of votes that Barnes had made in the state legislature sound objectionable. For four months Millner aired one negative ad after another. According to the old manual, this was good politics: define your opponent before he gets a chance to define himself.

For the most part, the attacks were factual. Barnes had made more than fifty thousand votes and each for a good reason, but the attacks were out of context. To the voters' credit they understood that. Millner's tactless campaign was defeated by 10 percentage points; he vows he will never run again. Millner was done in by not noticing that the electorate was changing.

This example does not herald the end of negative ads by any means. But the question now is, What is a negative ad? Is it negative to point out that an opponent truly wants to abolish the national department of education? Or to explain that an opponent supports school vouchers or does not?

Today's voter is much more responsive to what are called comparative ads. Eschewing screaming or name-calling, the best of the comparative ads simply put both candidates side by side and measure their records. Since today's wily voter refuses to believe an unsubstantiated charge, it is imperative to include documentation of every charge leveled. Indeed, 1998 focus group research taught professionals that using the banner of a newspaper headline in addition to the headline and article when substantiating a charge makes it more believable than just using the headline. The more information the better.

A candidate's gender has also largely become irrelevant. Both men and women must fully explain themselves, their platforms, and their charges. There was a time when spots for female candidates were softer or less aggressive, but those days are over, and voters see little difference between male and female candidates. For example, the 1996 Mary Landrieu for U.S. Senate campaign (Louisiana) presented a series of spots that featured women exclusively on daytime television. The idea was to run a gender gap by speaking about a couple of topics that resonated with women more than men. Democrats must run gender gaps to win in the South, and that sometimes requires specialized ads, but increasingly voters disdain pandering and want to know what the office-seeker will do for them.

THE RESEARCH IMPERATIVE

At one time, consultants created television ads with little more direction than a gut feeling or an idea from a friend or campaign employee. The lore of spots being written on the back of cocktail napkins is widespread. Single-malt whiskey often served as a muse, and a campaign's strategy would change with the moon. Those days are gone.

If a modern consultant tells a candidate he or she has a "hunch," this is a signal to find a new consultant. Creating television commercials has become as much science as art. Tens of thousands of dollars are spent on research before writing the first draft of a script.

First, there is an extensive interview of a candidate. Who is he or she? What makes her tick? What is he truly passionate about? Often this interview is taped on a home video camera and held for future reference. Then issues are discussed. Some candidates are willing to switch from unpopular positions, like opposing the death penalty. Others are resolute in their core beliefs and intransigent despite the risk of espousing an unpopular stance. Depending on the issue, such intransigence can cost a candidate a race. In a representative democracy it is imperative that a candidate share the views of the voters.

Following the interview, a media consultant will travel with a candidate—see how he or she moves and interacts with people and whether the campaign work is relished or endured. Speech patterns, intensity, delivery, and style are studied for days. The reason is simple: ultimately a consultant must capture a candidate's entire being on film. This is no easy task because people rarely play themselves well on television.

The next step, then, is opposition research conducted on the client as well as the opponent. Everyone is reluctant to expose skeletons and gaffes made over a lifetime, and even now many office-seekers naively assume "it won't come out." Often clients promise there is nothing in their backgrounds that could be used against them in a campaign. Generally the research indicates they are wrong.

Once the opposition research is completed, a poll questionnaire is developed. This is often done with the help of all consultants in a campaign. It takes three to six days to conduct a poll and another week or so for a pollster to write a report. This accomplished, the campaign's message is determined and a media consultant begins thinking about the direction the campaign's communications should take. Candidates and consultants alike must recognize this truth: *polls should drive the content of television ads.*

TELEVISION AND THE REAL WORLD

The decisions described above cannot exist in a vacuum: real-life campaigning is often a series of compromises with reality, especially when dealing with the monetary drain of television. A case in point is the candidacy of Rose McKinney-James, an African American woman coaxed into running for lieutenant governor in Nevada in 1998. She had never before run for office, and the political climate was tough for a left-leaning Democrat in a Republican state. But McKinney-James possessed a charisma that can't be taught, and she had the tools to become a very good candidate.

The great challenge for McKinney-James, however, was generating the necessary money and finding the motivation to make the enormous number of cold calls required to meet a financial goal. In raising money, candidates are competing against everyone on the ballot.

McKinney-James's opponent, Lorraine Hunt, was on the city council and managed to transfer some $400,000 from her city council reelect account to her account for lieutenant governor. That put McKinney-James behind the curve. And because the lieutenant governor has little power in Nevada, it was difficult to convince contributors to give the maximum allowed contribution of $10,000.

Cash, or the lack of it, determined strategy. A poll indicated that education was the most important issue facing Nevada. School discipline was the specific focus. A decision was made to run McKinney-James as if she were aspiring to be the state's principal. Rhetoric like "We can't let two bad children hold hostage the education of twenty-six good kids" became part of the campaign's lexicon.

Ideally, the campaign would have run two positive ads spelling out how McKinney-James planned to put discipline back in the schools. The positives would have been followed by two negatives to turn voters away from Hunt. Then the campaign would close the final days with a wrap-up spot more positive than negative. That plan would have cost some $500,000; McKinney-James had about $130,000.

In an attempt to overcome this financial deficit, the Democratic candidate's campaign employed a technique first created in 1992. Called the "10–20," it is a strategy of running two spots for the price of one. The format calls for a ten-second negative ad delivered by an announcer. The spot fades to black for a second and a half and a positive ad follows. Crucially, voters believe they are *two different* ads, which is important because the candidate is then not blamed for a negative ad. The problem with negative ads is that, although intended to drive up the unfavorable rating of one's opponent, they often slightly increase the unfavorable rating of the candidate running them as well.

In the Nevada race, the negative ad concerned Hunt's having voted to allow some restaurant owners to pay less than minimum wage. She was a restaurant owner herself, and the hope was that voters would find her position hypocritical. The positive portion of the ad featured McKinney-James speaking about putting discipline back into schools and holding students accountable. As she spoke, she walked across an office set, and as the camera panned, the governor moved into the shot to finish the spot by saying he strongly endorsed McKinney-James.

It was an attempt to run a negative, give a positive message, and offer an endorsement from the governor in thirty short seconds. Unfortunately, it violated the cardinal rule of trying to accomplish too many things in a thirty-second spot. The lack of money for communications coupled with Hunt outspending McKinney-James by more than two to one made the outcome inevitable. The final vote was Hunt 50 percent, McKinney-James 40 percent, and lesser candidates carving up the remaining 10 percent.

The outcome was more of a reflection of money buying elections than a failed spot technique. Indeed the 10–20 format worked in what has become a famous case. In 1992, a thirty-two-year-old woman named Blanche Lambert decided to move back to Arkansas from Washington and challenge her former boss in a Democratic primary. She had

Figure 10. McKinney-James for Lieutenant Governor video still

Courtesy Strother Duffy Strother

been a receptionist for Congressman Bill Alexander, who had served for twenty-four years. He did not take the challenge from the young woman seriously, and by the time he recognized there was trouble it was too late.

Like McKinney-James, Lambert raised only enough money for one television commercial in the primary. The problem was that the district, Arkansas's first, required buying three media markets to communicate properly: Jonesboro, Little Rock, and Memphis.

Lambert used the 10–20 format. The negative was a seven-second blip showing Alexander denying he had bounced any checks at the— now infamous and closed—House Bank. As cartoon music played, a screen dropped over his face reading that Alexander had bounced 114 checks. The following twenty-second positive featured Blanche smiling and shaking hands with the words HONESTY, INTEGRITY, THE FUTURE, flashing across the screen. She won with 62 percent of the vote.

Lambert got married, served two terms, and retired because of complications from a pregnancy with twins. In 1998, she decided to run for the U.S. Senate seat being vacated by Dale Bumpers. The primary had four major participants: Lambert-Lincoln; the sitting attorney general, who had also been the Democratic Senate nominee two years before, Winston Bryant; Nate Coulter, a young, handsome man who had barely lost a race for lieutenant governor just two years before; and a rich doctor who was running as the antipolitician.

Initial research indicated problems and opportunities. Focus groups told us that many older voters would not look favorably on a woman with young children taking a full-time job as demanding as a U.S. Senate seat. The extrapolation was that a third of the electorate would simply not support Lambert-Lincoln for this reason. But the focus groups also reported that the best way to overcome the concern was to show the candidate's husband and explain that he was a doctor and that the couple would raise their children together, as a team. The findings were incorporated into a poll, and spots were written from the information.

The research indicated that the best way to sell Lambert-Lincoln to the voters was to have her appear in person to speak to the camera. The budget of more than a million dollars for television allowed the campaign to run several different ads. In most of the spots, Lambert-Lincoln looked directly into the camera and delivered thirty-second pieces.

The ads worked: she ran first in the primary, won the runoff against

Bryant, and defeated a far-right Republican by 60 to 40 percent. Lambert-Lincoln won not with "gut feelings" or genius but by working hard and using research and polling to her advantage.

That is the reality of modern campaigning that unfortunately (and ironically) is little shown or publicized in mass media. The research, creative process, shooting, editing, and placement of television ads is a sober and clinical process—for good reason, because like war, people's lives and the country's welfare depend on it.

Don Walter | # NONBROADCAST VIDEO

Nonbroadcast video (NBV) is a general category covering the familiar commercial tapes that are in every home, from a copy of *Braveheart* ordered from Amazon.com for Christmas, to the Barney movie rented for the weekend from a video store, to the demonstration video mailed to a new Chevy owner. Surprisingly, however, NBV has only recently come to the attention of and been fully exploited by politicians. This is not for lack of opportunity or utility. For office-seekers, made-to-order and distributed videos can be used to build name identification, create images, outline agendas or plans, respond to an attack or inoculate against an expected charge, raise money—or just entertain. Moreover, NBV is in several ways superior to other media such as broadcast and cable television, print, and radio in enacting the principal objective of any political campaign: targeting *specific* people with an informative, entertaining, memorable message.

ADVANTAGES OF NBV

Voters actually watch NBV. Focus groups of various demographic mixes from around the country have found that voters are not only more likely to *watch* a video that they have ordered or been given than read a piece of direct mail but are also far more likely to *believe* and *remember* a video than either a thirty-second television spot or a mailer. Data have also indicated that older citizens—who generally also tend to be the people most likely to vote—undecided about their election preferences are the one group most likely to sit down and watch a video to get information about a campaign.

The reasons why recipients become viewers vary among different demographic groups. Older men, for example, will view a video at least once because, according to focus group research, they "want to keep the tape to record sporting events on." The campaign message in this case is not lost: the tape is watched at least once. Women, on the other hand, particularly older women, see these videos boxed in full-color sleeves, like any product purchased or rented from the neighborhood video store, as an item of value to be watched (again, at least once) and retained.

Finally, there is a good chance that the focus will be on the *message* rather than the distracting visual environments of most other media. Once the viewer hits the "play" button, he or she is engaged; there are no other channels to surf or pages to turn, or, as is the case with most Web sites, extraneous beeping, flashing, scrolling graphics, and words.

NBV offers superior information density. All voter groups have indicated that, compared to television ads, videos are a better format to learn about a candidate's record, experience, and future agenda. Most thirty-second television spots, while packed with visuals, actually give out very little information: the average speaking script runs no longer than eighty words. Radio ads may provide more talk, but the visual dimension is lost. Print ads offer more room for substance, but length and space considerations also apply.

An NBV is subject to no such restraints; if the candidate needs five, ten, or thirty minutes—or two hours—to describe a twenty-year voting record or a solution for Medicare, the tape allows the time. In 1994, Newt Gingrich's GOPAC, for example, sent nearly every Republican candidate for public office in the country a thirty-five-minute "how-to" video on campaign tactics. The compounded utility of the NBV format is that so much information can be disseminated to viewers who, if they wish, may replay the message at no additional cost to the sender.

NBV is targetable. Television ads, even when run on narrow-niche cable stations, may still reach tens of thousands of people for whom the information may have no connection or relevance. Those whom you specifically want to reach may ignore the ad. Direct mail is much more targetable, but there is the problem that people are inundated with mail so that they do not accord any special value to yet another miscellaneous item. Nonbroadcast video, however, combines the best of both worlds. It is specifically designed to address a limited group of people: blue-collar union women; homeowners who pay more than $3,000 a year in property taxes; retired Jewish senior citizens; rural evangelicals; suburban, professional African Americans; or the residents of a city with a prohibitively expensive television market. Once the audience is identified by mailing lists, the message, the information, everything the NBV says and shows can be designed to attract their attention, stimulate their interest, and, it is hoped, persuade them to support the cause or the candidate.

NBV is cost effective. The most compelling reason why candidates for public office and political groups employ NBV to deliver a message to targeted voters is that, at a cost between two and three dollars per tape, the production and distribution (including mailing) of NBV is inexpensive. What other options exist for a campaign to disseminate five minutes of message to twenty thousand targeted households for about $50,000? Only a handful of network television markets in the country would require less than $50,000 to achieve a reach and frequency to rival a five-minute NBV. Political campaigns would be hard-pressed to convince broadcast television stations to sell the consecutive time. Even if stations did make such time available, a political campaign would have to purchase almost 1,000 gross rating points (of a five-minute ad) to reach the same targeted viewers with a suitable frequency. It would be hard to justify the cost even in smaller markets. Similar comparisons to radio and cable television are easily made with the same conclusion.

NBV IN ACTION

The precise targeting of the NBV message is especially useful to down-ballot candidates with small targets but limited funds. In a recent case, Jeannemarie Devolites, a first-time Republican candidate for the Virginia General Assembly, calculated that, to beat the incumbent, she needed ten thousand votes. She could not afford television or even much radio, did not have a large campaign staff, and had no support from volunteer networks or trade associations. She did, however, possess a little money, was a telegenic personality, and had an enormously talented nine-year-old daughter who was unfazed at narrating a video documentary about her mother.

We produced a five-minute video and had sent them by bulk-rate mail to ten thousand targeted families. The response was tremendous. Although it had been incredibly difficult to earn media (get news coverage and free publicity) in the intense Washington, D.C., market, within days of distribution of the video, the campaign and "its slick new tactic" received front-page, sectional coverage in the *Washington Post*. Garnering 11,233 votes, Devolites achieved her goal (with the support of at least 536 Democrats) and won her campaign without going into debt simply by the targeted use of NBV.

Figure 11. Devolites for Delegate video back cover

Courtesy Creative Media Partners

After the victory, Devolites commented, "I'm convinced that my video not only inoculated me from my opponent's negative attacks in his direct mail but enabled me to deliver an uninterrupted message directly onto the television screens of my targeted voters."

Nonbroadcast video is also the format of choice for candidates who not only want to reach a targeted audience but wish to do so with a message that is visual, complex, and cannot be boiled down to the thirty seconds of a television ad. A case in point is that of Jack Cottey, the sheriff of Marion County, Indiana, who, in a recent election campaign, was interested not only in boosting his margin of victory in targeted precincts but also in leaving a lasting impression among the voters, the press, business and political leaders, and past and potential contributors. Cottey's five-minute video outlined the sheriff's vision of the future but also, by using black-and-white stills from his childhood and days in the U.S. Marine Corps—in a segment narrated by and featuring his mother—told a story about Jack Cottey that most constituents had never heard and that could not be expressed in a soundbyte or visbyte. More important, Cottey knew, was that long after most campaign commercials were a distant memory, his video, in its full-color sleeve, would remain in thirty thousand households across Marion County, next to *Great Bible Stories* and *Rain Man.*

It was as if Jack Cottey stuck a campaign bumper sticker on the wall next to the television set in thirty thousand family rooms.

Figure 12. Cottey for Sheriff video cover

Courtesy Creative Media Partners

For such reasons, nonbroadcast video is the message that never goes away and keeps on playing. In the future its format and distribution scheme may change—in four years we might be mailing out digital video disks or streaming video files through e-mail—but the concept and the cost effectiveness will remain.

Bud Jackson | **EARNED MEDIA**

Political campaigns rightfully invest enormous resources and thought into developing and executing a paid media strategy—everything from direct mail to television advertising—because it provides the opportunity to deliver an unedited and unfiltered message to voters. But many campaigns, particularly congressional, state legislative, and local races, often make the mistake of shortchanging a more subtle yet valuable opportunity commonly referred to as "earned media." Earned media is the art of generating or shaping favorable or tactically advantageous publicity in newspapers, magazines, columns, radio and television talk shows, and any other media vehicle available. Once known as free media, the new term reflects its growing importance; earned media is not free for the taking but is achieved by spending a substantial amount of time and effort.

RESEARCH FOR AN EARNED MEDIA PLAN

Before formulating a comprehensive earned media plan, a campaign must first study the media outlets that could potentially cover a campaign. This is not just a matter of accumulating a mailing list; the researcher must profile and qualitatively assess each potential contact, as described below.

Develop a media list of all newspaper, radio, and television outlets that could apply to a campaign. Further research the programming they offer their audience, noting the shows that might be useful avenues for exploitation. Media lists should include the contact persons' names, media deadlines, phone and fax numbers, and e-mail addresses.

Identify which reporters will be covering the race. If unsure, a polite introductory call should be made to the media outlet's editor or news director.

Study each media outlet's ideological leanings and get a sense of its general attitude toward politics. Past editorials and news stories are the best guide for potential future slant and interests. Who have they endorsed? Who have they reviled? Do they favor liberals more than conservatives? Do they approve of or oppose courses of action on issues relevant to a campaign? Have they written past stories on the opponent(s)?

Become acquainted with the columnists and talk show hosts. Research their past stories, columns, and shows to understand their individual biases and points of view.

Research "vertical" media outlets such as senior citizen and veteran publications and neighborhood association newsletters. These outlets could be useful for reaching targeted groups. News stories in these outlets are generally easier to place and are more likely to be written in a manner desirable for a campaign.

IMPLEMENTATION

Several methods can be used for enacting an earned media strategy; some consist of constructive activities, some are to be avoided. Understanding how and when to use these methods will maximize favorable coverage and will also minimize embarrassing mix-ups.

Press Releases, Video News Releases, Radio Actuality

To do:

• Send out an occasional press release. Press releases tailored to specific media outlets and their individual audiences will likely generate more stories. Develop a local angle or "hook" to entice journalistic interest. For example, if doing a press release about senior citizens who face rising prescription drug costs while living on fixed incomes, put the issue in the context of local senior citizens.

• When appropriate, submit video clips to news stations with a press release explaining the footage. Television news operations are limited by the number of cameras they have to cover a day's events. Sometimes they will use footage provided by a campaign to do a story. Higher-profile campaigns may even warrant an interview of a candidate or spokesperson from a satellite center, making it that much easier for a television news operation to cover a candidate or issue.

• Offer "actuality" clips to radio stations. A radio actuality consists of a thirty-second to one-minute audio clip of a candidate or spokesperson talking about a relevant issue. Typically, there is a brief introduction at the beginning of the clip stating who is speaking, what the topic is, how long the clip is, and then a three-second countdown to the start of the candidate or spokesperson speaking. Campaigns might then establish a dedicated telephone line with a machine that automatically plays the clip for radio stations to record at their leisure. The clips are typically included in radio news programs.

• Follow up with the appropriate people to make sure they have received the press release, clip, and so on.

• Hold an "announcement" event or send an announcement press release. Most media outlets offer every candidate or cause this introductory story.

To avoid:

• Do not send out a press release every single day. A constant dribble of press releases without any substantive news will damage the campaign's credibility among the media.

• Do not send a press release to the wrong audience. For example, a press release touting cuts in veterans' benefits should not be sent to a publication for veterans.

• Do not badger or anger reporters and editors for not doing a story based on a press release. Also avoid picking needless fights with the media. They have barrels of ink and hours of airtime to get in the last word.

• Do not call a reporter or editor minutes before deadline unless they have asked for a call.

News Conferences and Photo Opportunities

To do:

• Hold a news conference, providing there is a compelling reason to draw reporters to cover the news event.

• When possible, hold a news conference at a location that is relevant to a topic at hand. A news conference could also become a photo opportunity if conducted at a visually stimulating or issue-relevant location.

• Send out a media advisory alerting the press of an event. Follow up with phone calls.

• Have a campaign take its own photos and video of appearances and submit them to the media with press releases and captions.

*   *   *

To avoid:

• Do not hold news conferences or events that are in a remote location, too far away from the media covering the race.

• Do not plan to do many news conferences on local and district levels (unless the candidate and campaign staff want to be all alone at the conference).

• Do not plan a news conference or photo opportunity that is too close to important press deadlines.

• Do not plan marginally important news conferences on potentially busy news days. The press will be even less likely to attend.

Special Events and Speeches

To do:

• Have the candidate speak at special events such as public service club meetings, when appropriate. Make sure the remarks take into consideration the audience and that they will be warmly received to avoid public embarrassment—unless the point is to spark controversy by challenging the sponsoring organization.

• Invite the local media with media advisories from a campaign or group sponsoring the event.

To avoid:

• Do not hold or attend a special event or speech every week and expect to receive coverage each time. This applies even more to lower-level local and state legislative races.

Editorial Board Tours

To do:

• Request to meet with editorial boards. Use previous research to prepare and to understand their ideological leanings and positions on relevant issues before attending the meeting. Answer their questions and soften criticism by taking their biases into consideration.

• Bring a press kit with favorable clips, speeches, and campaign literature so they can better understand what a candidate or campaign has been doing. The content should be compiled with consideration of the individual media outlet's perceived biases.

* * *

To avoid:

• Do not get angry if an editorial board refuses to meet with a candidate or campaign. Simply send a press kit and a request for an endorsement if they choose not to have a meeting with a candidate or campaign.

• Do not go into an editorial board meeting until a candidate and campaign are knowledgeable enough about their own positions and relevant campaign issues to answer questions comfortably.

Talk Shows—Radio, TV, Internet

To do:

• Understand format and subject material, host biases, and program audiences for all local radio, television/cable, and Internet talk shows that are relevant to a campaign. Know their show days and times.

• Ask producers or hosts if a candidate or spokesperson can be a guest if the show is appropriate.

• Have people—but not paid campaign staff—prepared to call in to say positive things and ask easy questions, if calls are taken.

• Know the issues; put off a guest appearance until a candidate or campaign is comfortable with them.

• Instruct a candidate or spokesperson to expect the unexpected and not become unraveled when challenged by inhospitable hosts, panelists, or callers.

To avoid:

• Do not go on a show that has no tactical benefit or whose host(s) will probably try to embarrass or ambush a candidate or spokesperson.

Maintaining Relationships with the Media

To do:

• If there is a media outlet of particular importance, offer it a potentially newsworthy exclusive—with the up-front understanding that it will, in fact, do a complete story. (Generally, a campaign staffer, not the candidate, should contact them.)

• Offer exclusives only infrequently and only after carefully weighing the advantages and possible pitfalls of shutting out other members of the media.

- Have a good working relationship with the media outlet about to be propositioned.
- Keep in touch with columnists, talk show hosts, and producers who might be useful or supportive in the future.
- If there is an established *trusting* relationship with a media person, pass along *truthful* deep background information about the opposition which calls into question their credibility and deserves to be investigated further. Voters have a right to know some matters about which the opposition might not want them to be aware.
- Offer a story or column idea, even if it is not a political topic. The gesture will ultimately garner future goodwill from a grateful member of the media.

To avoid:
- Do not jeopardize the bond of trust you have cultivated with reporters, show hosts, editors, and the like by passing on false information or by failing to keep promised commitments.

Third-Party Endorsements

To do:
- Seek third-party endorsements that benefit a candidate or cause.
- Allow a third party to send out a press release on its own letterhead with glowing quotes about a candidate or issue campaign. That person could also hold a press conference, stage an event, appear on talk shows, and so on. Endorsements from a person or group not directly affiliated with a candidate or campaign carry greater credibility.
- Make an attempt to collaborate with a third party about the message. A unified effort means more effective publicity.
- Ask a group endorsing a candidate or cause to mail to their membership a letter announcing the endorsement. Ask them to release the letter to the press at an advantageous moment.

To avoid:
- Do not actively seek or encourage publicity about endorsements that do not benefit the campaign. For example, if a candidate supports the death penalty but is running in a very liberal anti-death-penalty district, do not publicize pro-death-penalty organization endorsements.

Op-Ed Pieces

To do:

• Submit occasional opinion pieces to be printed opposite newspapers' editorial pages.

• Pick a relevant campaign topic and consider how the piece could be used to achieve a political objective or support a paid media program.

To avoid:

• Do not annoy editorial page editors with several phone calls or call back in anger when they've turned a piece down for publication.

• Do not write anything that can be used against a candidate or campaign in the future. It is, after all, a public document.

Letters to the Editor

To do:

• Organize an effort to have people in the community send in letters to the editors of newspapers supporting a candidate or cause or criticizing the opposition.

• Help letter writers tailor their message in conjunction with what a campaign desires.

• Actually write the letters for willing supporters who agree with the content.

To avoid:

• Do not have people send in form letters or letters so similar in wording that it is obvious a campaign is orchestrating an effort. Editors will be even less likely to publish the letters.

• Do not encourage people who are considered strange or extremist or who are not well liked in a community to write letters.

Reader or Viewer Feedback, Phone-In Opportunities

• Have people call in to reader or viewer feedback phone lines whose numbers are often printed in the paper or played on-air.

EARNED MEDIA IN TODAY'S CAMPAIGN ENVIRONMENT

Two phenomena of the modern media age make earned media an increasingly valuable campaign tool. First, we live in an era of public cynicism about paid political information; people are conditioned to be skeptical of political, partisan-paid ads, spots, and other promotional items. In such a climate, earned media can be an important source of credibility for a campaign's message. A campaign's message is more likely to be believed when it is part of a news story, written by someone outside the campaign, or delivered by a radio or television talk show host. Endorsements, headlines, and quotes from the media add legitimacy to a paid media program and reinforce the campaign's overall message when included in television spots, radio ads, direct mail pieces, and other forms.

Second, there is the problem of channel overload. The expanding number of media outlets—from all-news stations to radio talk shows to Internet Web sites—have changed the traditional news environment. People now get their news from more sources than the network television news and the daily papers. News cycles that were once easily measurable are now far less obvious, and news is now being delivered virtually real-time into people's homes through computers and satellites. Consequently, campaigns have more media targets to reach, each with their own audiences and some with deadlines that are not daily but hourly.

It is increasingly obvious that a crucial step on the path to public persuasion—and victory—is establishing a comprehensive earned media strategy integrated with the overall goals of the campaign.

Trevor Parry-Giles **SPEECHWRITING**

Before polling, before direct mail and focus groups, before thirty-second spots and voter targeting, politicians were giving speeches and hiring experts to write them. The first known speechwriters were Corax and Tisias, two resourceful fifth-century B.C. Athenians who recognized the opportunities before them as the art of oratory was taking hold in ancient Greece. As humans began to give speeches—at ceremonies, in deliberative bodies, in the courts—the need arose for speechwriters. Prospective orators realized they lacked either the time or the ability to formulate a good speech, so they hired skilled practitioners and teachers to write their speeches for them.

Ancient speechwriters were called "sophists," a word that means "wisdom-bearer" in Greek, though its original meaning has changed considerably. Sophists soon began teaching their craft—the art of rhetoric—to future citizens and public leaders. Speechwriting and oratory came to dominate public life in ancient Greece and Rome.

In America, speechwriting is a time-honored art and science that remains in high demand in a political climate increasingly dominated by television and other mass media. Yet whatever its form, whoever does the writing or the speaking, or wherever it is practiced, speechwriting has certain basic principles that can be culled from historical precedent and applied to modern considerations.

SMART AND WISE

The Greeks and Romans believed that speechmaking could be used for significant advancement—that it was an indispensable practice for a community to perform in order to survive. They also feared that rhetoric could be manipulated and misused—hence Plato's castigation of sophists as eloquent deceivers. They believed that the way to prevent demagogues and liars from doing damage was to ensure that speechmaking and speechwriting were performed by learned, ethical people. This requirement survives to this day.

A good speechwriter is trained in what we might broadly call the liberal arts. Narrowly educated, technically trained people lack the expansive knowledge and understanding required to craft truly eloquent oratory. Unfortunately, college and university programs in public relations and journalism are insufficient in training effective speechwriters. The good speechwriter is someone who is well-read, has a deep understanding of philosophy, history, literature, economics, psychology, and art. This person understands and appreciates the power of language and the influence that eloquent uses of language can have on audiences. This individual values and appreciates the oratory of both Abraham Lincoln and Malcolm X. The good speechwriter recognizes just how Ronald Reagan and Barbara Jordan were able to use language and rhetoric masterfully and artistically to convince audiences of radically different ideas. And the good speechwriter treats the spoken language with respect and understands the ethical limits to which the power of oratory should be used.

LIMITED FORUMS AND GENRES

As they examined where and when speeches took place, the ancients realized that political speeches generally occur in three forums. Ceremonial speeches are the first type of speeches that politicians are asked to give—speeches that are presented at funerals, awards ceremonies, banquets, and the like. A second type of speech is a deliberative speech—the oratory that occurs in hearings, on the floor of legislative bodies, and the like. The final type of speech is a forensic speech such as is given in courtrooms and other legal settings.

A good speechwriter recognizes the differences between types of speeches. This awareness comes from effectively analyzing the situation facing the orator. Good speechwriters also have a keen awareness of previous examples of oratory in different settings. Speechwriters are students of public address—they've read the classic orations of our culture, which include many more speeches than just John F. Kennedy's Inaugural Address and Martin Luther King, Jr.'s, "I Have a Dream" speech. Learning how previous orators and speechwriters have handled different speech situations is a good way to discover the best ways to address a contemporaneous speech situation.

THE STEPS OF SPEECHWRITING

Step One: Invention. This step involves discerning the message, arguments, evidence: indeed, the very content of the speech.

First, get as much information as you can about the speech setting itself. Where will it be delivered? What time of day? Will your speaker be the only speaker at the event or one of several? What will be the layout of the speaking situation?

Second, learn as much as you can about the audience. Who are these people? What demographic characteristics do they possess? How do they feel about the speaker? How do they feel about the topic of the speech? Have they heard from the speaker on previous occasions? There are several sources for information about the audience. An important source is the organizers of the event itself—event planners, advance people, campaign staffers. Polling data may also be quite helpful in identifying the attitudinal profile of the audience. Consulting with local media outlets—newspapers or television stations—can offer insights as to what is important and pressing for a given audience.

Third, figure out what the predominant theme, argument, message, or idea of the speech will be. Consult with the speaker, if possible, or with his or her surrogates, concerning the speech and its message. What is the main idea that must be communicated? Is that idea likely to be received favorably by the audience? Can it be easily and clearly understood? Is the central theme capable of sustaining a full speech, or is it so complex that it can't possibly be discussed in a brief oration? And is the core message of the speech consistent with the overall communication strategy or narrative arc of the campaign? Note how the sample speech page (Figure 13) contains a clear and cogent central idea for the speech.

Fourth, gather evidence and information for the speech. Find compelling statistics, funny jokes, dramatic stories, and authoritative studies that will support the main idea you want to communicate to the audience. Notice how the sample speech makes use of a local narrative to illustrate the larger message of the oration. Ask members of the staff, local experts, media sources, and other knowledgeable people for information. And remember, it is always better to have too much information than not to have enough.

Step Two: Organization. Audiences generally are not very good at listening—especially to political speeches. One way to maximize the listening capacity of an audience is to structure clearly the speaker's message. Make certain that transitions are clear, structure is apparent, and repetition is frequent. A good outline is essential for a well-organized speech.

First, the introduction of the speech must be compelling and com-

The introduction may require additional acknowledgments of individuals or the nature of the occasion. There should be some recognition of the introduction.

This paragraph establishes a connection between the speaker and the audience. The speaker recognizes the accomplishments of the community. The paragraph also includes self-deprecation.

Thank you very much. Thank you. And thank you, John, for that very kind introduction.

Coming back to Centerville is always such a joy for me. I spent many warm summer days playing baseball here—and losing more often than winning. The Centerville Spartans are the titans of high school baseball in Ohio and Coach Howard Smith—well, he's a legend. We were always a little nervous about our chances whenever we came to Centerville and we had good reason to be scared. And whenever I was at bat, I felt more like Mudville's Casey than Babe Ruth when I faced those Centerville pitchers—and I wasn't all that mighty when I struck out.

This paragraph establishes the broad themes and values at the foundation of this speech. Of course, such themes and values should also reflect the overall message of the campaign.

Those were good days back then. For me, Centerville, like my own hometown of Granite Falls, represents the type of community that made America and Ohio great. The good people of this town are firmly grounded in their values and their commitment to community service. They care about their neighbors, they care about their town, they care about their country. And of all the towns in Ohio, Centerville has lost per capita more of its young people fighting for their country than any other community.

<u>Today, I want to celebrate Centerville's communal spirit, its dedication to duty and devotion, its belief in a better and brighter tomorrow</u>. I think it's time for all of Ohio, and the entire country, to return to the values that are represented so well here in Centerville. I think it's time we recaptured our uniquely American spirit of giving and volunteerism and dedicate ourselves to making a real difference in our communities.

This sentence expresses the specific purpose of the speech. Notice how the sentence uses parallelism and alliteration.

Many of you know the story of Mary Jones. I consider Mary one of my proudest accomplishments as your Congressman. Mary was a star student here at Centerville High. Her grades were great, she played three sports, and was president of the National Honor Society. She worked hard and played by the rules—and she wanted to go to college. But her family just couldn't afford it—even with loans and scholarships, they couldn't make it work.

The focus here shifts to a specific story. The story, in this case, is of a local individual, giving it greater resonance with the audience.

Mary wrote to me and asked if there was anything I could do to help. I put Mary in touch with the Americorps coordinator for Ohio. At that time, Americorps was still a new program. Few people knew it existed. I was proud that I voted in favor of Americorps (over stern Republican objections), and I was committed to making this innovative program work for Ohio's young people.

Mary signed up for Americorps and was able to afford a quality college education. But as she said to me, "I got more than a good education out of Americorps. I discovered the true joy of helping those in need, of making my community and my nation a better place. That's the real benefit of Americorps."

Our Congressman is able to weave his own public accomplishment/ vote for Americorps into the flow of the narrative—and even to highlight GOP opposition.

I'm proud of Mary, and my small role in her success, because she reflects what is truly unique and special about Centerville, and all of America—an optimistic belief that one person can make a real difference.

The quotation from Mary adds credibility and authenticity to the speech. If Mary is present, the Congressman should recognize her and acknowledge her support.

Figure 13. Sample speech

Courtesy Trevor Parry-Giles

plete; it should make appropriate acknowledgments and seek to secure the audience's attention. This may involve a joke, a meaningful narrative, a quotation, a startling statistic. Whatever is used, the introduction must command attention from the audience—if not, you can forget about the rest of the speech. The sample speech contains an introduction that involves the audience, highlights the speaker's credibility, and makes clear the central idea of the speech.

Second, offer the audience a well-defined sense of the purpose of the speech. Indicate what the core idea of the speech is, and demonstrate why the speaker is credible to discuss this topic. Even the most comatose member of the audience ought to know and remember what a speech is about.

Third, structure the main points of the speech clearly. Each of the main points should relate back to the central idea of the discourse and should be well supported with evidence, a story, or statistics. Each of the main points should also relate to the audience. And there ought to be evident transitions from one point to the next—help the audience to follow the progression of the ideas.

Fourth, develop a conclusion that "makes the sale." Reiterate the main points of the speech and make the case for why the audience should accept the argument and should vote for or support the speaker. Leave the audience with something meaningful, humorous, dramatic, or otherwise substantial; do not throw away the ending of speech. As they say, first *and final* impressions are the most lasting.

Step Three: Language. The language used to express the ideas of a speech is critical. Unfortunately, speechwriters are often more skilled at a written style of language than they are with a spoken style of language. Spoken language is clear, more concrete than abstract, more specific than general, shorter rather than longer, and more attuned to the ear rather than the eye. Capturing this difference is crucial if a speech is to be successful with an audience. The sample speech text contains illustrations of spoken language and language style that are useful for political speechwriting.

Imagine if John F. Kennedy had said, "And so my fellow Americans, I encourage you to ponder and inquire of yourself what you might do for your nation—don't simply demand to understand what the government can provide to you." Or if Ann Richards had said, "Poor George Bush. We must forgive him his inability to understand working Americans because he was born wealthy and never wanted for any need or requirement." Would we remember Ronald Reagan's challenge to Mikhail Gorbachev if he had said, "Mr. Gorbachev, the time has come to remove this Wall from our midst and allow peace and democratic freedoms to reign once again throughout the European continent?" Kennedy, Richards, and Reagan (and their speechwriters) were effective precisely because they understood the difference between language written to be heard and language written to be read.

Steps Four and Five: Memory and Delivery. Good speechwriters understand their speaker; they know how he or she speaks, what he or she can remember, the words they can't pronounce, the cadences they prefer. When writing a speech, the speechwriter should always try to write for the speaker in a way that will maximize not only the ideas they are communicating, but also the manner in which those ideas are uttered. For instance, a speaker without a strong sense of cadence should not be given a speech that includes a great deal of repetition or parallelism. The connection between the crafting or wording of a speech and its delivery before an audience must be foremost in the speechwriter's mind.

THE ROLE OF MEDIA

The rules and principles about public oratory from ancient civilizations are still relevant today. But our earliest speechwriters could never have envisioned a time when speeches would be broadcast to millions over radio and television or when oratory would be available simultaneously all over the world via telephone lines and the World Wide Web. Thus we need to adapt and alter our understanding of rhetoric and speechwriting for political life in the contemporary, mediated age.

Contemporary speechwriters must recognize that the speeches they write may appear on television. So while the speechwriter tries to account for the specific audience gathered to hear the speech, he or she also has to think in terms of soundbytes and the larger voting audience at home. This situation creates new demands and conditions in the speechwriting process. Most important, as New York University professor Mitchell Stephens concludes, we live in a time when the image is overtaking the word. Speechwriters, who deal almost exclusively in words, need to consider the power of images and the place and fit of their words in those images that define their candidate. The language of a speech is not separate from the image of the candidate as she or he delivers that speech. Bill Clinton's finger-wagging denial of an affair with "that woman, Miss Lewinsky," for example, will forever be etched in the public consciousness, as much because of the pictorial image of the president at that moment as for the words he uttered.

The rise of mass media and television has also made the public speech of even greater importance in a campaign and in political life. One slip, one gaffe, and a candidate will forever face commercials with the mistake and news footage of the error. Dan Quayle spelling "potato(e)" and Gerald Ford's assertions about Eastern Europe are just two examples. This is why political leaders and candidates take so much time to make certain that the speech is just right. Of course, the off-shoot of that attention is that speechwriters must be able to take criticism—to leave their egos at the door and adapt what might be fine oratory to the needs of the client. Arguably, this is one of the hardest aspects of speechwriting. The speechwriter will believe in the speech and the ideas it expresses only to be told to do it again by a fussy client or officeholder who is not quite able to articulate his or her complaints about the speech. Taking and adapting to criticism is a central requirement for an effective speechwriter.

The mass media also contribute to a punditocracy in which speechwriters lose their anonymity and invisibility. We've gone from the time of the obscure and unknown Judson Welliver (the first known White House speechwriter, hired during the Harding administration), to the era of Tony Snow and Peggy Noonan, where a stint as a speechwriter in the White House is but a stepping-stone toward future public and journalistic success as a public commentator.

This shifting in roles requires some potentially complicated ethical and philosophical juggling by the speechwriter. Do you protect the myth that effective oratory is merely an extension of the speaker with no credit due the speechwriter? Do you, like President Kennedy's speechwriters, refuse to take credit for effective, enduring language and lofty ideas? Or do you capitalize on your fame and write books or go on television to talk about the intricacies of the speechwriting process? Do you exploit your proximity to power and celebrity to enhance your own status? These questions reflect the dilemma, and are just a few of the challenges, facing speechwriters in the contemporary political age, dominated as it is by the mass media and twenty-four-hour-a-day television.

SUGGESTED READINGS

Aristotle. *The Art of Rhetoric*. Translated by John Henry Freese. Cambridge, Mass.: Harvard University Press, 1982.

Diamond, Edwin, and Robert A. Silverman. *White House to Your House: Media and Politics in Virtual America*. Cambridge, Mass.: MIT Press, 1995.

Gelderman, Carol. *All the President's Words: The Bully Pulpit and the Creation of the Virtual Presidency*. New York: Walker, 1997.

Jamieson, Kathleen Hall. *Eloquence in an Electronic Age: The Transformation of Political Speechmaking*. New York: Oxford University Press, 1988.

Noonan, Peggy. *What I Saw at the Revolution: A Political Life in the Reagan Era*. New York: Random House, 1990.

Ben Goddard | ISSUE ADVOCACY

Throughout most of American history, lobbying has been a restrained, behind-the-scenes exercise. Advocates and opponents of legislation preferred to work one-on-one with key legislators or regulators. While politicians might take to the "bully pulpit" to campaign for or against specific policies, private sector advocates generally stayed out of sight. Long-term relationships, campaign contributions, mutual favors, and quiet debates were the preferred tools of those who wanted to shape public policy. In the 1990s, that situation changed dramatically.

The seeds of this change were sown in the 1992 presidential campaign, when Bill Clinton made health care reform one of his key domestic issues. Shortly after his inauguration, the president appointed First Lady Hillary Rodham Clinton to lead the task force charged with health care reform, signaling the importance of the issue to his administration. He appeared to have broad-based support. Labor, public health organizations, seniors, and consumer groups all voiced their endorsement of the president's proposals for "guaranteeing health coverage with comprehensive benefits for all Americans." In a Gallup poll, 68 percent of the respondents said they were "very or somewhat confident" that the Clinton plan would succeed in "making health care affordable" for everyone in the United States. Given these highly visible allies and strong public favor, it seemed that Clinton's health care reform agenda was unstoppable.

In the flurry of early, positive publicity, however, the costs of the plan were little known and its mechanics little understood. As in so many cases in public policy issues, a special interest group first identified the problems and dangers: the plan would have literally put some three hundred medium to small health insurers out of business. Through their trade association, the Health Insurance Association of America (HIAA), these companies launched a campaign to defend their industry that would change the way public policy is debated in America. It was clear that a traditional "inside the Beltway" lobbying effort had small prospect of success given the powerful forces allied behind the president's plan. Instead, the association decided to mobilize

217

national grassroots support to put pressure on politicians to change or defeat Clinton's proposal. The effort included telephone contacts, direct mail, and organizing of grassroots opinion leaders. HIAA also hired public opinion pollsters to track the efficacy of its messages and formulate strategy. But the most important and prominent component was a $17 million television blitz of ads featuring "Harry & Louise," a mythical American couple who learned how they would be adversely affected by the Clinton plan. Harry & Louise went over the heads of policymakers and elected officials and appealed directly to the American people—especially to opinion leaders who were heavy watchers of news programs where most of the ads were carried.

The strategy worked: the HIAA campaign drove support for the Clinton plan into the low 30 percent range and opposition to nearly 60 percent. In a Gallup Poll taken in late 1993, only 8 percent of respondents said they thought they would be "a lot better off" under the plan. It died a slow and painful death in congressional committees, never making it to the floor for debate.

The success of Harry & Louise quickly led to "advocacy advertising" campaigns for issues as diverse as tort reform, global warming,

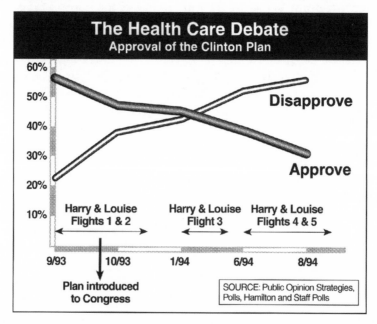

Figure 14.

Courtesy Goddard Claussen

and tax policy. Though few of those efforts have matched the scope of the HIAA campaign (one year and a total of $21 million), they have significantly changed the way public policy battles are waged in America. Advertising and grassroots activity outside Washington, D.C., are now staples of lobbying efforts.

THE AUDIENCE

The audience for an advocacy advertising campaign is not really "the public." The intended audience is, rather, those informed Americans who shape public policy debates. These opinion leaders make up no more than a quarter of the total population. They belong to organizations, go to meetings, write letters, and make political contributions. As a result, their voices are heard. Generally they are well-educated, upper-income professionals, entrepreneurs, business leaders, educators, elected officials, policymakers, and members of the press. But not all opinion leaders share these upscale demographic profiles. Union shop stewards, community organizers, and leaders of service or volunteer organizations also help drive public opinion in America. The one characteristic they all share, however, is that they are *involved* with American society and thus have a significant impact on how America thinks.

These "influentials" or "informed Americans" are not a new group in our society, but it was only in the late 1940s that polling by the Roper organization first began to identify them. Since then other researchers have expanded on this early work. In the early 1990s, Charlton Research began to segment the American public into four groups based on their level of information about public policy issues (see Figure 15). The majority of Americans are relatively uninformed about public policy and have little impact on it except at election time, when their attitudes and their votes generally follow those of the more informed. Those whom Charlton defines as "informed Americans" fall into three groups: the minimally informed, the moderately informed, and the highly informed. The sought-out opinion leaders make up the highly informed group and thus are the most important targets of any advocacy advertising effort.

As their name implies, informed Americans are avid consumers of information. They read newspapers, watch cable news networks, listen to talk radio, and are very frequent viewers of network and local television news and magazine shows. They consider themselves intelligent consumers of information and dislike being lectured to or having pre-packaged opinions fed to them in advocacy advertising. They prefer to be provided with information they can process and use to form their own conclusions, which then have a tremendous influence on the development of public opinion.

What becomes clear is that public opinion in America is largely driven by a continuously reinforced communications cycle. The media raise issues that catch the attention of opinion leaders. Opinion leaders process this information and develop opinions, which are communicated to elected officials and policymakers, who then tell the media what their constituents believe about an issue, which is reported in the media and reinforces or sometimes changes opinion leaders' attitudes. And the cycle goes on. The public opinion communications loop is shown in Figure 16.

The communications process can begin at any point in the cycle, although it usually starts with the media. The cycle is iterative and thus can fuel itself. It also consumes large amounts of information, so it needs replenishment. New information that is properly introduced

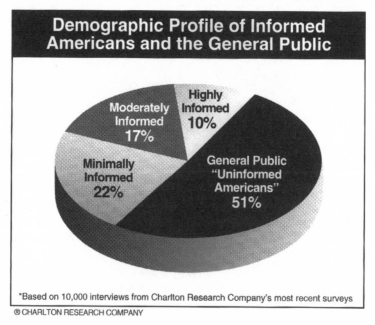

Figure 15.

Courtesy Goddard Claussen

INFORMED AMERICANS: ENGAGEMENT

Based on Charlton Research's database of 10,000 interviews from our most recent surveys, informed Americans tend to engage in the following activities:

	Highly Informed	General Public
Been registered to vote	95%	75%
Signed a petition	82%	25%
Attended a public meeting on community affairs	85%	16%
Been a member of an organization dedicated to improving your community	83%	16%
Written to your congressman/senator/ governor or other elected official	78%	14%
Served as an officer of any club or organization	75%	10%
Been a member of a group focused on improving government or changing government policy	66%	5%
Given a public speech	61%	6%
Written a letter to the editor of a newspaper or magazine	50%	4%
Worked for a political party or a candidate	50%	4%
Called in to a radio or television talk show regarding an issue	33%	4%
Written an article for publication	42%	N/A
Held a position in or run for political office	12%	1%

into the cycle can have a profound impact on the messages moving through the loop. This component, then, is crucial for an advocacy advertising effort. By crafting messages that are introduced into the loop through paid advertising in a vehicle that reaches opinion leaders, one can effect a change in public perception of an issue. The key is to add credible information to the message mix and use the cycle to create an alternative opinion.

DEVELOPING THE MESSAGE

Obviously, creating the desired change in opinions on a given issue requires communicating the right information. Unlike traditional politi-

INFORMED AMERICANS: PSYCHODEMOGRAPHIC POINTS

Informed Americans have the following characteristics:

	Highly Informed	General Public
Are white collar workers	73%	60%
Tend to be Republican	41%	33%
Tend to be strong environmentalists	47%	31%
Are middle-aged: 35–44	27%	21%
45–54	24%	15%
Tend to be well-educated: College graduates	36%	17%
Post-graduate	25%	6%
Tend to have higher incomes: $50K–$79K	26%	14%
$80K and above	15%	5%

Charlton Research has compiled a database of 10,000 interviews from our most recent surveys to profile informed Americans.

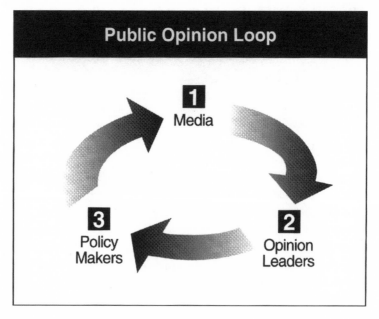

Figure 16.

Courtesy Goddard Claussen

cal advertising in which messages draw a conclusion about a candidate, advocacy advertising messages must provide information that helps the target audience draw its own conclusion. The essential task, of course, is to craft messages that lead to the conclusion the advertiser wants drawn. To do that, one must abide by the fundamental principle of advocacy communications, which is that *everyone acts in his or her own self-interest.* The messages, accordingly, must appeal to the self-interest of the audience in such a way as to draw its members to the proper conclusion. Research is the tool used to discern the proper message track.

Both quantitative (e.g., opinion surveys) and qualitative (e.g., focus groups) research tools are generally necessary to identify the messages that will actually move attitudes on public policy. To begin an advocacy campaign, focus groups help reveal how the target audience perceives an issue. This attitude will often shift dramatically if the question can be framed differently; if you define the terms, you win the debate. In the HIAA Harry & Louise campaign, for example, fully two-thirds of the American people were telling the president's pollsters they wanted "radical reform of the health care system." Clearly, arguing that reform was not necessary was going to be a very difficult debate to win. The HIAA campaign managers set out to determine just what "radical reform" meant to opinion leaders and discovered it was something quite different from what the White House was proposing. By "radical reform," opinion leaders meant guaranteed health care coverage, portable coverage that could move with people if they changed or lost their jobs, and coverage that was affordable. That understanding allowed Harry & Louise to focus the debate on elements of the proposal that did not appeal to opinion leaders: government-managed mandatory health alliances that might lead to rationing of some care. Throughout that campaign, the fictional American couple always agreed that health care reform was a desirable goal but argued there was "a better way" to accomplish it than the plan proposed by the president.

Once focus groups help define how the target audience perceives an issue, quantitative studies such as opinion polls are used to validate and further develop the arguments suggested by the groups. The goal of this research is to determine what message elements will "move the needle" on an issue. Where opinions are at the time of the research is of less importance than how various messages can affect those opinions. A national message development survey might test as many as two dozen message elements in brief statements, measuring how these statements move opinion with a variety of testing devices.

The messages that have been developed in groups and then refined in a survey must be tested in various forms of execution to determine what combination will have the most impact on the target audience. Messengers as well as messages must be tested, for often the messenger adds or subtracts credibility from the message itself. This research is best done using "animatics" or test spots in a dial group setting. Animatics are generally video storyboards—artists' renderings of the action that will appear in a television commercial, which are then photographed and transferred to videotape. Actors' voices play the parts of the characters in the commercial. Experience has shown, however, that test audiences respond better to sample ads that are closer in production value to finished commercials. Thus a preferable testing device, although a much more expensive one, is to create test spots by shooting sample commercials on a video medium such as High 8 or VHS.

The animatics or test ads are played in a focus group setting in which each participant uses a hand-held device to dial favorable or negative responses to what they are seeing on screen. Such tests provide a real-time measure of the audience's response to specific message points throughout the thirty-second commercial. At the end of the dial sessions, the test ads are played again and the group discusses what they have seen and heard.

Using these techniques, messages can be refined to accomplish the basic goals of an advocacy advertising campaign: they define the terms of the debate in the self-interest of the audience and lead them to the conclusion the advertiser wants. Now all that must be done is to deliver those messages successfully to the target audience and elicit a response that will move policymakers to action.

DELIVERING THE MESSAGE

Informed Americans are avid consumers of information. Thus the place to reach them with public policy messages is on information programming. All four commercial broadcast networks refuse to carry advocacy advertising—and it is not required that they do so under current interpretations of law—so network news and information shows, including the popular Sunday morning shows, will not be part of an advocacy advertising media plan. Cable news programming on networks such as CNN, Headline News, CNBC, and MSNBC generally forms the core buy of such a plan. Networks like Discovery, Lifetime, ESPN, and A&E also deliver a large audience of informed Americans and allow some additional targeting by gender, age, and income. Print publications like the *Wall Street Journal, New York Times*, and national newsmagazines are also efficient national buys for this target audience. *USA Today* is only slightly less efficient but has the advantage of making the print buy appear "national" to a greater degree than any other daily newspaper. Along with these more general media, it often makes sense to use industry or special interest publications to reach a specific segment of opinion leaders.

In addition to national advertising placement, many advocacy campaigns focus on the Washington, D.C., market and on congressional districts that are home to influential members dealing with a specific issue. Although network programs will not carry advocacy advertising, most stations in most local markets will. Using a combination of national cable and local information programming in a media plan creates the impression that the campaign is widespread and allows one to achieve frequent repetition with the target audience. Broadcast advertising in Washington, D.C., and print vehicles such as *National Journal, Roll Call, Congressional Quarterly, Weekly Standard,* and *The Hill* are useful to remind policymakers and their staffs that someone is talking to their constituents.

New media like the Internet are increasingly being used in efficient advocacy advertising campaigns as well—especially since the highly informed American is also one who is more likely to be online. Television commercials and print ads should carry a Web site address. An effective Web site can be linked to the sites of the campaign's sponsors, creating new opportunities to reach informed Americans. The Web site itself allows for the further development of the advocacy arguments and provides opportunities for sending e-mail messages to members of Congress, letters to the editor in local communities, sign-up forms for visitors to the site to become volunteer members of an advocacy organization, and other tools that actively involve informed Americans in a campaign to change public opinion.

Advocating public policy through grassroots and advertising campaigns will continue to play a critical role in American life for one simple reason: it works. The tools briefly discussed here will shape these debates for years to come. Although the methods of issue advocacy may evolve, one lesson is likely to be indelible: major changes in public policy will have to be "sold" to the American public (through opinion leaders) as much as are candidates in any election.

| *Diana* | PRO BONO WORK |
| *Daggett* | |

Virtually every corporate culture recognizes the importance (and rewards) of community involvement by employees. Pro bono service, the donation of professional services at no charge, is one of the most valued forms of volunteer service. The political consulting profession is no different. Many of us were introduced to our profession by volunteering. Because we are activists as professionals, we are natural candidates for activism in our communities.

What is often missing, however, is the next step. We volunteer but do not necessarily view our *professional* skills as a valuable commodity in our volunteer efforts. During our career development, we often lose the thirst for activism that initially drew us into politics. Because we travel extensively, it is easy to surrender our sense of community. Home is where the suitcases are; voluntarism is cutting a check. In addition, we are not generally tied to a corporate identity and have no annual review process beyond our win/lose record. There is little top-down professional inducement to get involved by serving on boards of nonprofits or offering our expertise on a pro bono basis. Résumé enhancement through community service does not have as obvious a payoff in our profession as it does for more traditional professional roles. There is no authority figure reminding us of our civic responsibility.

WHAT WE CAN DO

What we can easily overlook is the direct benefit pro bono service provides to our business and professional growth. Even more important, the highly specialized skills of political consulting are often indispensable in the world of nonprofits. You can make a measurable difference doing things you love to do, and it feels great. The skills necessary for these struggling nonprofits are precisely those that political consultants are trained to deliver. They include the following.

1. *The technical know-how of generating funds.* Familiarity with the mechanics of direct mail, the logistics of special events, and the

fundamentals of fund-raising are vital for a campaign veteran. In the world of nonprofits, that knowledge is the coin of the realm, but it is often met with skepticism or even fear. It takes a small leap of faith for people who are not politically involved to trust a system or practices that they have seen derided by the media.

2. *Overcoming the naïveté of nonprofits about fund-raising.* Many nonprofits routinely fall victim to scams or inflated fund-raising costs because they lack professional knowledge. They pay too much per piece for mail. They sign on to expensive product solicitations that provide little return. They invest too much in up-front costs and never recoup the investment. They become involved in telemarketing schemes that line someone else's pockets and damage the organization's public image. One nonprofit association, for example, became involved in a Bingo parlor that was initially profitable but started to lose money, although the parlor proprietors promised that it would turn around. It took months before the board members realized they were victims of a racket. Campaign professionals have the unique experience to provide expert advice and caution as well as encouragement. The most basic fund-raising knowledge can make a dramatic difference.

3. *Marketing and message development.* Knowing what sells, and how to sell it, is an art. It can also be a challenge. Imagine for a moment organizations in which the members are consumed by their issue and frustrated by their inability to invigorate others. No one cares the way they do. No one understands the way they do. No one feels as deeply. Helping these groups articulate their need and their mission to wider audiences who may not share their passion not only advances the cause but energizes the weary participants. The political consultant's ability to generate earned media, create public awareness, and provide purposeful movement rather than aimless motion can lend new resolve to people who may feel they are a voice in the wilderness. It is as simple as knowing how to do a press release, design a brochure, or create a public service announcement. These are basics for someone with campaign experience, but they can be a mystery to an activist going door-to-door.

4. *Built-in networks of fund-raising.* When first petitioned for advice on fund-raising, I replied, "It's simple: you ask." The reaction to this counsel—disbelief—was predictable. To prove my point, and to get the ball rolling, I mailed letters to some of my friends requesting a donation—in this case for autism research. With that initial effort we

raised $7,000 and proved two things. First, asking works. Second, and perhaps less obvious, was that there is no *harm* in asking. From this first experience we ventured cautiously into sending more donation request letters and holding a modest fund-raising event. No gimmicks, no tricks: just clear, honest communication where there was a need. At every step I took care to explain the process and predict the outcome. When the predictions came true, because they were based on solid fund-raising experience, confidence in these tactics grew.

5. *Built-in networks of political influence.* Unquestionably the most important and unique benefit a political professional brings to a nonprofit is that our clients are the people who make policy. We have the ability to help an organization articulate what it wants and then know where to get results. Simply determining which government body has jurisdiction on any issue can be a challenge. Often nonprofit organization members go to the elected official they know or have seen on television. They may be beating on the door of the city council to get state aid. Guiding them to the people who can make a difference is our special skill. Your senator cannot cure your special child, but she can ensure that the United States continues to offer a free and appropriate public education in the least restrictive environment and secure funding for medical research or guarantee the civil rights of all citizens, regardless of ability or circumstance of birth.

WHAT'S IN IT FOR US

This is what we can bring to the plate of nonprofits: our skills are our best donations. The personal benefits for ourselves are rich, but the *professional* benefits are also enormous. The political consultant's job is to feel the pulse of America, to tap into what moves people. Personal involvement in the community provides a window, an opportunity, to understand our people. It leads to insights and knowledge available in no other way. Listening is not enough. Getting your hands dirty and your cheeks wet with tears is the only way to understand.

Road warriors are easily isolated. At our worst, some who started careers stuffing and stamping now enter a headquarters, walk past the volunteers and staff, and go into the closed-door meeting with the candidate and manager to make important decisions. We analyze crosstabs, edit videotapes, dissect opposition research, reduce everything to thirty-second spots, and leave before the votes are counted. At our best, we cry with the candidate, celebrate with the staff, and share the war stories that invariably start with "Here's why I love America." By getting more deeply involved in communities, we keep those stories current rather than stowed in the ancient history of the beginnings of our careers.

But there's one caveat: they say all politics is personal. Similarly, good pro bono work always comes from the heart. Don't treat it as simply a civic responsibility—like jury duty, for example. Make a commitment to a cause you actually care about. In the long run, this wards off burnout and makes the "work" a pleasure, not just another job. Identify the issue you care most about: maybe you have a family member who suffers from a disease, or your community is involved in a quality-of-life issue related to the environment.

Find the group that is involved and offer your services. Be specific about your skills and your time commitment. You might offer a particular service, such as drafting letters, directing a media event, developing a message, creating a brochure, or organizing grassroots effort. Whatever your commitment, follow it to completion. Finishing the job is your most important obligation. When one task is achieved, evaluate the results and determine how or if you want to continue.

Keep a record of your pro bono services and include them in your professional materials. Your service sets an example that enhances the image of the industry. It can also be an effective marketing tool. Candidates value public service and will value it in professionals. Encourage your colleagues to get involved. Create action teams with diverse skills. Political consultants are generous people. A few are even prosperous!

All I can say in conclusion is that participation in pro bono service works. My involvement was inspired by my extraordinary daughter's diagnosis of autism in 1984. I was fortunate to find the support and experience of other parents in a chapter of the Autism Society of America. Their knowledge and dedication were miles and years ahead of mine; what I brought to the table was a little energy and an unusual professional background. I don't believe any of these wonderful parents had ever met a political consultant. They were intrigued but very skeptical. I was not certain that my skills were relevant or helpful. It was for this group that I wrote my first nonpolitical fund-raising letter. The experience stuck—I ended up serving four years as a board member of the society. For my efforts I was given the society's Pro Bono Award. I am convinced that the experience made me a better professional, and I hope I made a difference a time or two.

NEW TECHNOLOGIES

Lynn Reed | ONLINE CAMPAIGNING

The use of the Internet is one of the most rapidly changing and least understood aspects of political campaigning in the late 1990s. In 1992, the Internet was a little-known tool for scientists and academics. In 1996, major and minor party presidential campaigns ran Web sites as novelties that had little strategic value. By the end of 1998, we had seen dramatic growth in both the number of campaign Internet presences and the number of voters who consider the Internet an important source of political information, but we have not—yet— seen the "JFK of the Internet," the national candidate who is widely considered to have won his or her race by mastering the new medium. We have, however, witnessed a handful of federal and statewide candidates using the medium in strategic ways, as an organizing tool or as a tool for communicating with voters, to play a determining, but not decisive, role in their campaigns.

DEMOGRAPHICS

The upper limit of the power of the Internet as a campaign tool is largely determined by the number of voting-age adults with Internet access in a candidate's jurisdiction. Surveys indicate that 62 to 70 million U.S. adults, roughly one-third of the voting-age population, had Internet access, at work or at home, in 1998. And while those online Americans more closely resemble the nation's population as a whole in race, gender, age, education, and income than the Internet users of two or three years ago, they are still more likely to live in certain parts of the country than others and to be slightly younger, better educated, and higher income than the population as a whole.

While 82 percent of Web users indicate that they are registered voters, only 40 percent of those who actually voted in 1998 consider themselves regular Internet users. And within the subset of voters who are Internet users is the smaller subset of voters who use the Internet specifically for political information. Phone surveys conducted by the Pew Research Center in December 1998 found that 16 percent of voters used the Internet for political information, and only 6 percent considered the Internet their primary source of political information. Put a slightly different way, Wirthlin Worldwide exit polls indicate that 11 percent of voters found information on the Internet that helped them decide who to vote for, up from 9 percent in 1996. We have no data on whether the persuadable voters found this influential information on a news site, a political party site, a candidate's Web site, or e-mail from a friend.

These demographic realities suggest three main challenges for campaigns in developing Internet strategies: first, how to develop an Internet presence that attracts voters who are online to your campaign site where they can receive your campaign message; second, how to develop an Internet presence that also attracts the attention of the offline media, extending the site's reach to voters who watch television and read newspapers but are not online or reinforce campaign messages to voters who are online but also watch other media; and third, how to use the medium to get timely information to supporters and activists quickly and inexpensively.

The three campaigns discussed below found successful strategies for dealing with these challenges.

TAMMY BALDWIN FOR CONGRESS: ATTRACTING ONLINE VOTERS

In Wisconsin's second district, made up of the city of Madison and adjoining rural counties, Democrat Tammy Baldwin won a very competitive race to replace retiring Republican congressman Scott Klug, becoming the first woman elected to Congress from Wisconsin and the first "out" lesbian elected to Congress in U.S. history.

The Internet lesson in the Baldwin-for-Congress story comes out of her win in the Democratic primary in which she narrowly defeated two opponents. Baldwin's base of support was in the city of Madison, home of her state legislative district and home of more than thirty thousand students at the University of Wisconsin (UW). Her opponents, Rick Phelps and Joe Winneke, had their bases in the more conservative rural areas outside of Madison.

Baldwin needed an overwhelming turnout in Madison to overcome her opponents' strength in the other parts of the district. She anticipated strong support from UW students, but young (aged eighteen to twenty-five) voter turnout is notoriously low and considered undependable by most political professionals. Worse, UW students would be returning to campus for the fall semester a few days before the primary election. In that interval, freshmen would barely have time to locate their classrooms on the vast campus, much less find their polling place.

To strengthen her traditional organizing (rallies on campus, dorm captains, flyers), Baldwin employed an Internet strategy to reach out to UW students. A special "Students for Baldwin" section of her volunteer-designed Web site was constructed, outlining Baldwin's position on issues of concern to students and, most important, offering a list of student polling places, with addresses and photos of the buildings, organized by dormitory. The student section also outlined Wisconsin's same-day voter registration requirements, explaining that students could register at the polls on primary day by providing proof that they had lived in the district for ten days.

To further entice students to hit the Web site, and therefore direct them to the polls, a television ad, featuring a young woman in UW garb supporting Baldwin, was produced and placed on MTV and other programs students were sure to watch. The ad contained the Web site address, mentioned the same-day voter registration process, and directed students to the site for more information.

The student strategy was so successful that the *Capital Times* columnist John Nichols called Baldwin's primary victory a "youthquake," saying, "Bottom line: Baldwin could not have won Tuesday's primary without the votes of people between the ages of 18 and 30. And in a nation where low voter turnout among the young is an epidemic, that ranks as a remarkable statistic."

Baldwin's victory was not a result of the Internet alone, but the Internet (in synergy with traditional campaign media and methods) helped her target and turn out young voters who were key to her success.

BRIAN BAIRD FOR CONGRESS: ATTRACTING OFFLINE MEDIA ATTENTION

In Washington State's third district, Brian Baird defeated state senator Don Benton in a very competitive race to replace retiring Republican congresswoman Linda Smith. The Internet lesson in the Baird race

Figure 17. Baldwin for Congress Web page

Courtesy Lynn Reed, NetPolitics

concerns both the integration of the Internet strategy with the overall campaign strategy and the effective use of the Internet in illustrating an issue for the news media.

Late in the race, Baird polling and opposition research revealed that Benton's support declined when voters learned that he had missed over four hundred votes during his four years in the state legislature. Although the Baird campaign had established a main Web site earlier in the year, it now developed a second site, *www.missedvotes.com*, to illustrate this issue.

The site was launched October 8, 1998, when paid television ads on the same issue began to run in the district. The ads carried the site address and offered voters the opportunity to view for themselves all four hundred of the votes Benton had missed. At the same time, Baird raised the issue in a televised debate, and the campaign began to invite reporters to visit the site and view Benton's votes.

While the site received significant overall traffic, visits from the news media were most important. Consider what would have happened if the Baird campaign had distributed the information in the tra-

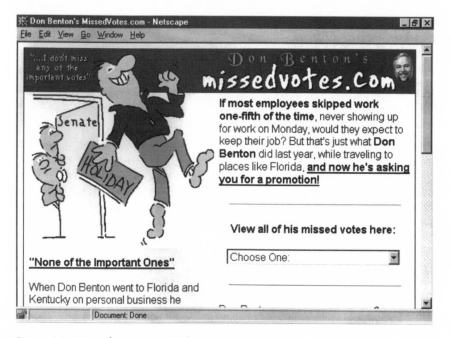

Figure 18. Missedvotes.com Web page

Courtesy Lynn Reed, NetPolitics

ditional manner—on paper. In all likelihood, a reporter would not take
the time to page through a list of four hundred missed votes and would
certainly not have printed the full list in the newspaper for voters to
see. With the Web site, reporters could quickly view the list by year,
by issue area, or even by "greatest hits."

As a result, Oregon newspapers wrote many articles on the issue, a
local television news piece on the issue and the Web site was aired, and
the *Portland Oregonian* endorsement of Brian Baird over Benton specifically noted: "Attendance is part of a legislator's job. A poor showing
in one office is no recommendation for another."

As with Baldwin, Baird's victory was not a result of the Internet
alone, but the Internet strategy raised the profile of the key campaign
issue with the news media, which in turn reached a much larger segment of voters than could have been reached on the Internet alone.

JESSE VENTURA FOR GOVERNOR: EFFECTIVE ONLINE ORGANIZING

Three days after election day, the *New York Times* online reported that
the surprise win of Reform Party candidate Jesse Ventura in the Minnesota governor's race was "a victory that some attribute to effective use
of the Internet as a tool for mobilizing volunteers and voters." Undoubtedly, with only one paid staff member and without a campaign
office until the final months of the race, the Ventura campaign was
forced to rely on e-mail and the Web site (along with phones and fax)
for the bulk of internal campaign communication.

Phil Madsen, the Ventura campaign webmaster, indicates that the
Internet strategy boosted fund-raising, recruited supporters and volunteers, and relied on those volunteers to perform office support tasks
such as data entry that would otherwise be provided by paid campaign
staff. For example, more than five thousand people filled out volunteer
forms at the Ventura booth at the Minnesota state fair. As Madsen explains, there were "no computers in the office and no money to hire a
data entry service." A private data entry Web site was established, an
e-mail appeal was made for volunteers to enter data, and within days
volunteers entered all the data.

During the Ventura "Drive to Victory Tour" in the final two days of
the campaign, e-mail appeals were also used. On October 26, an e-mail
and phone tree–mass calling from lists of those who had expressed in-

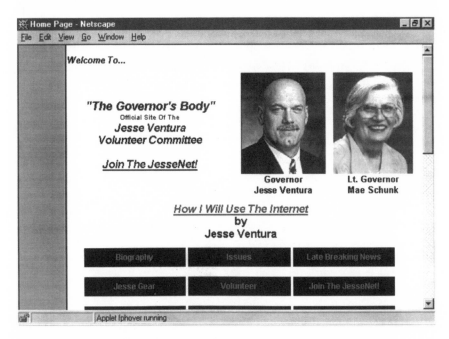

Figure 19. Ventura for Governor Web page

Courtesy Lynn Reed, NetPolitics

terest in the campaign announced an organizational meeting for the tour. Two days later, 250 volunteers showed up for the meeting. As Madsen explains, "the tour plan and volunteer positions were publicized" and "people rose to fill the tour volunteer slots and went to work organizing the local rallies." Throughout the tour, the public Web site was updated with video clips and digital photos from the rallies shortly after they happened. The Ventura campaign feels that this final tour was far more successful because of the Internet than it would have been without it. Ventura's momentum was sustained and his support grew in the crucial final days of the campaign.

Madsen summarizes, "While it's true that we could not have won the election without the Internet, we did not win the election because of the Internet." But in the absence of an office and staff, the Ventura campaign's use of the Internet stands out in sharp relief. A lack of traditional resources forced the Ventura campaign to integrate its use of the Internet more fully into all the operations of the campaign, with impressive, if not decisive, results.

*   *   *

If the Internet success stories of 1998 are any indication, the campaigns of the year 2000 will produce Internet campaign strategies that compellingly attract online voters, that illustrate key campaign issues to the press, and that more fully integrate campaign office functions with the Internet. It is difficult, however, to predict whether 2000 will produce the "JFK of the Internet."

SUGGESTED WEB SITES

Intelliquest (*http://www.intelliquest.com*)
CyberAtlas (*http://www.cyberatlas.com*)
PoliticsOnline (*http://www.politicsonline.com*)
NetPoliticsGroup (*http://www.netpoliticsgroup.com*)
Georgia Institute of Technology Graphics, Visability, and Usability (*http:// www.cc.gatech.edu/gvu/*)
National Journal's Cloakroom (*http://www.cloakroom.com*)
Wirthlin Worldwide (*http://www.wirthlin.com*)

Jay Perkins THE INTERNET AND
CAMPAIGN '98

The political Web site became a powerful tool for
several major campaigns in the 1998 election, but far too many candidates and campaigns still haven't "got it."

But they will by the year 2000, political observers say. And if those observers are correct, the interactive potential of the Internet will one day become as important to campaigns as media buys and polling.

It would be premature to assert that the Internet came of age in the 1998 elections. Even though almost all statewide campaigns had a Web presence—a survey by George Washington University's Graduate School of Political Management found major party candidates in 81 percent of the tightest races had Web sites—few of those sites were treated as part of the actual campaign. Most campaigns used their Web sites as an online brochure where voters could get a basic biography and a few issue papers. Some put up a Web page and promptly forgot about it. Others made no effort to integrate the Web site into the campaign strategy. And even of the few Web sites on which things were done right, the influence of the Web site was limited to a small number of voters.

Despite those caveats, it would be fair to say that in several races, the Internet showed its potential in helping to organize a campaign, in getting out the vote, in collecting campaign funds, and in helping a campaign influence the media's perception of the race. Two campaigns that accomplished these goals were that of Jeb Bush for governor in Florida and Barbara Boxer for U.S. Senate in California. These campaigns as well as several others provided a few lessons:

Political astuteness is more important than technical abilities, particularly in this early period of development when consultants are just figuring out what works and why. "Political astuteness is needed right now while they sort out the different features that work on a political site," said Rick Alber, who oversaw development of the Boxer Web site. "Those are political questions. The technical aspects, they're not that tough."

Rapid response is a necessity for a political Web site. "In the commercial world, if a commercial client gives you an update, you get it up in a week to ten days, that's good performance," said Mike Connell, president of New Media Communications, the Cleveland-based firm that created the Bush Web site. "In a political environment, they want an update made in an hour. The Internet is rapid response like we've never seen before."

A Web site must accurately reflect the campaign's message and personality as well as the campaign's goals. The Bush Web site, for example, had a serious but playful air as it hawked everything from position papers to Jeb Bush campaign buttons and clothes. The Boxer campaign viewed the Web site as enhancing Boxer's image as technically savvy. "One of the goals was to demonstrate her technical understanding of the Internet and be consistent with and improve her image as a tech person," said Alber. "Representing Silicon Valley in California, she needs that image."

Campaigns can raise money through Web sites. Although the totals collected in the 1998 campaign were small, both the Bush and Boxer campaigns reported receiving $1,000 donations over the Web from people using their credit cards.

Campaigns can attract human resources through Web sites. Probably the greatest single achievement of the Internet in 1998 was in allowing campaigns to attract volunteers quickly. The Boxer campaign picked up 673 volunteers—over half of the total number of volunteers used in the campaign—from forms submitted online. The Bush campaign picked up over 1,000 volunteers online.

The Internet's ability to organize campaigns and to interact with supporters may be the area of greatest potential. The Boxer campaign experimented with chat rooms where supporters could meet online—a virtual campaign headquarters, so to speak. The Bush campaign made it easy for visitors to send personalized pro-Bush e-mail postcards to their friends.

The Web provides an effective means of dealing with conventional media. Although reporters will continue to call the campaign manager for comments, they also will make good use of position papers and press releases collected over the Web. "Using the Internet with the media is still the most underutilized part of the process," says Phil Noble, the founder of PoliticsOnline. "The interesting thing about big dumb animals—not to say the press is a big dumb animal—is that they look to those who are feeding them first. So if you are providing them that information . . . they'll look to you for information, they'll look to you for ideas, they'll look to you for sound, for video. . . . As anybody in politics knows, you want to frame the issues, you want to define what the election is all about. "

The demographics of the Web make it effective for reaching younger voters. Both campaigns provided forms online to make it easier for Internet visitors to register to vote. The forms did not actually register the voter—Florida, for example, requires voters to submit a signed form and swear an oath—but they got the process rolling. The Boxer campaign form directed visitors to the National Voter Registration form from the Federal Election Commission. California allows registration by mail and accepts computer printouts of that form.

UNDERSTANDING THE USERS

Clearly, Internet usage—and its impact—is growing exponentially. Surveys by IntelliQuest and Nielsen in 1998 estimated total adult Internet users in the United States at 73 million and 79 million, respectively. That would put between 27.8 percent and 30 percent of the population over sixteen years of age online. In 1995, just three years earlier, Nielsen estimated total Internet users in the United States at 6.7 million.

Survey Date	Number of Adult Internet Users	Percentage of American Population	Data Source
1995	18 million	6.70	CommerceNet/Nielsen
June 1997	51 million	19.17	IntelliQuest
February 1998	62 million	23.0	IntelliQuest
October 1998	73 million	27.8	IntelliQuest
August 1998	79 million	30.0	CommerceNet/Nielsen

More important to campaigns, however, is *who* is using the Internet. A 1997 survey of Internet users by Chilton Research Services found 53 percent of the sample in the eighteen-to-thirty-four age group and 25 percent in the thirty-five-to-forty-four age group. The Chilton survey also found that 78 percent of the Internet users had some college education and that 53 percent reported income of more than $50,000 a year.

Since younger adults tend to vote less frequently than their older counterparts, the Internet clearly represents a potentially fertile area.

In addition, the higher-income, better-educated voters on the Internet are more likely to be receptive to the depth of campaign materials the Internet can provide.

The problem, of course, is getting those voters to a campaign Web site and keeping them there. A survey by Don Goff and David Duleo of American University found that Web sites for specific campaigns were hard to find in the 1998 campaign and that most Web sites had few visitors. "Senators were receiving hits in the range from only about 3,000 to 6,000—not even the margin of error in a close race," they wrote. "House seats received substantially fewer hits."

The number of hits was not a problem for Bush's and Boxer's campaigns. The Bush campaign went from 50,000 to 60,000 hits a week in summer to 150,000 hits per week three weeks before the election. "The week before the election, it went up to about 250,000 hits a week," Connell said. "Two days before the election, on Monday and Tuesday alone, the Web site took over a half million hits." The Boxer for Senate campaign in California recorded 554,814 hits from 32,668 user sessions (individuals) in October 1998.

Measuring the effectiveness of a Web site is a problem. Because computer log files show the user's originating domain, the Boxer campaign could identify only 6,269 of those users in October as being in California. In contrast, the log files recorded 10,552 users in the same period from Vienna, Virginia. Those users were not necessarily residing in that suburb of Washington, D.C.—the totals simply reflected the traffic coming from Vienna-based America Online (AOL).

Two of the more encouraging statistics on Internet usage are the time visitors spend on a campaign Web site and the type of pages they access.

The Boxer log files showed that visitors spent six minutes and forty-five seconds before leaving for another site. The two most visited pages outside of the entry page dealt with issues. Users spent an average of fifty-three seconds on the page showing Boxer's position on issues and two minutes and fifty-five seconds on a page that compared her position with that of her Republican opponent, Matt Fong.

GOPAC, the Republican organization, studied the computer logs of twenty Web sites maintained by Republican candidates for statewide races such as senator or governor and came up with similar results. GOPAC's study found that voters tend to stay with a campaign Web site for eight minutes and thirty-two seconds and that much of that time is spent looking at pages that might help them decide who to vote for—candidates' biographies, their stands on issues, and articles comparing one candidate to another.

Another measure of the Internet's potential is shown by a survey by Wirthlin Worldwide that found that 11 percent of the voters surveyed in the 1996 election said they received information from the Internet or from services such as AOL or MSN (MicroSoft Network) that helped them decide for whom to vote.

THE WEB AS POLITICAL NETWORK

Clearly, 1998 was a year in which politics took note of the Internet, even if great numbers of voters did not notice political Web sites. A survey by *Campaigns & Elections* magazine in late July and early August showed that 84 percent of the 270 campaigns surveyed had a Web site already on the Internet or planned to have one. Campaigns for statewide or congressional offices had a far greater presence on the Web (71.7 percent) than campaigns for state district, local, or municipal office (55 percent). Nearly 86 percent of those campaigns with budgets of more than $1 million had Web sites online at the time of the survey.

The survey also showed that few campaigns really understood or were harnessing the potential of the Net. While 97.1 percent of all sites surveyed had biographical information on the candidate and 89.9 percent had issue papers and policy statements, only 52.4 percent had interactive communications that allowed the candidate and voter to communicate by polling or other feedback mechanisms. Only 4.1 percent had chat rooms where the voters could chat electronically with the candidate at prearranged times.

Internet consultants usually cite three areas of potential when discussing the growth of the Net: fund-raising, attracting volunteers, and communicating internally with other campaign workers and externally with dedicated voters.

Both the Boxer and Bush campaigns attempted to raise money through online credit card transactions. The Boxer campaign collected over $25,000 through a Web credit card form—a drop in the bucket when compared to the overall spending of about $13 million. The Bush campaign collected more than $10,000.

The Boxer campaign's form was so sophisticated that it could instantly check the validity of the credit card number. "I'm convinced that online fund-raising was really cutting its teeth in 1998," said Connell. "I think we're going to see that expand greatly in 2000 and beyond. People need to get used to the notion of using a credit card online."

A second area of Internet ability frequently cited is the ability to mobilize volunteers. Both the Bush and Boxer campaigns picked up substantial volunteers through online forms that allowed voters to volunteer for the campaign by filling in a few blanks.

Connell called this new ability to mobilize volunteers one of the most important factors in the early stages of the campaign, when Web site hits were low but volunteer interest was peaking. Alber said he believed the ability to raise volunteers was the most important result of the Boxer Web site.

GOPAC's study of twenty Republican campaigns also found that the Internet is turning voters into volunteers. It surveyed more than a thousand volunteers in the 1998 campaign to see who these people were and how they were using the Internet to volunteer. Nine out of ten Internet volunteers in the GOPAC survey said they were not recruited by the campaign in any way and 55 percent of those volunteers said they had never before worked in a political campaign.

The third area of Internet potential is in the ability to communicate

Figure 20. Boxer for Senate Web page. One page of the Boxer Web site was devoted to getting people involved in her campaign.

Courtesy Rick Albers, Barbara Boxer for Senate Campaign

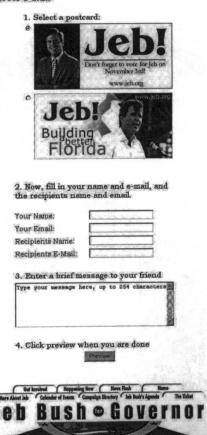

Figure 21. Bush for Governor Web page. The Bush campaign made it easy for supporters to bring in other supporters. All they had to do was fill in the boxes and the campaign Web site automatically sent in illustrated e-mail to their friends.

Courtesy New Media Communications, Inc.

internally and externally. "This is the one area where I think the Internet has the greatest potential for campaigning that was largely untapped in 1998, and that is the ability to use the Internet to basically coordinate campaign activities," Connell added.

Both Bush and Boxer maintained interactive Web sites encouraging supporters to fill out forms online on ways they could help the campaign (see Figures 20 and 21).

Both campaigns hawked campaign buttons and shirts to supporters on their Web sites, encouraged supporters to send campaign materials to friends online, and set up forms to help unregistered voters become eligible voters.

Yet despite the successes and the uncovered potential, the Internet is far from becoming a major part of the media mix. "Most candidates don't really understand the Internet yet," Noble told a seminar sponsored by American University's Center for Congressional and Presidential Studies. Even worse, he said, is that consultants, particularly older ones, don't understand the Internet either.

Jon Katz, the First Amendment Center scholar at the Freedom Forum, calls the Internet "by far the most political" of all media and adds that "because of its immediate, inexpensive and intensely communicative infrastructure, the Net will inevitably transform politics, once there are enough politicians around with the brains to understand and use it."

Connell and Alber believe that campaigns must learn to integrate the power of the Internet into their organizations. "You need to have the Internet as part of the media mix," Connell said. "You've got to make it mesh with the rest of your campaign organization, you need it in synch with all the messages that the campaign is pushing out. What makes it work well on the political trail is if you embrace its qualities, and those qualities are that it is an extremely rapid response medium, it is highly interactive and it gives us the ability to communicate directly with the masses like never before, unfiltered (by conventional media) messages to and from the base, the voting public, and the media."

Matthew M.
Reavy

EVALUATING POLITICAL
WEB SITES

Political candidates have been seeking new ways to
reach out to voters for as long as there has been an electorate. In modern society, the Internet offers a unique opportunity for these candidates to communicate with the citizenry, bolstering and perhaps even
helping to guide participation in the political process. The equation is
a simple one. The Internet gives candidates the ability to disseminate
information about themselves. Citizens who possess knowledge about
their politicians play a more active role in determining which of those
politicians shall govern and which shall be governed. It follows that
those who gain information from the Internet and the World Wide Web
are more actively engaged in the political process than those who
do not.

Recent studies bear out this syllogism. A review of the 1998 campaigns by Edlund observed that "the Internet turned interested voters
into informed voters and informed voters into volunteers." As citizens
and activists grow more familiar with the concept of "cyberpolitics,"
it becomes increasingly important for candidates and their consultants
to pay attention to the role of so-called new media in the political
arena. Perhaps the most salient focus for this attention is the World
Wide Web, a subsegment of the Internet that has come to embody the
nature of the medium.

The 1996 presidential elections gave political birth to the Internet.
Evaluations of candidates' Web sites at the time found that, although
the quality of information varied considerably, the sheer quantity of
the data enabled voters to conduct political research online. Since that
time, researchers have worked to create standards for evaluating the effectiveness of World Wide Web sites. Although no definitive standard
has emerged, a review of the available literature suggests several key
issues that must be addressed when evaluating the effectiveness of a
Web page. These may be adapted to political Web sites and organized
under the acronym CAPITAL—Content, Audience, Purpose, Interactivity, Timeliness, Appearance, and Linkage.

Content usually dominates the process of developing or evaluating
a Web page. One should remember, however, that the form of a Web

site must always follow its function. To determine what a Web page should contain, one must first examine the audience and purpose of the site. Because the other aspects of effectiveness also play a role in determining content, it shall be addressed throughout.

The perceived audience of the site determines both its content and its appearance. A candidate's site should be geared toward at least three audiences: undecided voters, volunteers and other supporters, and the media.

A campaign Web site should have a clear purpose. In general, this purpose will be fourfold: to communicate the candidate's message; to enhance the candidate's image; to organize the campaign (primarily volunteers and donations); and to reduce the impact of the opponent's communications or other material negative to the campaign.

The term *interactivity* refers to the back-and-forth transactions between a Web site and the person using that site. It is what differentiates the Web from other media. People, by and large, do not interact with their newspaper, radio, or television. But they can interact with their computer while perusing the World Wide Web. Interactivity can be used to entertain, to educate, or even to generate "virtual proximity"—the feeling that the person or persons with whom you are communicating are somehow nearer than they really are. The extent to which a Web site makes the candidate available to visitors depends on the strategy of the campaign, although proper use of virtual proximity can add momentum to any campaign. In general, the more interactive a Web site, the better it will be received.

Timeliness refers to the perceivable gap between the moment a user views a message or document and the time when that message was last updated. Most basic media writing texts recognize that current information possesses greater value than dated information. One sign of a poor site—especially to Web-savvy journalists—is the existence of outdated information. It is crucial that a candidate's site keep up to date with the campaign. New items should be placed online as soon as they are received. Old items need to be removed as soon as they lose their value. A good site is updated daily, a great one hourly.

Communication scholars have long recognized that information with a strong visual component tends to gain and hold one's attention. A campaign site is a reflection of the candidate. Sloppy or disorganized sites suggest similar qualities about the candidate. If the site is slow to load on a typical computer using a typical modem, the candidate will appear to be out of touch with the citizenry. If the site lacks visual continuity, users may feel as though they are jumping around on the Web rather than navigating through one contiguous location. A good campaign Web site is neither dull nor flashy. It is pleasing to the eye yet always maintains the goal of enhancing access to the site's information content.

Many sites feature links to other locations on the Web. Candidates often feel compelled to provide links to their party's home page, as well as to other sites that share their philosophy on certain issues. Some operate under the assumption that a large number of links will draw more users to their page. This is a fallacy. Links are exits from a site, not entrances to it. A good site limits links to a few specific items on the Web, such as favorable stories about the candidate. Even then, these links should be controlled through technology such as frames, which display Web pages through "windows" on the candidate's own site.

The World Wide Web is a new form of communication that incorporates the characteristics of both mass and interpersonal communication. The average Web navigator visiting a site accesses essentially a form of mass communication or "wholesale politics." Many intriguing interpersonal elements have already begun to appear, foreshadowing a resurgence of "retail politics" that allows candidates or their avatars (virtual selves) to interact directly with potential voters.

One can imagine a time in the not-too-distant future when users visiting a site will be welcomed personally by a video image of the candidate that addresses them by name and can answer any question asked, calling on examples that allude to items of specific interest to that user. For example, a question about an upcoming tax hike could draw a different response depending on whether the end user is an educator, an environmentalist, or a member of the military. Simply reading data from the user's own e-mail address can already provide Webmasters with a "best guess" as to their affiliations. Considering that very little personal information remains private today, it is not inconceivable that a person logging into a site might soon be cross-referenced with a database containing vast amounts of data about his or her likes, dislikes, group memberships, and financial situation. If not in the next presidential election, such sites will surely appear in the one to follow.

SUGGESTED READINGS

Browning, G., and D. Weitzner. *Electronic Democracy: Using the Internet to Influence American Politics.* Wilton, Conn.: Online, 1996.

Edlund, M. "Campaign '98." Explanation of study findings available online at http://www.campaignstudy.org, 1998.

Fairley Raney, R. "Online Campaign Contributions Still a Promising Experiment." *New York Times,* November 22, 1998. Available online at http://www.nytimes.com/library/98/11/cyber/articles/22campaign.html.

Hill, K., and J. Hughes. *Cyberpolitics: Citizen Activism in the Age of the Internet.* Lanham, Md.: Rowman & Littlefield, 1998.

Reavy, M., and David Perlmutter. "Presidential Web Sites as Sources of Information: The Next Knowledge Gap in the Making?" Paper presented August 9–14, 1996, at the annual meeting of the Association for Education in Journalism and Mass Communication in Anaheim, California.

Tony Paquin | SOFTWARE FOR
POLITICAL CAMPAIGNS

Despite the immense sums that are spent each year on political campaigns in the United States, most of the nearly five hundred thousand individual campaigns run each election cycle operate on a shoestring and with little or no advanced software technology. This is not for lack of need to streamline and manage complexity. Campaign expenses include myriad overhead costs such as offices and salaries, fund-raising expenses such as direct mail and events, and advertising costs and other voter contact activity expenses. The paperwork of financial reports, contribution records, voter lists, and other record-keeping needs threatens to bury eager volunteers and sidetrack the candidate from the business of campaigning. Yet, according to a study of campaign spending in the 1990 U.S. House and Senate races, an average of just 1.6 percent of the total campaign budgets was spent on computers and office equipment, including campaign software. The top five campaign management packages (Campaign Manager III, Desktop Candidate, Vote Tech, Trailblazer, and Governet) have only about five thousand users combined.

The 1998 election showed that politicians were relying increasingly on technology and the Internet in their campaigns. Some campaign software products, like Netivation.com's Governet, contain direct links to the company's Web page, where users have access to a variety of political services and sites. Aristotle Publishing, producer of the top-selling Campaign Manager III, maintains a database of all 138 million registered U.S. voters and sells the information from that list to politicians. Candidates of the future will be unable to run competitive campaigns without integrating technology into their management plan.

WHY USE POLITICAL CAMPAIGN SOFTWARE?

Between 225,000 and 250,000 political campaigns are run every year. This number includes primary elections, ballot measures, and bond elections, as well as runoff and final elections for offices ranging from local school boards to the presidency of the United States. A single open office may draw a half dozen primary candidates from each of the two major parties and an equal number of independent candidates. Term limit laws are having the effect of increasing the number of political candidates as more and more contests are for open offices. Ballot initiatives are becoming a more important part of the American political process and are some of the most expensive campaigns.

At the same time, many of those thousands of candidates who run each year are taking increasing advantage of the growing amount of technology available to them. Those campaigns that use technology to help them sort through the paperwork are the ones that are staying organized and focused and are winning elections.

Campaigns have numerous record-keeping needs, including voter contact lists, volunteer coordination, contribution records, expenditure records, profiles of contributors and key supporters, mailing lists, and correspondence.

Campaigns also must regularly file financial reports with the Federal Election Commission (FEC), state agencies, or both. Financial reporting compliance requirements for political campaigns are increasing at both state and federal levels. Mistakes or irregularities in such filings may even damage the campaign's image, as the media pay particular attention to any hint of "scandal" or "error" in the finances of a campaign. The campaign with the ability seamlessly to integrate its voter contact records, financial reports, and direct mailing efforts is the campaign that ultimately has the best shot at success.

WHAT SHOULD POLITICAL CAMPAIGN SOFTWARE DO?

Political software is designed to allow users to automate many of the campaign record-keeping processes that tie up the time and energy of both paid staff members and volunteers. When selecting a campaign software product, users should look for a variety of features:

Database management. Smooth, seamless database management will allow the user to profile voters, organize volunteers, and produce trouble-free direct mailings. Contact records promote proactive campaign management by tracking all activity.

Ease of use. Because of the relatively short duration of campaigns, as well as the generally large number of staff members and volunteers who must be able to access the program, campaign software must be easy to learn and easy to use. Manuals should explain features in clear, nontechnical language. The software designer should provide reliable, fast support services and, if required, on-site training.

FEC reports. The top software products integrate a campaign's financial records with preloaded FEC forms to produce financial disclosure reports that conform to the strict federal financial reporting guidelines. Most states also have reporting requirements; thus campaign software should include the ability to produce custom forms for a variety of needs.

Faxing/e-mail. The ability to fax, e-mail, or both directly from the computer database, whether on an individual or mass basis, is essential for organized, direct contact with voters and campaign workers.

Customizable features. Campaigns differ in the way they profile voters, coordinate volunteers, and track financial information. The software must be customizable to handle those differences.

Internet integration. Some software products, like Governet, interface directly with the Internet. This feature provides integration with other Internet-based resources; access to updates, fixes, or add-ons on a 24/7 basis; and "real-time" linkage to parallel sites or other bases of the campaign (from other city or county headquarters in a statewide race to party headquarters in Washington).

Picture storage. The "see what I mean" feature allows for easy identification of key donors, volunteers, and others connected with the campaign. Campaign media managers can also distribute stills and videos for planned ads through the Web.

Product interface. Some software products easily interface with other Windows' applications such as MS Office, Microsoft Excel, or Lotus SmartSuite.

THE PRODUCTS

A variety of campaign software packages are available to candidates, ranging from systems that are little more than word processors to robust products that feature full Internet integration. Despite the variety of systems and prices, only a small percentage of campaigns in the country use software created specifically for political campaigns. According to *Campaigns & Elections* magazine buyers' guide, only a little over 1 percent of the five hundred thousand political campaigns conducted every election cycle use specifically designed campaign software. Tailored software packages range in cost from free of charge to $1,000 to $12,000.

Campaign software generally falls into one of two categories: campaign management or financial tracking—although individual software packages may overlap. In general, campaign management software includes voter and other contact database management, financial tracking and FEC reporting capabilities, fax and/or e-mail capabilities, and customizable reporting functions. Financial tracking software generally offers integrated accounting, contribution and expenditure tracking, fund-raising records, and FEC and state financial disclosure reporting capability.

Listed below are some of the most widely distributed campaign software products.

CAMPAIGN MANAGEMENT

Campaign Manager III (Aristotle Publishing, Inc. 800–296–2747)
Campaign management software approved by FEC and state campaign finance offices

DeskTop Candidate (Trillium Systems, Inc. 310–442–9222)
Manages voters, volunteers, contributors; bar-coded reports for data entry; imports digital voter databases

Governet (Netivation.com, Inc. 888–580–1010)
Campaign management software with FEC reports, contact database, Internet integration

Trailblazer (Aspen Software Corp. 800–446–1375)
Campaign management software offers supporter tracking, voter communication, integrated accounting, FEC reports

VoteTech (Data + Imagination, Inc. 818–985–6100)
Campaign management software with voter database, training; FEC reports, autodial telephoning

FINANCIAL TRACKING

Race-trax (Race-trax 317–842–4348)
Prints ready-to-file forms and schedules for all FEC committees; state versions

Campaign Craftware (Statecraft, Inc. 800–984–6789)
Manages campaign contributions, expenditure and fund-raising activities; generates figures and forms for state and federal races

Donor Works (Star Soft Technologies, Inc. 509–327–1476)
Donor profiting, gift entry/receipts and pledge management, reports

Elect Fundraising (Elect, Inc. 800–254–1205)
Tracks contributions, disbursements, generates thank-you letters, some disclosure reports

FAT Cats (Aristotle Publishing 800–296–2747)
A single CD-ROM with the name of every individual and PAC who gave money from your district, city, or state

Fund-Master (Master Software Corporation 800–837–5800)
Maintains information on donors, prospects, alumni, campaigns and gifts; detailed reports

The next generation of campaign software will integrate the power of the Internet with the user's desktop application. Netivation's Governet is currently the only product that connects political campaigns to the wealth of information and opportunity on the Internet. In the future, online fund-raising will become the norm, with Internet firms acting as the credit card clearinghouse, charging the campaign a small fee for each transaction. Online fund-raising and the campaign software's integration with that process will quickly become the least expensive means of fund-raising available to political campaigns.

CONSTITUENCIES

Donna L.
Brazile

THE AFRICAN AMERICAN VOTE

During the 1994 midterm election campaign, African American voter turnout in some congressional districts fell to its lowest level since the passage of the Voting Rights Act of 1965. This phenomenon—the flip side of the more publicized heavy turnout of Christian Coalition voters and "angry, white males"—directly led to Republicans seizing control of both the House and the Senate for the first time in half a century. The reasons for lack of motivation among black voters were understandable: Democrats took their votes for granted and the Republican Party ignored them. In addition, the Democratic Party relied—ironically—on a "trickle down" approach to energizing the African American vote: headlining national leaders like Reverend Jesse Jackson, Sr., but giving little or no assistance to local party leaders or operatives. In reaction, many African American leaders called on the Democratic Party to refocus its efforts and energy on targeting one of its most loyal and dependable groups of voters. The 1994 results were thus a turning point not only in American political history but in the strategies and rules of black politics.

TAKE BACK THE HOUSE

After 1994, members of the overwhelmingly Democratic Congressional Black Caucus (CBC), led by senior representatives Charles Rangel (New York), Maxine Waters (California), and John Conyers (Michigan), teamed up to work closely with the House Democratic leadership to develop a comprehensive plan to motivate African American voters to participate in future congressional midterm elections. The strategy was simple:

- *Raise money to attract and support high-quality candidates.*
- *Identify a coherent message to motivate African American voters.*
- *Register and educate African American voters on the importance of the midterm congressional elections.*
- *Allocate resources early in key races where planning, organiza-*

tion, and coalition building would enhance the Democratic Par-ty's ability to target and turn out its base voters of African Americans and Hispanics.

The plan was so simple that the Democratic Congressional Campaign Committee (DCCC), under the leadership of Representative Martin Frost (Texas), decided in early spring 1998 to adopt the CBC's "Take Back the House" plan to make voter participation and turnout a top priority for its fall campaign strategy. The DCCC decided that grassroots organizing and base vote participation in 1998, unlike in the 1994 and 1996 electoral cycles, would be a significant part of every major campaign it supported in the fall. The decision was endorsed by the House Democratic leadership, the Clinton White House, and the Democratic National Committee (DNC), and the plan was implemented immediately in selected competitive races across the country.

TARGETING AFRICAN AMERICAN VOTERS

Democratic candidates have often taken the constituency of African American voters for granted. For example, many candidates have not given African American leaders and institutions sufficient financial and political support to enhance their ability to target and turn out the vote. The tradition has been to turn to these leaders and institutions two weeks before election day asking them to support the Democratic Party nominee.

In 1998, the pattern shifted; to convince Democratic leaders of the crucial role African Americans play in selected local and state-wide campaigns, many campaigns adopted a new seven-part Voter/ Campaign Assessment Program designed to identify, motivate, and energize African American voters in a targeted district. The plan's components were campaign structure, campaign endorsements, campaign staff, campaign consultants and vendors, field operations, earned and paid media, and get out the vote (GOTV).

Some components, including field operations, earned and paid media, and GOTV plans, were emphasized more than others because they are essential in helping a campaign get off the ground and become competitive. Each campaign manager was asked to identify a *local* African American person to serve as a full-time member of the staff to assist with scheduling, developing the field plan, and recruiting volunteers for GOTV activities. Candidates were also advised to work closely with African American opinion leaders in each district, especially those with media contacts. These local leaders would lend credibility and guidance to the campaign, as well as serve as advisers to the candidate on issues important to the district. This new "bottom-up" way of thinking about "black politics" in the Democratic Party became a model for future campaigns.

The information gathered from each of the targeted districts through direct campaign/voter assessments and past voting patterns and behavior of African American voters provided the Democratic Party, through the DCCC, the ability to analyze individual campaigns. In turn, this enabled the party vastly to improve turnout of African American voters in a nonpresidential election cycle.

MESSAGE, MOTIVATION, AND MEDIA

While the campaign assessment provided the DCCC and the party with information on African American involvement in campaigns in specific targeted districts, the Democratic National Committee, departing from past customs, conducted a major nationwide poll in the summer of 1998 of African American voters on their attitudes about Democratic candidates and the party's overall message. The survey was distributed to 1,217 registered and likely African American voters. All respondents were screened and said they would vote in the midterm congressional elections. The survey, which had a margin of error of plus or minus 2.5 percent, was designed and supervised by Ron Lester, who specializes in polling for African Americans running in majority white districts.

The 1998 poll's results showed that African Americans, like their white counterparts, were responding positively to the Democratic message of providing better schools, protecting Social Security, raising the minimum wage, and providing high-quality health care. Unsurprisingly, a high percentage of African Americans identified with the Democratic Party and approved of President Bill Clinton. The data further suggested that the strong "rise in party identification was fueled by the sense that Democrats were on the side of African Americans in the partisan struggle unfolding in Washington, D.C." Only 6 percent of likely African American voters agreed that the Republican Congress, led by former House Speaker Newt Gingrich, "deserved to be re-elected."

This important set of data, gathered at a crucial time in the Democratic Party planning, led senior African American lawmakers to press the DNC and the DCCC to target twenty-five congressional districts in which the African American vote could result in the margin of victory. For the first time in recent history, the party committed significant resources to motivating African Americans to vote on Tuesday, November 3, by making a direct appeal to African American political, religious, labor, and civil rights leadership at the grassroots level. In essence, the party went back to the basics of identifying its core supporters and targeting them for important campaign activities, such as advertising on African American radio stations featuring members of the CBC, President Clinton, and First Lady Hillary Rodham Clinton; direct mail programs that identified drop-off voters in nonpresidential election cycles; phone bank programs that used the voices of prominent African American leaders and President Clinton; and old-fashioned door-to-door canvassing five weeks before election day. Finally, in addition to raising funds to support campaign activities in the African American community, members of the CBC "adopted" key congressional districts and served as surrogate speakers to help enhance voter contact with the grassroots African American community.

The results of the grassroots and hands-on approach in the November election were unambiguous. A surge in African American participation, especially in the South, helped Democrats win key statewide and congressional races, including the governorships of South Carolina and Alabama and the senatorial seat in North Carolina, all strong Republican-leaning states where Democratic Party strength has declined in the recent past.

A second effect was to revive the old progressive "big tent" alliance of African Americans and labor Democrats (who in recent years turned to the GOP). This renewed coalition allowed the Democratic Party to reclaim many state legislative bodies—a crucial victory, looking toward the census reapportionment in the year 2000.

But perhaps more important for the nation as a whole, the campaign message also "provided healing" in the Deep South. Democrats tried to appeal to positive issues and agendas (such as safeguarding Social Security and improving schools) popular with both black *and* white voters. In contrast, many African Americans (and many whites as well) perceived that in the past the Republican Party had promoted negative wedge issues such as busing, crime, and affirmative action.

THE OUTCOME OF 1998 AND THE FUTURE

In 1998, for the first time in American electoral history, African American voters and leaders were accorded respect as political players, and key precincts were targeted for early planning and involvement. Beyond the traditional two-week, trickle-down approach, candidates participated in forums held and sponsored by local African American communities, and the CBC led a major bus tour in the Midwest to stimulate more grassroots involvement. As a result, the Democratic Party picked up five additional seats in the House and retained key seats in the Senate. The Congressional Black Caucus retained its membership in the House—thirty-eight Democratic members—and the Republican Party decided to elevate its only African American congressman to one of its top leadership posts to help "expand" its outreach and message. In short, the problems of 1994 were addressed in 1998: Democrats and Republicans now understood that the black vote counted but could not be automatically counted on.

It is important to note that six African American members of Congress were reelected in majority white districts after being strongly targeted by the Republican Party for defeat. They included Representatives Mel Watt (North Carolina), Julia Carson (Indiana), Sanford Bishop and Cynthia McKinney (Georgia), Corrine Brown (Florida), and Barbara Lee (California). (The other African American to represent majority white voters is House Republican conference chairman J. C. Watts of Oklahoma.) Despite the loss of the only African American member of the U.S. Senate, former Illinois senator Carol Moseley-Braun, African American voter turnout made the difference in key Senate races in South Carolina (Ernest Hollings), New York (Chuck Schumer), North Carolina (John Edwards), Nevada (Harry Reid), California (Barbara Boxer), Wisconsin (Russ Feingold), Arkansas (Blanche Lincoln-Lambert), and Maryland (Barbara Mikulski). Other key congressional races in which African American voters made a significant difference are listed in the table.

African Americans also scored several significant middle and down-ballot victories across the country. For example, Thurbert Baker of Georgia will become the first African American attorney general elected from the Deep South. Baker will serve with Michael Thurmond, an African American elected as insurance commissioner of Georgia. So, as the important 2000 presidential election approaches,

Candidate	State/District	Percentage of African American Voters
Ronnie Shows	Mississippi/4	36
Bob Etheridge	North Carolina/2	28
John Spratt	South Carolina/5	28
Nick Lampson	Texas/9	22
David Price	North Carolina/4	20
Jim Turner	Texas/2	15
Shelley Berkley	Nevada/1	10
Dennis Moore	Kansas/3	10
George Brown	California/42	10
Joe Hoeffel	Pennsylvania/13	6
Rush Holt	New Jersey/12	5
Maurice Hinchey	New York/26	5
Dave Phelps	Illinois/19	3
Lane Evans	Illinois/17	3

African Americans are poised to make significant gains, not only in key congressional races but in state races across the country.

At the core of these voting trends is the Clinton factor. In the Lester poll and in many other national surveys in recent years, African Americans have consistently expressed sympathy and support for this president—stronger than any other constituency in the nation. Clinton, despite his personal problems, was able to appeal directly to African American voters by going on the radio and sending a letter to key African American religious and political leaders across the country. He also found and readily sought out black audiences and organizations that had always enthusiastically and warmly welcomed him. In each contact, by media or in person, his list of legislative accomplishments for African American voters, his strong defense of civil rights, and his sincere empathy for the problems of the poor and disadvantaged resonated with audiences and renewed their support of the party. He literally embodied the new hands-on approach to seeking black support.

Nevertheless, in practical political terms, Clinton's personal appeal will not mean much after he leaves office. Thus candidates seeking to improve their outreach to the African American community will have to develop strategies to show that they too are serious about working to improve the conditions and addressing the specific concerns of all Americans. Slogans and sympathy will not be enough.

As the race for the year 2000 presidential contest gets under way, African American leaders and voters will be looking to both major parties to lobby for their support. The traditional view that African Americans are solid Democrats is extinct. African American voters will have to be courted and solicited like every other American voting group; and like any constituency, if they are ignored and taken for granted, they will stay home. The real lesson of 1998 was that African Americans showed the party that they would vote in record numbers if they were listened to, respected, and motivated as are other major national constituency groups. Their vote would make the crucial difference in competitive congressional races where winning or losing would be determined by the party's ability to turn out its base voters. The 1998 midterm election became a season of new beginnings on how to navigate race politics in America.

Wayne
Parent

RACE ISSUES AND POLITICAL CAMPAIGNS IN THE SOUTH

Political pundits and media workers outside the Baton Rouge, Louisiana, area were stunned when the race for the apparently safe seat of six-term incumbent Republican congressman Richard Baker became a 1998 election cliffhanger. Indeed, Baker beat his newcomer Democratic challenger Marjorie McKeithen by less than three thousand votes. Racial issues were never mentioned. It was banker (Baker) versus lawyer (McKeithen), business versus labor, established incumbent versus novice.

McKeithen set the tone for both campaigns when she started running ads accusing Baker of being "in the pocket" of big New York banks. Indeed, McKeithen appeared to have pulled even in an election that showed Baker with a twenty-point lead in September because she used the classic James Carville-esqe "it's the economy, stupid" Democratic theme of little guy working person opposing establishment monied elite. Nothing in the campaign indicated that the election was anything but a standard New Deal–like party shootout that could have been run almost anywhere in the country. Despite this, and despite the fact that neither candidate was African American, the dirty little secret was that, in the end, race politics probably determined the outcome and the closeness of the election.

One of the main reasons that the district was ripe for a Democratic challenge was that it had been redrawn in 1997, resulting in an increase in the proportion of African Americans from about 22 percent to almost 30 percent of the district's voters. This was the first contest in the more Democratic-friendly district, and McKeithen knew that a fundamental building block of a winning coalition was strong African American support. She enlisted the help of one of the most prominent African Americans in the state, a former congressman and gubernatorial candidate, state senator Cleo Fields. McKeithen also hired Fields's sister Darlene to a key position in the campaign. The strategy worked well. Black support and mobilization were strong, and although there were almost no public polls to show the race tightening, the intense, steady drumbeat of television ads and counter ads indicated that the race had become competitive.

The Sunday before the Tuesday election, the Baton Rouge *Sunday Advocate* headed its front page with a story about Cleo Fields and his election mobilization effort. The story characterized Fields as perhaps the most important person in the race, even though his name was not on the ballot. On Sunday, Monday, and election day Tuesday, the Baton Rouge television stations ran several stories showing the Fields voter mobilization effort. The stories were, of course, legitimate. African American turnout had been historically lower than white turnout and, if Democrats are to win in Louisiana, high African American turnout is key.

Indeed, African American turnout was one of the primary explanations widely used for the Democratic successes nationwide. The high turnout in the African American community undoubtedly helped Democrat McKeithen. Yet the publicity about Cleo Fields and African American turnout almost certainly had a counter mobilization effect in the white community and helped Baker secure his victory. Ultimately, though black turnout was high, white turnout was higher and the Republican won a squeaker. This election demonstrates that *reaction* to black mobilization in the white community can be as galvanizing to a campaign as black mobilization itself. Racial consciousness is an obviously polarizing factor in southern elections.

(VOTING) SEGREGATION IN THE PAST

The seeds of this racial consciousness in politics can be found in two related revolutions in southern politics in the past fifty years. The first was the civil rights revolution that resulted in a dramatic change in the racial makeup of the voting electorate from as low as less than 5 percent black to over 30 percent in some states. The second was a partisan revolution, from a time before World War II when Republicans were virtually shut out of southern politics, to today when they are the dominant party in southern national politics in a hefty majority of southern states and are highly competitive in the remaining ones. It is the interconnectedness of these two revolutions that has been the lifeblood of racial politics in the South.

The irony of the present race-and-party-politics dynamic is striking. Republicans—the party of Abraham Lincoln and the Emancipation Proclamation—receive majority support from southern white voters, including most white voters who oppose the black political agenda.

Democrats—the party of Theodore Bilbo, Orval Faubus, George Wallace, and Lester Mattox and most of the best-known segregationists and race-baiters of the earlier part of this century—receive the support of blacks. With notably exceptional individuals such as current Republican conference chair congressman J. C. Watts of Oklahoma and civil rights moderate Winthrop Rockefeller, the first Republican governor of Arkansas, blacks in the South almost uniformly support Democratic candidates. Most exit polls in southern states show African American support for Democratic candidates starting at 80 percent and moving upward to more than 90 percent.

Racial polarization has continued in part because of the clear evidence of racially divided partisanship. After all, elections are run by consultants who base strategies on existing evidence. It is, therefore, understandable that campaign messages—especially voter mobilization messages—involve some appeal to racial consciousness. Democratic consultants know that a sure way to increase Democratic shares of the vote in southern elections is to mobilize black voters. Republican consultants likewise know that a certain way to increase Republican vote in southern elections is to ensure that white voters turn out at higher levels than black voters. Therefore, a crucial element in understanding the continuation of racial politics in the South is to recognize that raising white or black racial consciousness is an easy way to help a candidate win an election. In a business whose success depends on winning elections and in which racial politics can secure a win, race will naturally play a major role in elections.

Arguably, racism in the same Baton Rouge district that began this discussion played a central role in the evolution of the partisanship of racial politics in the South. It was in Baton Rouge where a young Hubert Humphrey, studying for a master's degree in political science at Louisiana State University, learned firsthand of the appalling particulars of racial discrimination. That knowledge enabled him to fire up the 1948 Democratic convention with a speech that convinced the delegates to include support for an end to racial discrimination in the Democratic platform. That position set in motion a series of events that left segregationist southern Democrats disenchanted with the Democratic Party, creating a Dixiecrat revolt. In 1964, Republican presidential nominee Barry Goldwater declared his opposition to the Civil Rights Act and Voting Rights Act and gained enough support from disenchanted southern white Democrats to give Republicans a presidential victory for the first time in Mississippi, Alabama, and

South Carolina history and for only the second time in Louisiana history.

Thus began the new order of racial politics. The combination of Democratic support for the African American agenda and Republican Goldwater's opposition to it had an even more demonstrable effect on black voters. With the national victories by the Democrats, these issues culminated in passage in the Kennedy and Johnson eras of two preeminent pieces of antidiscrimination legislation. This resulted in almost unwavering African American support for the Democratic Party in national and even state and local elections.

(VOTING) SEGREGATION FOREVER?

The evolution of racialization of partisan politics varies widely by state. In Mississippi, racially polarized partisanship is most transparent. Mississippi is the home of the largest proportion of African American voters in the United States, and it is also the state in which Republicans have seen incredible success in national elections. In 1964, Goldwater received more than 87 percent of the Mississippi vote. As recently as 1992, Republican George Bush received his largest statewide win in Mississippi. Mississippi's two senators and governor are all Republicans and win with comfortable margins. Given that Mississippi is a state where Republicans win statewide elections in record numbers despite containing the nation's largest proportion of African American voters—who vote solidly Democratic—racial polarization of party politics is obviously evident.

In other states in the south, the growth of racial partisanship has taken some detours but remains vibrant. Alabama's racially polarized partisanship was stunted by the dominance of Democratic segregationist George Wallace. Wallace (and his wife, Lurleen, when the Constitution barred him from running) held the governorship from 1962 until 1978 and won again in 1982. After Wallace's departure from office, party politics in Alabama became more starkly black and white. In Georgia, even though Democrat Lester Mattox used his fried chicken franchise to promote segregationism in the 1960s, the influx of non-southerners into metropolitan Atlanta has served to soften some of the racial rhetoric. The most recent example of this was the 1998 race for governor, when the Republican candidate criticized the support of the Democratic candidate by black majority Atlanta and this criticism backfired (the Democrat won). In South Carolina, Dixiecrat standard-bearer Strom Thurmond became a Republican the same year that Barry Goldwater declared his opposition to the Civil Rights Act and the Voting Rights Act. Democrats learned the importance of mobilizing black support in order to win. Republicans learned from prototypical political consultants Harry Dent and Lee Atwater that subtle racial messages can work for Republicans. While North Carolina's research triangle and economic boom in Charlotte projects an image of a state that is beyond race politics, the Helms-Hunt and Helms-Gantt races for the U.S. Senate provided probably the best-known examples of racially charged campaign ads.

Even in a state like Louisiana, where biracial coalitions maintained Democratic control of both U.S. Senate seats and helped the Clinton/Gore ticket win easily in 1992 and 1996, racial polarization is a campaign strategy that can galvanize voters. Louisiana Republican and former Grand Wizard of the Ku Klux Klan David Duke is the most prominent recent racial polarizer. Duke was elected to the Louisiana House of Representatives in 1989. In 1990, he received more than 60 percent of the white vote in his bid to unseat incumbent Democratic senator J. Bennett Johnston. In the 1991 race for Louisiana governor, Duke outpolled incumbent Republican governor Buddy Roemer before he lost to Democrat Edwin Edwards.

There are some distinct differences between the racist politics of the southern states of the recent past and the more subtle racial politics of today. Cries of "Segregation Now, Segregation Forever!" seem silly and outdated. No politician can publicly repeat the prophetic words of George Wallace when he lost an election for governor running as a racial moderate: "I'll never be out nigged again" (or "out segged again"; there is some dispute over the exact words). Even a teenager new to politics, however, will notice, just as did teenagers in the 1960s, that these days, when results of elections in the South are reported by precinct in the newspaper the morning after any election, an unmistakable pattern appears: black precincts vote almost uniformly for one candidate while white precincts, although slightly less uniform, almost always vote for the other candidate. In the 1960s, this polarity reflected factions in the Democratic Party. Today it is a partisan split. Voters know it; candidates know it; political consultants know it. And all can use that knowledge to perpetuate it.

Armando
Gutiérrez

THE HISPANIC VOTE

As recently as 1970, there were but 9.2 million Latinos* in the United States. By 1990 the number had increased to some 22 million. By 2000 the number is expected to reach 32 million. But in spite of these impressive absolute numbers, Hispanics have not been recognized as a force in American politics. Why? The general answer to that question is that in American politics it is not the absolute number of people that counts, it is the number of voters. And until the last few elections, Latinos had far underperformed in voting. This has been so historically for a variety of reasons.

Citizenship. A significant portion of the nation's Latino population (38.5 percent) is foreign born. Most of these immigrants have historically chosen not to become citizens, thus precluding them from voting.

Age. Compared to the general population, Latinos are overwhelmingly young. Latinos' median age is twenty-five, compared to thirty-four for non-Latinos. It is well recognized that there is a direct and positive correlation between age and voting participation.

Income. The rate of poverty for Latinos is roughly double that of the general population. There is also a correlation between poverty and lower turnout.

Educational attainment. Hispanics far underperform the general population in educational attainment. Some 34 percent of Latinos over the age of twenty-five have less than a ninth-grade education, compared with but 7 percent of non-Latinos. Like the above variables, education is positively correlated with electoral participation.

Although the above data paint a rather bleak picture of Latinos in the context of American politics, the situation is improving. First, recent changes in immigration laws have created incentives for immigrants to become citizens. That, combined with aggressive efforts by voter registration groups to register these new citizens, created a sig-

---

*For present purposes and as a general rule, I use the terms *Latino* and *Hispanic* interchangeably to refer collectively to those Americans of Mexican, Puerto Rican, Cuban and other South and Central American, (Spanish) Caribbean, and Spanish descent.

nificant boomlet among Latino eligible voters. In 1996, for example, roughly 1.5 million new Latino registrants were added to the rolls, and some two-thirds of these were new citizens. This trend is likely to continue for the next several years.

Second, as those young Latinos move into early and mid-adulthood, their voter participation rates should increase as well, as they do for other population segments. What's more, the census expects that every year for the next two decades, 750,000 Latinos will turn eighteen. The pool of Latino voters will continue to be filled for many years to come.

Third, Latinos have begun to make impressive strides in income, significantly narrowing the gap between themselves and the larger Anglo population. In particular, when you extrapolate the most recent immigrant population, Latinos stack up fairly well with respect to average household income.

Fourth, although Latinos have yet to "catch up" with the general population in educational attainment, there is clear evidence of advance. The gap between Hispanic and non-Hispanic educational attainment decreases yearly. This trend should also add to Latino participation.

In all, it is beyond doubt that, while the current numbers and rate of turnout easily signify that Latinos are central to electoral fortunes in many key areas, the future is virtually limitless. The parties and candidates must prepare now to incorporate Latinos fully into all that they say and do.

MARKET

Several factors are important to consider when undertaking outreach to the Latino voter.

Country of origin. About 65 percent of all United States Hispanics trace their origins to Mexico. Puerto Ricans (12 percent) and Cuban Americans (4 percent) make up the next largest groups. The remaining 19 percent of Latinos trace their origin to one of the many other Latin American countries and Spain (see table). There are significant differences in these groups' history, ancestry, traditions, language (colloquialisms, inflections, words), art, music, and customs. When reaching out to these segments, the intelligent use of these nuanced differences can be vital.

Native born versus foreign born. Four of every ten Latinos in the

HISPANIC POPULATION
by Country of Origin, 1990

Country	Number	Percent of Total
Mexican	13,496,000	61.3%
Puerto Rican	2,728,000	12.4
Cuban	1,044,000	4.7
Other Hispanic	9,888,000	21.6
	27,156,000	**100.0%**

Source: "Current Population Reports: Population Characteristics," *Hispanic Americans Today* (Washington, D.C.: Economics and Statistics Administration, Bureau of the Census, U.S. Department of Commerce, 1993), 23–183.

United States are foreign born. Although they have much in common, there are differences between native and foreign-born Latinos. In particular, the first group is loath to be called an "immigrant" population. Many of these native born trace their family roots back four hundred years. Until quite recently, for electoral purposes, the foreign group could largely be dismissed. This has changed dramatically in California and promises to see similar changes in other states in the near future.

Regionalization. Populations of both country of origin and native and foreign born are not randomly distributed throughout the country. Latinos of Mexican origin tend to reside in the Southwest and West. Puerto Ricans are still found heavily along the Northeast coast, while Cuban Americans are concentrated in Florida. Only Illinois, with 47 percent Mexican and 27 percent Puerto Rican, enjoys a large mixture of groups. Immigrant communities are also heavily concentrated in but a few states, with California, Texas, New York, Illinois, and Florida having the largest groupings.

Gender. The now famous gender gap of American politics also holds for Hispanics. Fifty-five percent of all Latino voters are women. They also tend to vote more strongly for Democratic Party candidates. In 1996, for example, 78 percent of Latinas voted for Bill Clinton, compared with 65 percent of Hispanic men.

Location. Over 92 percent of the nation's Hispanic population is concentrated in the states of California, Texas, New York, Florida, Illinois, New Jersey, New Mexico, Arizona, Colorado, Nevada, Washington, and Oregon. These states account for 247 electoral votes, just 23 shy of the number needed to win the presidency. In only two of these states, California and Texas, 56 percent of all Hispanics are found.

Party identification. All but one country-of-origin group, Cubans, tend to have similar political views and identification. When asked to identify their political party, 18 percent of all Latinos identify themselves as Republicans, 37 percent identify themselves as Democrats, 36 percent call themselves Independent, and 9 percent say they do not know. When asked which party they feel closer to in terms of policy and ideology, fully 52 percent say the Democrats and 29 percent say Republicans. In Florida, however, with its preponderance of Cuban Americans, some 46 percent identify themselves as Republicans and 59 percent report that they are philosophically closer to the GOP. This tendency is largely due to the particular political heritage of Americans of Cuban descent, who are either the sons and daughters of or are themselves escapees from their homeland's Communist regime. Traditionally, thus, Cubans have found greater affinity for the more conservative anti-Communist message of the Republican Party.

MEDIA

In the "core" states listed above, there are more than 200 Hispanic television stations, 350 radio stations, and over 200 newspapers. Emerging populations also can now be found in such states as Idaho, Utah, North Carolina, Tennessee, Mississippi, Ohio, Connecticut, and Massachusetts. While still relatively modest in absolute numbers, they can be significant to local and hotly contested races. A good indicator of these trends is the emergence of Hispanic media (usually radio) in the marketplace. Each of the newly settled states now has at least one radio station that broadcasts in Spanish and some have local newspapers. Arbitron and Scarbrough measure Latino radio listening habits, and there are audited newspapers as well. In addition, the United States enjoys three Spanish-language television networks: Telemundo, Galavision, and Univision Television Network. All have growing audiences, but only the last uses Nielsen rating.

Television. Like other Americans, Hispanics do not watch television, they watch shows, and certain shows attract more citizens than others. When reaching voters, music shows are of particular importance because they tend to draw heavily from second- and third-generation Hispanics and from citizens.

Radio formats. Radio is an excellent and inexpensive medium for reaching Latino voters. Remember that Hispanic radio has a multitude of formats just as English radio does and that each format draws distinct demographic and psychographic audiences. Arbitron ratings do not tell the whole story. A highly rated station may attract mostly noncitizens. Be careful in selecting the right (defined as those that attract citizen, voter listeners) radio stations.

Language. Except for recent immigrants, most Hispanic voters will have some fluency in English. Never underestimate, however, the *symbolic* importance of the Spanish language. The candidate's spots should be done in the language (Spanish, English, or bilingually) that best fits the on-air personality of the station. If the candidate cannot speak the language, do not force the issue; employ testimonials from Spanish-speakers, either the "man (or woman) on the street" or celebrities.

Print choices. Many communities have Spanish-language tabloids or English-language newspapers aimed at Hispanics. Many are good choices for reaching Hispanic voters. Remember, however, that some are geared for immigrants and thus are not a good use of valuable resources. Choose carefully.

Outdoor. America today is more residentially segregated than in 1960. This means that those sections of the city where there are heavy concentrations of Hispanics are usually readily identifiable. Outdoor advertising along those corridors that Hispanics travel can be effective at raising a candidate's name recognition among Latino voters.

Direct mail. Modern printing equipment easily and inexpensively allows a campaign to tailor a direct mail piece for specific targets. This is a great way to speak to Latino voters about issues that they care most about.

MESSAGE

Much has been said in recent years about the issue orientation of Hispanic voters. Indeed, the recent Republican Party push to woo Latino voters is generally rationalized in terms of the so-called natural fit between Latinos' social conservatism and the philosophy of the GOP. Certainly, on such issues as drugs, crime, education, personal responsibility, family, discipline in the classroom, and the like, Hispanics are rather conservative, just as the vast bulk of their fellow citizens (including African Americans) are.

But Hispanics are a complicated lot when one delves into the details of issues. For example, on the most oft-repeated issue on which Republicans hang their hats in Latino outreach, abortion, Hispanics are ambivalent. Only 13 percent of Hispanics, in spite of being 71 percent Catholic, are *opposed to all forms of choice*. Hence 87 percent of Hispanics support some form of choice. Hispanics are also much more inclined to support prison rehabilitation programs, certainly a more "liberal" position, than is the general population.

On economic issues, Hispanics are generally much more liberal. For example, eight out of ten support hikes in the minimum wage and support labor unions. A similar percent support affirmative action and bilingual education programs and oppose English-only laws. The rationale behind much of this support is the effects of such programs on economic opportunity for Hispanics and other minorities. As a general rule, Latinos seem to believe that government has a key role to play in creating and managing opportunity for those historically locked out but that once this opportunity has been created, it is up to each individual to make the most of it.

Another issue area on which Republicans are likely to find resistance among Latinos is that concerning the role of the different *levels* of government. Part of modern-day Republican policies is devolving power back to the states and localities. For Hispanics, however, this is highly problematic. Hispanic voters still remember that it was local and state government that most resisted the integration of minorities into the economic, political, and educational mainstream of America. It has been the federal government that has opened doors closed at the local level. Latinos are aware of these historic roles.

As in all political advertising, a campaign's Latino message should parallel and complement but not contrast or conflict with its general market message. Most important, the *application* of the message should be on issues that touch Hispanic voters. This should be kept in mind: when a campaign talks about the great things that the candidate or the party is doing for people, do not assume that Latinos automatically believe that they are included in the good news. Hispanics are aware of far too many instances in which good things were happening for others, while they were left behind.

In 1996, for example, President Clinton made one of his central themes the fact that a record number of jobs and new businesses had been created during his first term. Latinos did not necessarily assume that they had been the recipients of a significant number of those jobs or of the new business creation. The campaign's Latino media consultant created television, radio, and print ads that spoke directly to that issue, telling Latinos that they had benefited in a big way from the president's policies, with record low unemployment for Latinos and a record number of new Hispanic-owned businesses. *That* was something the Latino voter could relate to and get excited about.

Political consultants must also be aware that for Hispanic voters as much as any other group the validity of a message is affected by the validity of the messenger. Those folks who speak with authority to the society at large may or may not have any legitimacy whatsoever with Latinos. Polling and focus groups and even anecdotal data can go a long way in determining which messengers carry weight with Latino voters.

MOBILIZATION

It is elementary that the degree to which Latino voters will be energized to turn out in great numbers and vote overwhelmingly for one party or candidate is a function of how connected they feel and how important they see the outcome of the election as being. The intelligent and strategic use of the previously discussed campaign elements will heavily influence that mobilization.

But even more basic to a campaign's fortunes with Hispanics than the strategic use of media is the structure and attitude of the campaign itself. If the Latino vote is determined to be vital to a successful outcome, then Hispanics should be incorporated vertically and horizontally into the entire campaign structure from the get-go. That is, *Latinos should be a part of the campaign from the day it is organized.* The Latino voter should be incorporated into every facet of the campaign: voter contact, door-to-door, field, media, direct mail, fund-raising, schedule, surrogates, theme, message, issues, literature, press, research, speechwriting, and everything else. In short, there is no magic bullet that is unique to Latino voter turnout and performance. A successful outcome requires all of the essential elements of any campaign—only nuanced for the specific and unique proclivities of Latino voters.

With respect to campaign structure, and more specifically related to media consultation, production, purchase, and placement, it is vital that Latino and general market media budgets, and who handles them, remain *separate*. For example, if a campaign's total media budget is $500,000 and $100,000 of that is to target Latino voters, then that second amount should be considered as a separate budget item rather than as part of the overall media budget. To lump all media dollars together is to invite conflict between the general market and minority media agencies. Finally, there is no general market media agency in the country with a demonstrated track record of accomplishment in targeting Hispanics. Hire a separate agency with expertise on Hispanic voters. Not incidentally, that hiring should also be used as a political public relations tool.

SUMMARY AND SPECULATION

At present the Latino vote is in a state of flux, if for no other reason than that it is being courted as never before. Nationally, some 50 percent of Hispanics identify with and vote consistently for the Democratic Party and its candidates. Another 15 percent identify with and vote in the main for Republicans. The remaining 35 percent are best characterized as swing voters, who change from election to election. For that third of the Latino electorate, party loyalty is of little meaning because they generally identify themselves as independents or of no party. They are also key to election outcomes.

Empirical evidence tells us that those Latinos who steadfastly identify with one or the other political party do so based on a reasoned consideration of issues and stances. To be sure, Latinos are no better informed than most voters, and they certainly are not particularly ideological, with a clear, well-thought-out set of ideas, analysis, and vision. But they do know enough about their own objective conditions and the stances of the political parties to make an informed decision based on what they perceive to be in their individual and collective best interest. Those who argue that Latino voter patterns are largely a function of inertia and tradition vastly underestimate the intelligence and understanding of Latino voters. Put simply, Latinos vote their interests, and they know what their interests are and who best serves them. Parties and candidates would be well-served to realize this as they embark on a program to attract Latino votes.

Charles H.
Cunningham THE RELIGIOUS
CONSERVATIVE VOTER

WHO ARE RELIGIOUS CONSERVATIVES?

Religious conservatives are not, as unfortunately characterized by the *Washington Post*, "poor, uneducated and easy to command." They are, rather, everyday Americans who, as Ralph E. Reed, Jr., put it, "desire a good society based on the shared values of work, family, neighborhood, and faith." Reed, former executive director of the Christian Coalition, wrote in his first book, *Politically Incorrect: The Emerging Faith Factor in American Politics!* that religious conservatives seek "safe neighborhoods, strong families, schools that work, a smaller (less costly and intrusive) government, and lower taxes."

Religious conservatives are people of faith who have a personal relationship with God and who turn to him to help make decisions in their daily lives. The demographic model is a married couple with children who regularly attend church. They vary from Orthodox Jews to Roman Catholics, but numerically, religious conservatives come primarily from evangelical and fundamentalist Protestant congregations. They are predominantly white, but many black churchgoers share their conservative views on a variety of issues, particularly on gambling, school choice, and crime. A majority of religious conservatives are female, at about a 60–40 ratio. They are spread among all grades of education, occupations, and levels of income.

Religious conservatives share the beliefs of other modern-day conservatives (or classical liberals) who support limited government, individual rights, free enterprise, strong national defense, and traditional family values. Although many were raised in Democratic families, most started voting Republican when Ronald Reagan was elected president in 1980. That trend, more or less, has continued to this day for candidates for national office and, during the 1990s, has even gone down the ballot to state and local races. This is indicated by the number of Republicans being elected to statewide, state legislative, even local offices. Religious conservatives are not, however, bound by party loyalty. Results from recent elections show that if conservative candidates do not present a cohesive agenda and clear message, many religious conservatives will revert to the voting pattern of their roots.

Religious conservatives are particularly concerned about the moral and social slide of this nation. Activities and behavior rarely discussed only twenty-five years ago are now part of daily news reports: illegitimacy, abortion, divorce, homosexuality, violent crime, drug abuse and addiction, poor education in public schools, religious bigotry, and, most recently, a lack of character and integrity in our elected officials. Religious conservatives are among the overwhelming majority of Americans who believe that things in our nation have gotten off on the wrong track morally. They are concerned about the unraveling fabric of our society and the future for their children and grandchildren.

Religious conservatives want commonsense, rather than trendy, solutions to problems. Midnight basketball followed by midnight curfews to stop youth criminal activities; gun control and drug legalization to reduce violent crime; free condoms and needle exchange to combat sexually transmitted diseases—examples of government's best efforts—are not popular among religious conservatives.

ISSUES THAT MOTIVATE RELIGIOUS CONSERVATIVES

Life. Although prohibiting abortion except in limited circumstances remains a goal, recent emphasis has been on banning abortion for gender selection and partial-birth abortion; stopping taxpayer funding of abortion and abortion providers; requiring parental notification or consent for abortions performed on minors; requiring informed consent (knowledge of surgical risks, fetal development, and abortion alternatives) before obtaining an abortion; imposing a twenty-four-hour waiting period for abortions; prohibiting physician-assisted suicide; and prohibiting human cloning.

Education and parenting. Religious conservatives support school choice allowing parents to afford sending their child(ren) to any school—including private and parochial schools—through tuition tax credits, education savings accounts, or vouchers. They oppose feelgood, do-nothing schemes such as outcome-based education, which place less emphasis on student achievement and teaching the "basics" and more focus on the self-esteem of students. They support prohibition of the distribution of birth control devices without parental consent and oppose mandatory sex education and sex education curricula that stress "safe sex" rather than abstinence and teach that homosexuality is an acceptable lifestyle. They want clarification of "the right of parents to direct the upbringing of their children," including their education, health care, discipline, and religious training; efforts to return control over education to localities, with more of current funding returning to the classroom for instruction; and emphasis on student achievement and higher academic standards combined with more accountability of administrators and teachers.

Taxes and spending. They want no new or higher taxes because government—at all levels—is confiscating and spending record amounts of taxpayer dollars; a federal balanced budget Amendment; a simplified tax system with a flat rate; a legislative supermajority or voter approval to raise taxes; increased dependent child tax exemption; repeal of the federal marriage penalty tax; and repeal of the inheritance or estate (death) tax.

Religious freedom. Religious conservatives prefer public (but of course nonintrusive) expression of religious faith, including voluntary prayer in public schools, and sanctions against nations that persecute people based on their religion.

Traditional family values. Religious conservatives believe in not granting sexual preference or behavior a protected minority status under existing civil rights laws; prohibiting open homosexuals from serving in the military; not recognizing homosexual marriage; prohibiting adoption of children by homosexuals; no government requirement for recognition of and benefits for "domestic partners"; restricting the availability of pornography on the Internet; prohibiting possession of any child pornography; and eliminating taxpayer funding of obscene, pornographic, or antireligious "art."

Government reform. They feel there should be less government involvement and interference in individual and family decisions by allowing citizens to save and invest (without tax penalty) money in education savings accounts, medical savings accounts, individual retirement accounts, and the like; less dependence on and intrusion by government and more reliance on voluntary associations and organizations, even those that are faith-based, to solve social problems; voluntary involvement in the political process as compared to taxpayer funding of candidates and campaigns or compulsory union dues for politics; eliminating government departments and agencies that exceed the constitutional mandate for that level of government; defunding programs and activities that are beyond the role of government; returning

Congress to a part-time citizen-legislature; and reducing the "perks" of government officials, both elected and appointed.

National defense and sovereignty. The government should have a strong national defense capability and military readiness; antiballistic missile defense; resistance to social engineering in the military, including homosexuals in the military and women in combat; greater emphasis on foreign policy to protect our national interest and security rather than participation in global governance. They also prefer maintaining American sovereignty in any treaties or trade agreements; prohibiting U.S. troops from serving under United Nations command; and reduction in funding for foreign aid and subsidy of the International Monetary Fund and World Bank.

LOCATING AND COMMUNICATING WITH RELIGIOUS CONSERVATIVES

Like all groups of voters, religious conservatives can be identified by mail and telephone, then communicated with through mail and mass advertising. Lists of pastors and churches that advertise or subscribe to various Christian publications, such as *Charisma*, *Christianity Today*, *New Man*, and *World*, are available for purchase. Also, Christian radio stations are an effective means of narrowcasting a message to religious conservatives.

The best way of locating and communicating with religious conservatives is at the grass roots—through pastors and their churches. Whether a candidate is seeking election to an office statewide or in a district, he or she can ask to speak in person at church services about policy issues or his or her religious faith. An effective message is one that mixes philosophy and faith and then reminds the church of the Christian and civic duty to participate in the political process, to preserve and restore common ideals such as traditional family values.

Many pastors will invite candidates for public office to speak before their congregations. In addition, churches are legally able to conduct nonpartisan voter registration; distribute nonpartisan (nonadvocacy) voter education materials such as voter guides that compare the positions on various issues of opposing candidates; host candidate or issue forums; allow elected officials to speak at church services; and remind citizens of the importance of voting and encouraging the congregation to turn out on election day or vote by absentee ballot.

Churches under tax-exempt status may not, however, endorse candidates directly or indirectly from the pulpit on behalf of the church; contribute funds or services directly to candidates or political committees; distribute materials that clearly favor one candidate or political party; allow candidates to solicit funds while speaking in church—this is what got Vice-President Al Gore in trouble at a Buddhist temple; or establish a political committee that would contribute funds to political candidates.

THE PERIL OF IGNORING RELIGIOUS CONSERVATIVES

Issues matter and ideas do have electoral consequences. Voters are willing to cross partisan and union affiliation lines to support a candidate who agrees with them on key issues. For instance, many blue-collar workers who are usually pushed by their union upper leadership to support liberal Democratic candidates will vote for a Republican opponent because of a pro-life or pro-gun stand.

Candidates who run colorless, issueless campaigns and fail to draw a distinction on key issues with their opponent are rarely elected. Ronald Reagan once admonished fellow Republicans to "present bold colors rather than pale pastels." The 1996 presidential campaign of Bob Dole and the 1998 congressional elections were classic examples of the latter.

During the 1980s through 1994, Republicans consistently gained seats and eventual control of Congress by distinguishing themselves from their Democratic opponents, in many cases campaigning on the voting record of incumbent congressmen. In the 1996 and 1998 election cycles, however, Republicans were unwilling or unable to present a cohesive agenda and clear message about the differences between their nominees and Democrats. Accordingly, many religious conservatives (among other voter groups) either did not vote or reverted to their earlier pattern of voting for Democratic candidates.

The Christian Coalition contracted with various vendors to conduct national election night polling (samplings of one thousand individuals who voted [with a margin of error of +/− 3.2 percent]) in the 1994, 1996, and 1998 election cycles. In 1994, Luntz Research found that 33 percent of the electorate were self-professed religious conservatives and that two-thirds (67 percent) of them voted Republican while only one in five (20 percent) voted Democrat. In the next midterm election held in 1998, Shandwick Research International found that 28.6 percent of the electorate consisted of religious conservatives and that barely more than half (54 percent) voted for the Republican congressional candidate—down a full thirteen points from 1994—and nearly one-third (31 percent) voted for the Democratic candidate for Congress, up eleven points from 1994. The comparison between 1994 and 1998 showed that fewer religious conservatives participated in the latter election and that there was a total swing of 24 percent in the religious conservative vote for congressional candidates between those elections. Since voters were largely prevented from comparing real differences between opposing candidates, many—including religious conservatives—were not motivated to turn out on election day and vote for a candidate whose positions on key issues clearly contrasted with those of an opponent. Moreover, many religious conservatives returned to their Democratic roots, something they had not done since 1980.

For another comparison, the religious conservative vote in the 1996 presidential election cycle was a smaller percentage of the electorate than in the midterm election two years earlier. Wirthlin Worldwide found that 29 percent of the electorate in 1996 were religious conservatives; the same group made up 33 percent of the electorate in 1994.

Clearly, religious conservatives are not a wholly owned subsidiary of either political party. Candidates seeking to be elected should actively appeal to them by stressing certain issues and clearly delineating the differences in their own and their opponents' positions on those issues. Religious conservatives are not a voter group that can be taken for granted.

In turn, Democrats in 1998 appealed to the electorate by focusing on public policy issues such as Social Security, health care, and education reform while Republicans followed the strategy of trying to run out the clock and ride into office solely on anti-Clinton sentiment. The Clinton scandal was a push for many voters, but no message for real change in the future on many key issues provided a pull for them.

More revealingly, in some cases, Democrats recruited pro-life and pro-gun conservative candidates to run in various congressional districts, primarily in the South. In virtually every case, those Democratic candidates won because, in very large part, even Republicans who chose to run aggressive campaigns highlighting the differences on issues were less able to do so because there were significantly fewer actual contrasts. Examples of such congressional races include those won by Dave Phelps in Illinois (Nineteenth District), Ken Lucas in

Kentucky (Fourth District), and Ronnie Shows in Mississippi (Fourth District).

Some GOP moderates, in an attempt to spin the 1998 election results to leverage the Republican presidential ticket and platform in 2000, suggested that moral issues somehow backfired at the polls and that a "moderate" agenda is the salvation for success of the party and its nominees. Such claims were illogical and inaccurate. In fact, the problem was that almost without exception the Republican Party and its nominees offered religious conservatives no coherent agenda or clear message in the 1998 election cycle. Despite this poor presentation, religious conservatives remained the largest voter group (albeit in smaller numbers than in previous elections) most loyal to Republican candidates. In a news conference on the day following the 1998 election, Christian Coalition executive director Randy Tate stated, "Some message beats no message every time." Democrats did not campaign as liberals and Republicans did not portray themselves as conservatives. Just how was a voter passionate about a variety of timely and relevant issues to decide for whom to vote on election day?

After the 1998 election, *U.S. News & World Report* columnist John Leo declared that it was wrong for pols to use religious conservatives as their political scapegoat: "The religious right is larger and more varied than the stereotype forced on it by the media. 'Morally conservative' evangelicals, mainline Protestants, and Catholics are said to account for half of the U.S. population. They don't always vote together, and they don't always vote Republican. But it's too important a constituency to write off, no matter what the media elites think."

The lessons of past elections are that distinctions on many issues between opposing candidates should be emphasized rather than blurred. In most cases, Republican candidates put themselves at a disadvantage by presenting themselves as Democratic Lite when voters usually prefer the real thing. To be successful on election day, conservative candidates should not run from or hide their ideals but communicate effectively and wisely with religious conservatives that they share their values and will work, if elected, to enact pro-family public policy.

SUGGESTED READING

Reed, Ralph E., Jr. *Politically Incorrect: The Emerging Faith Factor in American Politics.* Dallas: Word Publishing, 1994.

Steven R.
Avellino

INFORMING INSIDERS:
THE POLITICAL NEWSLETTER

Studies show that newsletters, whether they are for *Star Trek* fans or Republican legislators, are more likely to get read than any other print media. They are, after all, delivered to a self-selected group with a strong interest in the specialized subject. If successful—in other words, reaching subscription saturation of the target audience—a newsletter can also become a valuable platform, information source, venue of advice, and bond for any community. Nevertheless, newsletters can and often do fail for many reasons, including technical considerations of readability and design. The political newsletter must take even greater care because its audience of political consultants and workers, officeholders, and journalists are among the most information-saturated in the world. To draw their sustained interest (and renewed fees) is a continual challenge. For a publisher of a newsletter, the "big five" considerations are to determine objectives (what to accomplish?), content (what will be in it?), frequency (how often to publish?), target audience (who will pay to read it?), and "source ethics" (how will you get your information?).

OBJECTIVES

The sophisticated newsletter reader will instantly know when a publisher has not clearly determined what to communicate. Do you wish to educate, inform, or motivate? After targeting our audience, we at *Electoral[ly] Speaking* decided it was in the best interest of (and would be most interesting to) our readers to attempt all three. It was also crucial to the success of our newsletter. Veteran political campaigners never send out a generic fund-raising letter when they can target a specific group and tailor the letter to them. The same concept applies with the political newsletter, but with an exponential leap in difficulty. You must target multiple audiences, or subgroups, without compromising the newsletter's coherence. This is impossible to accomplish until you have determined a clear objective.

CONTENT

Once you have determined your objective you can craft a clear and concise message. The first message to be related to your readers (and potential new subscribers) is your objective, which is placed directly underneath the newsletter nameplate. In our case the nameplate is *Electoral[ly] Speaking* and the subhead directly underneath is "Republican Political Strategy" (see Figure 22). These three words are a continual reminder to the readers about what to expect and to the staff about what to produce. We have several basic criteria or guidelines that determine which articles we solicit and accept:

• During a campaign year, we concentrate more on strategy and tactics. We also engage in prognostication—can we help the insiders predict trends, events, and issues that will affect their success in the election to come?

• During off years, we tend to address party-building and motivational topics: for example, the renewal of the party; building a national strategy; the need for grassroots outreach.

• We tend to reject articles or do not print information that is overplayed in national media (such as the impeachment scandal).

• We also, because we are an insider newsletter, reject pieces that attack, by name or by implication, groups within the "family" (that is, other Republicans).

FREQUENCY

Another important aspect of the publication of your political newsletter—and the biggest challenge—is the timeliness of your information. After all, you may research and print an article in your publication that ends up in a subscriber's mailbox two days after the *Times* or the *Post* has printed the same story on page 1, it has been the topic of *Nightline*, and has been the punch line of a Jay Leno monologue joke. To give a small example, we once researched a political group and went to print with the issue. Before we could get it in the mail, *U.S. News & World Report* ran the same story. We mollified ourselves by noting that ours took a slightly different perspective, but from the readers' point of view, we got beat. *Electoral[ly] Speaking* was at best a copycat publication and at worst a plagiarist. Since we publish every six weeks, we know that if we cover certain stories we will get scooped.

Figure 22.

Courtesy Steve Avellino, Electoral[ly] Speaking

The keys to overcoming the drawbacks of a monthly or quarterly publication schedule are good research and identifying the needs of the target audience. As Sun-Tzu wisely noted, every battle is won before it is fought. Newsletters going up against the "Nightly News," *Time*, and *Newsweek* are heavily outgunned and so must be clever. Before you even consider an article, you have to decide which battles should be fought and, more important, which battles can be won. If you target your audience, perform the research dictated by its wants, and cast a different "spin" on an article, you cannot be scooped by the dailies, even if they publish a similar story first. Be best by giving the audience what it can't get on the newsstand for fifty cents.

AUDIENCE

A new subscriber sends a check because he found something in the newsletter that was relevant to him personally. If subsequent newsletters do not maintain the same relevance, he will not resubscribe. Of course, readers subscribe for different reasons: our audience is not monolithic and can be broken down into subgroups. Some of our subscribers, for example, look to *Electoral[ly] Speaking* for campaign strategy and tactics, others for prognostication and election analysis.

This said, how does one determine relevancy for the individual subgroups while maintaining the newsletter's coherence? Once again, we must return to our objective and our target audience. For us it is hardcore Republicans, but this group can be broken down into United States legislators, party activists, state legislators, political consultants, major donors, the media, and so on. In turn, we strive to be thematic with each individual issue and follow a geometric progression—top to bottom. A political newsletter should be relevant to all members of its readership—from presidential candidate to school committee candidate, from party activist to major donor—while still maintaining its coherence.

For example, one issue of our newsletter was built around the idea of "A New Beginning for the Republican Party." The issue was published *after* the poor showing of Republican candidates in the 1998 midterm elections; obviously, *Newsweek* would not have had the same headline! On page 1 our Strategy Session piece was "The Perception of a New Beginning." This article targeted all of our readers and began to cement the theme. Three articles contributed by a prominent

Republican activist, House member, and governor addressed a grass-roots perspective, a legislative perspective, and a state/national perspective, all with the New Beginning theme in mind. An article on year 2000 Senate races continued the theme. A Social Security article and a piece on the mind-set of 1998 losing candidates followed the same cue. Every one of these articles adhered to one theme; all were inextricably tied to one another in an effort to garner the interest of our readers. Each too elicited an emotional appeal: although mainstream media were concentrating on the failings of the party, we tried to offer hope, direction, and concrete solutions. Our multiple subgroups were satisfied, and our newsletter's coherence remained intact for another issue.

SOURCE ETHICS

Another aspect to consider when publishing a political newsletter is what your conscience dictates to be "rules of propriety." These rules include respecting the wishes of your sources. We at *Electoral[ly] Speaking* do not like to burn bridges. For example, when we inadvertently found discrepancies in the Federal Election Commission reports filed during the 1996 Republican presidential primaries, we contacted the two campaigns in question but were not given satisfactory answers. We then contacted the FEC, which investigated and determined that no illegalities had occurred. It was merely creative bookkeeping, which would not be allowed in the future. When we went to print we did not identify the campaigns involved. It was not in our best interests or those of our readers.

We have also had run-ins with different government agencies, but we handle them delicately. Once again, your message must be dictated by your objective. If your objective is to expose, then by all means do so, but if it is not do not get overly excited when you stumble across a juicy item. If released, it can come back to haunt you.

Finally, in the case of newsletters, unlike mainstream media, your writers are also your readers. When you edit a contributor's article or conduct a phone interview, make sure the person in question receives a copy of the final product before you go to print. It's common courtesy. Follow this advice and you will always get a repeat article or interview. If you are fair and accurate, even people who don't like what you write about them or how you edit them will keep talking to you, writing for you, and (paying to be) reading you.

PHILOSOPHIES

<table>
<tr><td>

John
Franzén

</td><td>

CONSULTANTS AND
CLIENTS

</td></tr>
</table>

Political consultants are an unruly lot. We view our-selves as professionals and maintain a professional association, yet literally anyone can call himself a political consultant and start soliciting clients. Although several universities now have programs in campaign strategy and management, most consultants have no academic training in the profession, and many would scoff at the notion that it could be learned in school. We have emerged, unlicensed and largely unregulated, from a thousand campaign headquarters, congressional offices, newsrooms, software shops, and commercial ad agencies, united only in our conviction that we can successfully coax the electorate in the right direction, as we see it, and make a buck in the process.

Of course, not everyone will succeed. Political consulting is a Darwinian world, one of the few remaining truly free markets, where fortunes can rise and fall with breathtaking speed. No one can rest long on his laurels here, with a perpetual swirl of upstarts promising to do it better, faster, or cheaper. And it is in this boisterous, jostling marketplace that politicians go shopping for professional assistance.

Politicians, as well, live in a state of nature. They succeed more by perseverance and cunning than by any formal training, and they can rocket even more spectacularly to fame or into oblivion. Facing the absolute reckoning of election victory or defeat, they seek professional guidance with a keen awareness of the stakes—an awareness that sharpens the judgment of some but leaves others pathetically vulnerable to flimflam. Mostly by word of mouth, the smart politicians look for a record of election success and other objective evidence of the consultant's experience, creativity, and judgment. The others get caught up in gadgetry and giveaways or simply go with who's "hot."

The result is that for consultants and clients certain essential tensions arise from the act of cooperation.

WHO GETS THE LIMELIGHT?

We live in a carnival age. The same culture of celebrity that turns ball players into role models and actors into icons can also make stars of consultants. We have seen the awesome ability of television to turn our political clients into household names. It is hardly surprising that many consultants would put this magic to work for themselves.

That a consultant appears on TV or is quoted in the paper is not inherently wrong; we all need to market ourselves. But something in the nature of political consulting makes this public commenting and pontificating dangerous. Our job is to make stars of our clients. We are paid to make them look good, to give them the credit, to advance their ideas and careers. How is it, then, that some consultants have become more famous than most of the people they work for?

The late, great movie director Alfred Hitchcock had a playful habit of appearing briefly in his own films. We glimpse him in the background, missing a bus in *North by Northwest* and winding a clock in *Rear Window.* But in a troubling number of political campaigns today, old Alfred just keeps showing up—and takes center stage. He explains at great length to the audience how he directed the actors, wrote their best lines, and thought up most of the plot; he becomes the star and his wizardry is the message.

The consultant as commentator is not a problem in all cases. The practice crosses the line when the consultant comments publicly on the campaign of his own client, and particularly when that campaign is still *under way.* Each public utterance by the consultant in this context becomes a reminder to the television viewer or newspaper reader that the candidate in question is a creature of his handlers. Getting this kind of attention is easy for the consultant—it plays perfectly into the journalist's desire to reveal what's going on "behind the scenes"—but it reinforces the suspicion among voters that nothing the candidate says or does in public can be taken at face value. It actually insults and devalues the candidate and breeds further cynicism toward the political process.

As obvious as this problem ought to be to any thinking individual, many politicians continue to hire and rehire consultants who discredit and disrespect them in this fashion. A more logical approach would be to demand that the consultant remain essentially anonymous in the context of the campaign. And most political consultants do keep their tongues in check as a matter of professional pride. I personally assure my clients that I'll pay them $1,000 cash any time they see me quoted on the subject of their campaign without their specific authorization. Very often the most effective thing we can do, as stage hands, is simply to disappear.

CLIENT OVERLOAD

The sins of political consultants, alas, don't end with self-aggrandizement. Perhaps our most common failing is to take on more work than we can handle. Horror stories abound in political circles of candidates who hired the big-name firm and then couldn't get that big name on the phone or found their TV spots were being produced by college interns. In an industry where the work is so seasonal and where success builds so rapidly on success, getting overextended is a serious occupational hazard.

Client overload is driven, in part, by price competition, which has become far more intense in recent years as more and more consultants have gotten into the business. Consultants who sign up clients by low-balling their prices generally have to make their profit through volume, and the candidates who think they're getting a great deal generally, as the saying goes, get what they pay for. The thoughtful candidate shops for quality and is willing to pay for it, particularly if it comes with a guarantee that the consultant won't bite off more than he can chew. The basic step is to look at the consultant's list of clients and do a little division: how many campaigns are divided by how many principals, leaving how many days in the week for you?

THE QUALITIES OF THE CONSULTANT

What does quality look like? The consultant's election success rate is a pretty good indicator, but it's not the only measure. A lopsided win/loss record doesn't mean much if the consultant has worked only for safe incumbents. A lost election may sometimes be viewed favorably, if the loss was narrow and the odds were long.

It is also wise to scan the consultant's client list for patterns of repetition. If other politicians have rehired the consultant election after election, that tells you something, just as it's a danger signal if you see a lot of skipping around. The candidate seeking a consultant should also contact the consultant's former clients—the winners and the losers—and ask for their frank opinion. Many candidates don't bother to do this or don't do it systematically.

Often, candidates focus with particular concern on the size of the consulting firm. Is it big enough, they wonder, to be able to handle their campaign and give them the support they need? This is a good question, but it can't be answered simply by counting heads. Along with the number of individuals in the firm, one has to consider the number of other clients who will be competing for the firm's attention. Also, it is important to remember that a consulting business can be run quite effectively by assembling teams of freelance talent on a project-by-project basis.

This more free-form approach to the management of a consulting business has particular advantages if the consultant works in many different parts of the country. Why, for example, should a media consultant based in Washington, D.C., fly his own employee to California to scout locations for shooting when California has hundreds of talented location scouts who know the territory? As a firm believer in the small-is-beautiful approach to political consulting, I've developed working relationships over the years with dozens of such freelancers all around the country to whom I can turn on short notice. This allows me the flexibility to move quickly into a new situation and hit the ground running, and it lets me turn a profit without having to charge an arm and a leg to cover substantial permanent overhead.

The most important factors in judging the quality of a consultant are also the hardest to quantify. In particular, there's the matter of creative talent. Like pornography, it can't really be defined but we recognize it when we see it—or at least we ought to recognize it. Candidates and campaign managers do have an unfortunate tendency to talk about "media" as if it were an undifferentiated commodity, like soybeans. To achieve a certain effect, it is said, you need to air "this many" gross rating points of media. But we know very well that some TV and radio ads have no impact at all, no matter how many times they are aired, while others can shift public attitudes dramatically with only a few repetitions. The candidate who hires mediocre creative talent to save a little money is generally wasting money by the bushel.

Finally, there is the consideration of personal chemistry and trust. The candidate hiring a consultant is placing a very large part of his life and career, and a whole lot of money, in someone else's hands. He'd better feel some basic confidence in that person's character and judgment. Together, they will walk through fire.

Although there is no foolproof way to evaluate a consultant's integrity, the careful checking of references is obviously a must. The candidate should also check to see whether the consultant is a member of the American Association of Political Consultants. Every AAPC member has pledged in writing to abide by the organization's code of professional ethics, which covers basic matters such as truth in billing and client confidentiality.

FOIBLES OF CANDIDATES

A campaign can be reduced to misery or penury not only by inept or unprincipled consultants. Candidates and their staffs are human too, and their failings are just as numerous. The extraordinary pressure of an election campaign, with political life or death looming at the ballot box, often quite literally drives candidates crazy, particularly if it's the first time around.

A common syndrome is the compulsive refusal to delegate decisions. Any candidate should insist on signing off on the big ones, such as which issues to run on, but a depressing number of candidates just can't resist rewriting the radio scripts or niggling endlessly over the logo. I once had a candidate who personally had to choose the type fonts for the campaign brochure. At some point in such situations the consultant has to stop and ask, If you think you can do it better yourself, why did you hire me? And if the problem persists unabated, the consultant should be prepared to resign. In an election campaign the most precious commodity, after money, is the candidate's time. It has to be conserved and directed toward things that only the candidate can do.

The other extreme—more rare—is the candidate so stricken with the fear of defeat that he throws himself blindly on the expertise of his handlers, expecting to be told at every turn what to say and do and believe. In my twenty years in the business, I've had only one such case. This candidate asked me up front simply to create an image for him that would sell and he would go along with it. I did my best for him but the voters knew better, and he lost.

There are still other candidates who get into a campaign and realize they hate it but can't bring themselves to back out. They decide instead to lose, and they proceed, either consciously or not, to do stupid and self-destructive things toward that end. I've had three such candidates in my time. Two of them succeeded in losing. The other we were able to surround and protect from himself. Once in office, he decided he liked it and became a pretty good legislator.

A variation on deciding to lose is the candidate who refuses to raise money. This is a far more common syndrome and one with which I can sympathize. I wouldn't trust a candidate who actually enjoyed begging for money from people who generally want to see some specific benefit in return, and I think our campaign finance system should be radically reformed to break the hold that big contributors now enjoy. But until we achieve that goal, candidates must work within the system we have and must face the fact that contributors expect to be asked by the candidate. It is standard procedure in any campaign to assign large, daily blocks of time on the candidate's schedule to fund-raising, but simply putting them on the schedule is no guarantee that the calls will be made. The reluctant candidate can find endless excuses to avoid them. In campaign after campaign, in my experience, staff members and fund-raising consultants have had to dog the candidate endlessly to make those calls happen.

The unpleasantness of this exercise can lead candidates and their fund-raising assistants to resent the staffers and consultants who get to spend the money. Why should you have all the fun, they seem to say, while we go through this ordeal? They often harbor the suspicion, in fact, that the money they have raised through blood, sweat, and tears is being wasted—a suspicion that unfortunately is sometimes justified.

MONEY TROUBLES

With campaigns having grown so expensive, it is not surprising that many of the difficulties that arise between consultants and their clients revolve around money. Misunderstandings can often occur simply because the terms of the relationship have not been spelled out clearly in advance. Therefore, it is important for the candidate to have some understanding of how the consulting business works.

A media consultant is essentially an advertising agency, and we tend to charge for our services in the same three ways that agencies do. First, there are creative and consulting fees. Some media consultants will bill these fees on an hourly basis or a fee-per-spot basis, but most will simply set a fixed creative fee at the beginning of the campaign, payable in regular installments, sometimes with a victory bonus. Second, there is the commission on the airtime buy. The standard agency commission is 15 percent of the gross airtime cost—the station bills the agency based on the gross rate and expects payment of the "net," which is 85 percent. But that 15 percent differential isn't written in stone, and high-dollar campaigns can often persuade the consultant to reduce his commission and plow the savings back into the campaign. Finally, there are production mark-ups. It is a common practice for ad agencies to mark up their production and other expense reimbursement billings by a factor of 17.65 percent (which yields 15 percent working backward from the total), although some agencies will conveniently neglect to identify this mark-up as a line item. In my own firm, we generally don't charge candidates a mark-up at all. Some consultants do but manage to hide it.

There is no one "right" way to structure the compensation package—the three ways of billing should be seen as interdependent variables—but it is essential to understand the options and to spell out the arrangement in writing.

Of course, difficulties over money don't end with a written contract. The spending of large amounts of cash very rapidly in what amounts to a life-or-death struggle is inherently stressful. While every good campaign begins with an agreed-upon budget, that's only a starting point. Modern political campaigns are tremendously fluid, requiring dozens of revisions of the budget based on fast-breaking political developments and uneven rates of fund-raising success, and these decisions must always involve a certain amount of guesswork. All the more important, then, that the candidate hire a consultant who has been through this experience before and whose former clients can attest to his skill and judgment.

GETTING PAID

A common money problem for consultants in campaigns is the basic matter of getting paid. A signed contract indicating the consultant will receive X dollars on a given schedule does not guarantee payment. Again and again one hears of the consultant who gets caught up in the spirit of a difficult campaign, extends some credit and then some more, and in the end the candidate loses. At that point, the candidate can't raise money, the campaign committee shuts down, and the consultant is left high and dry.

How is it possible that so many consultants who seem otherwise bright and resourceful get caught so often in this position? The principal reason may be that most people in political consulting simply aren't motivated, or at least weren't motivated originally, chiefly by business considerations. This notion, of course, runs counter to the stereotype of consultants as sharks and high-rollers. But the truth is, most of us got into politics to advance a particular cause or point of view, and we discovered only later and to our astonishment that people might actually pay us to do this. Because we entered from that direction, it is not surprising that we sometimes have trouble with the realities of operating as a business.

At any rate, the wise consultant will take steps to assure payment. He'll arrange, for example, to get some part of his fee in advance and will structure the subsequent installments in such a way that the final payment is due before the end of the campaign—before the last of his work is done. Then he'll at least have some leverage for prying loose that final payment, which is often the big one. He'll also insist on receiving payments in advance to cover major expenditures such as television production. The process of obtaining an advance, which generally involves the presentation of a budget, will also help to ensure that the client really understands what's involved in the production effort—he won't be complaining at the end of the line that he didn't approve a particular item or didn't know it was going to be so expensive.

But perhaps the most effective way the consultant can ensure that he will get paid is to get the personal signature of the candidate on the contract. Losing campaign committees generally go out of existence; losing candidates don't. The smart consultant always insists on having the candidate's own commitment, in writing, that he'll fulfill the payment terms if the committee is unable to do so. This little addendum to the contract has a wonderful way of focusing the candidate's attention on the committee's payment obligations and can actually help motivate fund-raising.

Sometimes a consultant doesn't get paid because the client sincerely believes that payment isn't deserved. The work was shoddy, perhaps, or it arrived late, or the consultant mishandled funds. Occasionally, too, an unprincipled client simply decides to stiff the consultant—persuades him to spend money, for example, by saying the check is "in the mail" when it isn't. Far more often, however, the client who fails to pay the consultant fails with the best of intentions. It's simply a matter of the dynamics of the campaign having gotten out of hand, with the campaign manager or the consultant or both having allowed their high hopes to overrule their better judgment. In the well-run campaign, the manager and the consultant make regular reality checks and adjust their spending plans accordingly to keep from falling short.

Such prudence averts bad publicity as well: reporters are quick to sound the death knell for campaigns that leak money troubles.

WORKING TOGETHER

A campaign is a collaborative enterprise, and it is far more likely to succeed in an atmosphere of mutual trust and respect. The odds of maintaining such an atmosphere are greatly increased when lines of decision-making authority have been clearly established up front and when consultant, candidate, and campaign manager have a clear appreciation of each other's roles and responsibilities.

There is a natural tendency for on-site managers and other campaign staff to feel some resentment toward the consultant who comes in from the airport and tells the locals what to do. The locals, very often, are working outrageous hours for very low pay, while the consultant makes comparatively big bucks. But if the candidate and his staff don't believe the consultant is worth the cost, they should hire someone else who is, not go around griping about the unfairness of it all. They should also bear in mind that the consultant works long hours, too, and has to pay rent, staff, and other overhead that continues beyond the election. Many consultants end the campaign season feeling quite fat but are starving by the start of the next one.

The great sweetener, of course—what smooths out the bumps and heals the bruises of a stressful, exhausting campaign—is the prospect of ultimate victory. Achieving that goal makes everyone a hero and has a wonderful way of erasing bad memories of turf battles and arguments over money. Working together and giving all you've got to succeed in a noble cause may not be the only objective in life, but it does beat everything else.

Rob Allyn | # THE GOOD THAT POLITICAL CONSULTANTS DO

Our political ills—dishonesty, attack ads, low voter turnout, weak candidates, the reduction of issues to soundbytes, influence-peddling—are routinely blamed on campaign managers, media strategists, pollsters, direct mail gurus, press handlers, and fund-raisers of the television age. Of course, in any profession, there are both good and bad, efficient and incompetent, and honest and thieving practitioners. But political consultants differ from insurance agents, bakers, and computer programmers in that, for the most part, they do much good that goes unnoticed, unrecognized, and, ironically, unadvertised.

WE GET THE PUBLIC'S ATTENTION

Common wisdom holds that today's voters are turned off by attack ads, slick mail campaigns, and high-tech phone banks—all fueled by special-interest money. Yet consider the mechanisms engineered by the political industry: the focus group to determine what moves voters; the humorous attack ad with wry voice-over and mnemonic-device visuals; the creative mailer with its intriguing cover and zinger inside; the fund-raising letter with a stirring call to action and mail-back card; the predictive-dialing phone call reminding one to vote. All are designed to catch voters' attention and persuade them to take action. The result belies the myth of voters' disengagement: big-spending, hard-fought races tend to drive *up* turnout, while low-spending contests with little give-and-take tend to be ignored.

For example, hard-fought elections for governor of Texas in 1990 and 1994—legendary $50 million shoot-outs featuring all the tricks in the political consultant's handbook—caught the public's attention and produced record turnouts. In contrast, George W. Bush, Jr.'s, reelection as governor in 1998 was a gentlemanly contest of positive ads, earnest discussions of issues and an old-style, grassroots, door-to-door campaign by the challenger, the sort of election contest idealized by political scientists and editorial writers. The result? A record low turnout.

304

Were Texans so complacently assured of the popular governor's reelection that they didn't bother to vote? Possibly. Or perhaps they simply weren't agitated by the negative ad, alerted by the last-minute mailer on an issue that counted, or called away from watching *Monday Night Football* and reminded that their vote mattered.

WE MAKE COMPLEX ISSUES EASIER TO UNDERSTAND

In the mythic Garden of Eden of American democracy, the professional political consultants of the late twentieth century are the serpents who give out the bad apples. In this idealized version, Americans were an idealistic breed of yeoman farmers who read their newspapers by feeble candlelight and in the autumn dutifully packed up wives and children on the buckboard to attend a six-hour Lincoln-Douglas debate, there soberly to consider weighty issues facing the republic.

In fact, I suspect that while a few lawyers and bourgeoisie may have listened to Lincoln debate Stephen A. Douglas, the yeomen were over watching the bear wrestling across the midway. Americans have always been at least marginally interested in politics, but it is unclear if that ever translated into a deeper understanding of issues. In fact, through much of our history most Americans could not read or had little access to information about questions of the day. Many could not legally vote: women, minorities, folks under age twenty-one, people who didn't own property or couldn't pay a poll tax. Even today, with almost total enfranchisement and copious data and analysis about issues available through many media, including most recently the Internet, there is no evidence that the average voters actually take the time or devote the attention to truly understanding what and for whom they are voting.

The basic problem is that most of us (politicians included) find the issues of salvaging Social Security, reforming health care, or reining in deficit spending too intricate to understand in detail. But voters have remarkably good sense about the basics. Good consultants do service to democracy by putting complex issues in a form voters can grasp.

For example, in 1993 and 1994, political professionals helped crystallize America's nagging doubts about one-party control of government in the early days of the Clinton administration. The average voter may not have understood the health care debate, the reckless management style of the early Clinton White House, or the seeming inability of the presidency and Congress to control the growth of federal spending, but across America, GOP challengers and their consultants engineered tough, smart, well-funded campaigns that put those complex issues in terms that resonated: "Your congressman is too much like Clinton." "He voted to raise your taxes." "Congress is out of touch and doesn't care how it spends your money." "They wanted to put government in charge of choosing your doctor." "We need term limits." "It's time for a change."

Simplistic, perhaps, but it worked, as simple ideas usually do. Contrary to popular wisdom, Newt Gingrich and the Contract with America did not single-handedly win the 1994 Republican Revolution. Surveys at the time showed that only a fraction of those who actually voted had even heard of Gingrich or the contract. The 1994 upheaval was the product of bright, committed candidates with the courage to tackle entrenched incumbents; intelligent, skillful professionals who articulated a well-researched, simple, and creatively delivered message against Clinton and tax-and-spend incumbents; and the money to pay for it all.

If lauding the simplification of messages sounds patronizing to voters, it's not. In today's busy and complex world, citizens have more than politics on their minds. A recent *Wall Street Journal* poll indicated that Americans rank politics as the fourth most important thing affecting their lives, well behind, say, advances in medicine. Citizens are right. Viagra or monoxidil probably will affect one's life more than gays in the military or the capital gains tax (at least for those of us approaching middle age). But politics matter, and today's political consultants make democracy, however unpleasant the process, work on an everyman level, a valuable leveling service to the system.

WE HELP WEED OUT BAD CANDIDATES AND CAUSES

A little-known truth of the political system is that few of the potential candidates for any given office make it to the starting gate. Before running for mayor or president, Congress or judge, candidates make the rounds of movers and shakers—contributors, bigfoot journalists, party activists, and elected officials—who generally will advise them to get a good consultant.

The best consultants are gatekeepers for the republic. Karl Rove, Governor Bush's lead consultant, when asked what made his business successful, replied: "Good candidates." A great candidate is gold to a consultant. They say the right things, raise money, present solid qualifications, and become a permanent cottage industry for the consultant, rising higher and higher and referring other good clients.

Conversely, consultants hate to be saddled with bad candidates. They say the wrong things and hide skeletons in their closets that can cause embarrassment later. They won't make their finance calls, can't make up their minds about copy, and can blemish a win-loss record. Professions have different ways of handling their mistakes. Doctors bury their dead; architects plant vines; in politics, they just leave the ad off the reel.

It is true that this winnowing process can be put to evil uses. Perhaps there are a herd of Mr. Smiths out there waiting to go to Washington, thwarted by PAC-funded political pros who won't give them the time of day. But generally, the best candidates and causes are the ones that engender widespread affection, that people *want* to vote for, not have to be corralled and pushed to vote for. These are, of course, the very men and women we seek as clients.

WE TELL TRUTHS THAT THE SYSTEM HIDES

Modern consultants take blame for negative advertising, but the tactic is as old as the republic. Which U.S. vice-president was wanted for murder in New Jersey? Aaron Burr, who killed Alexander Hamilton in a duel over a mudslinging pamphlet about an illegitimate child. Bill Clinton wasn't the first president charged with draft-dodging and adultery; Grover Cleveland played around *and* paid someone to take his place in the Civil War.

The point is not that personal muckraking is necessary but that negative advertising can make a positive contribution. The Thirteenth District of Texas stretches improbably from Amarillo nearly to Dallas, larger than a typical New England state. Congressman Bill Sarpaulis served three terms there from 1990 to 1996. Labeled a "dim bulb" by local media, he masqueraded as a moderately conservative Democrat who believed in guns, farm price supports, and limited government, in that order. Texans who took the *Washington Post* or attended a town hall meeting might have tumbled to the surprising knowledge that Bill Clinton had persuaded him to switch his vote and support billions in tax hikes in 1993, but the vast majority of his constituents had no idea.

Thanks to a tireless and highly ethical rancher named Mac Thorn-berry and a brilliant manager named Sylvia Nugent, the 1994 Republican campaign did not travel the usual path of mudslinging and personal attacks against Sarpaulis. Instead, they had us create television ads introducing Mac Thornberry to the district and showing real citizens articulating their anger at Sarpaulis's betrayal.

"I've always been a Democrat, but Sarpaulis . . . he's just lost me," said one farmer in a feed store. "Changing his vote at the last second, just so Clinton could get his taxes." That farmer was shocked when we asked him to do a second take. "Heck, this TV stuff is just like farming," he said. "Just go over and over the same field in your tractor all day long."

At a filling station, we filmed the wife of an unemployed truck driver. She pretended to memorize the script and then rewrote it orally, giving us a perfect thirty-second ad in her first try. "Seven cents a gallon may not seem like much if you're a congressman making a hundred thousand a year," she said, waving curtly at the pump sign announcing the gas tax hike. The shot cut to her bumper sticker with our candidate's logo: "I'm making a change to Mac Thornberry."

Thanks to a hardworking challenger and generous supporters who helped get his message on the air in a professional fashion, the voters got information the incumbent was trying to hide. Today, the district has a congressman who reflects its views, and the nation has a balanced budget for the first time since the 1960s. That makes a good day's work.

WE KEEP CAMPAIGNS ON THE HIGH ROAD

Here's the myth. Young and idealistic candidate, in shirtsleeves, is presented with nefarious political dirty trick by unkempt, unctuous campaign manager. "Senator, we gotta hit him about his kid getting busted for dope, or we lose," says the manager.

"I'm just not going to do it," says the candidate, horrified. "Someone's got to stand up against this sort of thing." Campaign manager winces: "It's your funeral." Candidate does right thing. Somehow triumphs anyway. Wife is darn proud. Fade to black.

Here's how it really works. Candidate's spouse calls consultant at dawn. "Have you seen the papers? They're killing us! We've got to hit back! Where's the file on the brat with the hash habit?" Calls come from the candidate, the candidate's lawyer, the precinct chairs, even the media: "When are you going to use that stuff?"

As public distaste for mudslinging grows—and professionals see campaigns knock themselves "off message" by launching personal attacks—today's best consultants are the ones holding back the reins, counseling clients to rise above and stick to message discipline. The better campaigns and consultants seem to be the ones running positive ads and keeping negative ads issue-oriented, while weaker candidates and rotten consultants fairly revel in the mud.

In our firm we employ a twofold standard: first, is it true? and, second, is it relevant? If it meets these two tests, it's fair game. It may be true that a candidate sends his children to private school, even while braying against vouchers—but is it relevant? (No, don't use it.) It's true that the opponent voted for a tax hike—purists say it was only a procedural vote—but clearly it's relevant. (Heck, yes, use it!) The result: political consultants winnow the muck too—we keep much more negativity off the air and out of campaigns than would erupt if we weren't around as professional voices of reason and experience.

WE CHECK THE FACTS

Good political consultants don't lie. They poll to find out what the public likes and highlight those positives; they use focus groups to find out what the public dislikes and either avoid it or turn it into an asset, as when Ronald Reagan promised that if Walter Mondale wouldn't make an issue of his age, he wouldn't make an issue of Jimmy Carter's inexperience.

Indeed, we are terrified of being caught in a lie—it's bad for our clients, for our reputation, and for present and future business. We must face the press year after year; in the era of media "ad watches" and opposition countercharges, we know that our commercials, brochures, letters, and press releases will undergo withering scrutiny. Careful firms often require written verification before airing attacks: the record of the tax vote; the bankruptcy filing; the signed issue questionnaire. In addition, it's wise to release documents along with the advertising, buttressing the ads against counterattack.

Our firm has learned to press for details even of positive information, for example, asking for written proof of past successes we are to tout. What happens if you don't? In 1992, Lena Guerrero, a rising star of the Texas Democratic Party, resigned in disgrace when it was discovered that, instead of having been awarded the Phi Beta Kappa key, as she had claimed for years, she had flunked out of college.

Because we have immediate access to the candidate's past and a burning motive to get the facts, good consultants can verify, correct, delete, or talk the client out of a staggering amount of misinformation every election year, helping the public get accurate information in a way that the media cannot.

WE PERSUADE CITIZENS TO DO THE RIGHT THING

In the end, the service political consultants provide to the public is that we help elect good candidates, pass good laws, and persuade the public to that which is good for our communities: grand breakthroughs like a balanced federal budget to guarantee our children a strong economy and freedom from debt; less dramatic changes like the right to choose their doctor or join a not-for-profit credit union; local issues like allowing a mayor to unite a city rent with racial woes or construct a sports arena and chain of lakes to spur economic growth in a decaying downtown area.

Consultants, then, like democracy, are not perfect, but it is destructive to focus only on what's wrong with the system and ignore its positive benefits and their chilling alternatives. Winston Churchill once said, "Democracy is the worst system devised by the wit of man, except for all the others." As political professionals, it is our job to make it better.

Tom King | # CANDIDATES AS FUND-RAISERS

> *My partner Peter Fenn likes to tell a story about Frank Church's 1980 Senate campaign. Peter gave Senator Church a list of twenty people who had given to the party in the past and asked him to call these potential donors and request $1,000 from each. "I can't do this," Church said. "I don't know them." The next day, Peter returned with a list of twenty of the senator's friends and told him to call and ask for $1,000 each. "I can't ask these people for money," said Church. "They're my friends!"*

FEAR OF FUND-RAISING

Fund-raising is the worst part of the political consulting business. Everyone—from the candidates to the consultants—dislikes it. Unfortunately, it is a necessary evil. Campaign costs have risen significantly in the past several years because of the increasing rates of airtime buys as television becomes more important to campaigns and for other reasons. According to the Center for Responsive Politics, winning congressional candidates in 1994 spent an average of $516,126. By 1996, this figure had risen to $673,739. There are no indications that such campaign budget inflation is easing.

Most of this money comes from individuals. The best person to do the tapping for contributions, of course, is the candidate. But nobody becomes a senator (or an alderman) just so that he can call people and ask for election money. The result is that fear and loathing of fund-raising are pandemic among American politicians. Journalists and scholars have estimated that candidates spend 85 percent of their time raising money. What this really means is that candidates are spending 85 percent of their time thinking about raising money—but much less time actually doing it.

Part of the problem is that most politicians are "people persons" and "problem solvers"—they like to talk to constituents and others and feel good about solving their big and small problems. The question of money puts a sour spin on such encounters. Consider that there are four groups of people who routinely give money to political candidates:

Friends or relatives. These donors support the candidate because of personal relationships.

Special thanks to Noah Cole and Jeremy Goodwin for their assistance with writing and research.

Ideological supporters/party supporters. These potential contributors may not have met the candidate personally, but they agree with the candidate's positions on the issues and believe in supporting candidates from that political party.

Those who think this candidate will win.

Those who want something. The latter two groups are interconnected. These people are usually motivated to give because they believe that the candidate, if elected, will be in a position to help them in some way; alternately, they give money (often to both sides in a race) so as not to alienate the candidate even if they aren't very happy with his or her voting record.

All of these people have one thing in common from the point of view of the candidate: the contact can be successful (money is obtained) but unpleasant (money is discussed). The problem is that, because the candidate may find fund-raising distasteful, she or he may do it badly, not treat it seriously, or not allocate the required campaign resources and brainpower to the task.

FUND-RAISING AS A BUSINESS

It is clear, then, that fund-raising cannot be an ad hoc activity. Initially, 75 percent of the candidate's time should be allocated to raising money. Although this target may be impossible to achieve, it is important to start the fund-raising effort with a significant investment of time. If it is treated as a business, the experience will be less onerous and more efficient. The crucial steps are to begin setting up the fund-raising schedule, staff, and goals early; then more time can be spent on the other aspects of campaigning. In addition, the sooner fund-raising mechanisms are in place, the more likely the campaign will have sufficient capital for use throughout the race.

Although not all campaigns hire fund-raising consultants, all campaigns should have a staff member whose sole responsibility is to raise money. This person's first step is to devise a fund-raising plan that will define a strategy to locate contributors, from individuals to PACs.

Time spent making random, untargeted phone calls is time wasted; therefore, a key task is to identify all possible donors. First, the candidate should compile a list of friends and relatives who can be approached, and no stone should be left unturned. A good place to start is the candidate's Rolodex and Christmas card lists. Next, donor lists should be assembled. The most likely contributors are people who have given to the party and to similar campaigns in the past.

A crucial caveat for political candidates when raising funds is to *stay within the letter of the law!* A good organization that expends sufficient effort can raise all the money needed while observing the laws. Campaign finance law has its own gray area; however, any questionable procedure should be avoided.

When soliciting donors, it is important to have an amount in mind. One should always ask for more than the donor gave in the past but not request an undue amount.

The actual process of soliciting donations itself consists of five main techniques.

Individual solicitation. This is the best way to raise money. It is also, however, a time-consuming and candidate-driven process generally consisting of individual phone calls or personal meetings. Candidates are directly involved by personally soliciting potential givers, usually targeted at the largest donors: one call that nets $1,000 is better than five that earn $100 each. Also, unfortunately, small-money pledgers have a higher rate of welching (never sending the money) than larger donors.

Fund-raisers. A steering committee within the campaign organizes fund-raising events. Again, the candidate is directly involved: the campaign must set aside blocks of time in which the candidate is focused on raising money. A nominal amount of entertainment or food may be provided, but the cost of attendance really goes toward the chance to spend "face time" with the candidate. Interestingly, at all levels of campaigns, the nature and content of fund-raisers do not change significantly, from living-room coffees in support of a small town's school board candidate to the famous White House coffees of 1995. An important follow-up step to these events is to track attendance; participants may become the targets of future solicitations later in the campaign.

Finance committee. This is an extension of the individual solicitation technique but does not involve the candidate directly. Dedicated supporters of the candidate—from business and community leaders to ordinary activists—agree to go out and solicit funds on their own, to reach some individual total. Their fund-raising tactics may be focused more on personal ties to friends and associates than ideological appeals.

Direct mail. This is the method of fund-raising that all campaigns like because no one is required to ask for money personally. But it can be expensive, especially for challengers who don't have time-tested lists of likely donors' addresses handy. In addition, printing and mailing the materials is costly. Direct mail solicitation is least effective for little-known challengers or middle-of-the-road incumbents. The technique is most successful for famous candidates with strong ideological identification (for instance, Oliver North or Ted Kennedy), whose supporters may be moved to write a check with a piece of mail as the sole inducement.

PAC contributions. More than any other form of fund-raising, this is dominated by a candidate's ideological stand and his chance of winning the race. PACs don't give money as a personal favor. Also, a candidate will tend to attract more PAC dollars if he or she has already been successful with fund-raising from other outlets. The best-financed candidate is often seen as having a better chance to win the election. A campaign with a big bank account will always see its funds increase at a larger rate; campaign dollars attract PAC dollars. But this form of campaign fund-raising is viewed negatively by the public, provides potential targets for the opponent's attack advertising, and can invite press scrutiny. Thus a campaign must decide if the PAC money is worth the notoriety it may attract; the answer is usually that it is.

DISCIPLINE FOR DOLLARS

Anyone can come in off the street and use the tactics suggested above to raise money. It only takes a quarter to make a phone call. But what makes one candidate more successful at fund-raising than another? There are three overriding factors: discipline, discipline, and discipline.

Money does not guarantee an election (e.g., Ross Perot or Michael Huffington), but the bottom line is that it is difficult to win without it. And though it is not the only factor, a larger bank account is definitely an advantage; the more money a campaign has, the greater chance it has to disseminate its message. Obviously, not everyone has the right message to win, but the message must be heard to be effective. In the 1998 Minnesota governor's race, for example, Jesse Ventura didn't have enough money to hire a media consultant until mid-October. Once he did, however, it took two weeks for him to rise from third to first in the polls and ultimately win the election.

Former Speaker of the House Tip O'Neill used to tell a story about his first campaign. He ran for the Cambridge, Massachusetts, City

Council and lost. Shortly after the election, his next-door neighbor told him that she wasn't surprised he lost. He was amazed to hear this because he had often shoveled her walk and taken care of her children. "Did you vote for me?" he asked. "I did," replied his neighbor, "but I knew you were going to lose because you never asked for my vote." As Tip found out, if you don't ask for support, people assume that you don't need it. The same principle can be applied to fund-raising. In Boston, they say it takes three things to win a race: money, money, and money. Just as you can never be too rich or too thin, when it comes to campaigns you can never have too much money or too much support.

RESOURCES

Lynda Lee
Kaid

THE POLITICAL
COMMUNICATION CENTER

The Political Communication Center (PCC) is an interdisciplinary unit at the University of Oklahoma that coordinates academic degree programs in political communication, facilitates research projects, sponsors conferences, oversees archival collections, and provides service to academic and professional communities interested in political communication, political advertising, and political debates.

The archival collections of the PCC serve as important historical repositories for political materials. Containing over sixty-six thousand items, the Julian P. Kanter Political Commercial Archive is the world's largest collection of political radio and television commercials. The major purpose of the archive is to preserve these valuable historical materials and to make them available for scholarly and professional use.

Originally founded in 1956 by a private collector, Julian P. Kanter, and housed at the University of Oklahoma since 1985, the archive collects, preserves, and catalogs an ever-increasing number of political commercials and related materials. The archive maintains a strict preservation and access environment for the materials it preserves, including climate and humidity controls for preservation and adherence to Library of Congress cataloging standards. The collection has operated for many years with the endorsements of the National Archives, the Library of Congress, the American Film Institute, the American Association of Advertising Agencies, the Republican and Democratic National Committees, and the American Association of Political Consultants.

The PCC also maintains collections of other political communication materials, including an archive of televised political debates, a collection of international political television programs, and a small number of print political advertising items.

CONTENTS OF THE COLLECTIONS

The commercials in the archive date back to 1936 for radio and 1950 for television. All levels of races are included: presidential, U.S. senatorial, U.S. congressional, gubernatorial, state legislative, other statewide offices, county and municipal, judicial, school board, and so on. The archive has materials from all fifty states and some foreign countries. It also contains advertisements for and against ballot issues (or propositions) and an increasing number of advocacy commercials that deal with public and social policy questions, commercials by political action committees, and advertisements sponsored by corporations and special interest groups on public issues. Many of the items in the archive are one-of-a-kind copies and are no longer available from any other source.

The commercials vary in length from very short spots to program lengths of thirty or sixty minutes. The original masters of the spots are on a variety of formats, including audio tape, 16mm film, 2-inch videotape, 3/4-inch videocassette, 1-inch videotape, and 1/2-inch videocassette.

The televised debate archive contains copies of debates from all presidential elections, as well as from many state and local campaigns. The international collection includes political programs and debates from Great Britain, Germany, France, Italy, Romania, Bulgaria, Japan, Korea, Chile, Poland, Russia, Turkey, Thailand, and many other countries.

ACCESS TO THE COLLECTIONS

Users can locate items in the collections in one of three ways. First, the PCC publishes a printed catalog. This catalog is also available on the Internet at the PCC's web site: [www.ou.edu/pccenter]. Second, the PCC sends electronic versions of its holdings, according to Library of Congress cataloging standards, to the OCLC Union Catalog. These listings of the contents of the archive are available in libraries throughout the world and via Internet access. Third, the PCC maintains an on-site computer database for more detailed analysis of each item in the collection. While the catalog and OCLC access provide general information on the holdings for a particular candidate or entity, the on-site database details the characteristics of each individual commercial or program by candidate, political party, year, state, type of election, type of commercial, issues contained in the commercial, gender of the candidate, and many other attributes.

Because the University of Oklahoma is a public educational institution, its collections are open and available for use on-site during the normal operating hours of the University of Oklahoma. The archive does, however, adhere to restrictions placed on the access to specific materials by the donor of the materials. Very few archival holdings are subject to such donor restrictions.

For most users, access is available only to copies of the materials and primarily on-site. No originals are available for routine usage. For this reason, advance consultation with the archive staff is recommended for information on the most efficient methods of providing access for a particular user's needs. This is particularly true if a user's needs involve extensive compilations of materials that span several time periods or campaigns. In unusual cases, copies of materials may be rented to off-site users at a cost necessary to cover staff time, equipment usage, and supplies. All usage and copying of archive materials are subject to adherence to federal copyright laws.

When the archive provides materials for use, the user is given rental copies of the materials only, and these copies must be returned within the specified time. The user must provide assurances to the archive that materials will not be used in any unauthorized ways. It is the express policy of the archive that its materials will not be used in any way to bring disrespect, ridicule, or misrepresentation to the candidates or producers of the commercials it preserves.

For further information about the Political Communication Center or the archives, interested users should contact

Lynda Lee Kaid, Director
Political Communication Center
University of Oklahoma
Norman, OK 73019
tel. 405–325–3111
FAX 405–325–1566
e-mail: LKAID@OU.EDU

Carol Hess | # RESOURCES FOR POLITICAL CONSULTING

A vast array of resources are available for political consultants and students of practical politics. The reference materials listed here are organized into three categories: publications, schools, and the Internet.

PUBLICATIONS

Most readers will be familiar with the mainstream sources of political information. The list below includes less commonly referenced material. The directories, national and state journals, and newsletters focus on practical politics. They deal with securing information or analyzing campaigns, elections, and politics in particular states or regions.

Publication	Phone	Web Address
Almanac of PACs	703-525-7227	http://www.pacfinder.com

Almanac of PACs
Directory of political action committees with detailed financial and background information.

American Political Report   301-664-8430
Newsletter on American politics, published by Kevin Phillips.

Ballot Access   415-922-9797   http://www.well.com/conf/liberty/ban
Newsletter on legal and political aspects of ballot issues.

Bill Shipp's Georgia   707-442-2543   http://www.billshipp.com
Newsletter on government and politics in Georgia.

California Journal   916-444-2840   http://statenet.com
Monthly journal on government, policy, and politics in California.

California Political Week   310-659-0205
Weekly newsletter on California state and local government.

Campaigns & Elections   202-887-8530   http://www.camelect.com
Monthly magazine for the professional political industry. Many "how-to" articles.

Capitol Business   717-238-2701   http://www.capitolbiz.com
Newsletter on political and legislative issues in Pennsylvania.

Cook Political Report   202-789-2434
Newsletter analyzing congressional, gubernatorial, and presidential elections.

Empire State Report   518-783-0001   http://www.empirestatereport.com
  Monthly magazine on New York politics, public policy, and government.

Evans-Novak Political Report   202-393-4340
  Biweekly newsletter on local, state, and federal politics.

Headway Magazine   281-444-4265   http://www.headwaymag.com
  Monthly political, conservative, black magazine.

The Hill   202-628-8500   http://www.hillnews.com
  Weekly newspaper focusing on Capitol Hill.

Indiana Legislative Insight   317-817-9997   http://www.ingrouponline.com
  Newsletters on Indiana.

Inside Michigan Politics   517-487-6665
  Biweekly newsletter covering Michigan politics.

National Journal   202-289-8400   http://www.cloackroom.com
  Weekly journal analyzing national government and politics.

Political Pulse   916-446-2048
  Newsletter on California politics and government published twice monthly.

Political Resource Directory   800-423-2677   http://PoliticalResources.com
  Over 3,300 political products and service providers. Includes description; cross-
  referenced by specialization, state and principals. AAPC annual directory.

Politics in Minnesota   612-293-3911
  Newsletter on politics in Minnesota. Twenty-two issues/year.

Roll Call   202-289-4900   http://www.rollcall.com
  Twice-weekly newspaper chronicling the activities of Congress.

Rothenberg Political Report   202-546-2822
  Biweekly newsletter on House and Senate campaigns.

Southern Political Report   202-547-8098
  Biweekly newsletter covering southern politics.

State Legislative Sourcebook   785-232-7720
  Resource guide to legislative information in the fifty states.

Texas Weekly   800-611-4980   http://www.texasweekly.com
  Weekly report on Texas politics and government.

SCHOOLS

Several academic institutions offer either degree programs or specialized courses in practical politics. The following is a selected list.

School	Phone	Web Address
Graduate School of Political Management, George Washington University	202-994-5852	http://www.gwu.edu/~gspm

Women's Campaign School at Yale University	800-353-2878	http://www.yale.edu/wcsyale
Political Management Institute, University of California-Davis	530-757-8643	
Suffolk University	617-573-8126	http://www.clas.suffolk.edu/berg/grad.html
Regent University	888-800-7735	http://www.regent.edu
Campaign Management Institute, American University	202-885-6251	http://auvm.american.edu/~ccps/

ON THE WEB

The political resources that are available on the World Wide Web are almost infinite. The following list provides several comprehensive sites with general information, election coverage, and legislative and party information. Most have extensive links to other political sites. In addition, Political Resources publishes *Political Web Notes*, a free monthly e-mail newsletter highlighting interesting political Web sites.

General Sites	Web Address
Center for Responsive Politics— campaign reform	http://www.crp.org/
Project Vote Smart—extensive links, tracks congressional votes	http://www.vote-smart.org
THOMAS—immense compilation of legislative information on the Net	http://thomas.loc.gov/
Policy—links to issue sites	http://www.policy.com
Politics I—links to presidential, gubernatorial, and congressional sites	http://www.politics1.com
Political Resources Online— consultants, practical political information	http://PoliticalResources.com
National Confederation of State Legislatures—information on the state level	http://www.ncsl.org/

Political Party Sites	Web Address
Democratic National Committee	http://www.democrats.org/
Libertarian Party Site	http://www.lp.org/

Reform Party	http://www.reformparty.org
Republican National Committee	http://www.rnc.org
U.S. Taxpayers Party	http://www.ustaxpayers.org/

Voter Information Sites	Web Address
Federal Election Commission (FEC)	http://www.fec.gov
FedInfo	http://www.tray.com/fecinfo
State Boards of Elections	http://PoliticalResources.com/

Associations	Web Address
American Association of Political Consultants (AAPC)—a membership organization providing conferences and networking opportunities	http://www.theaapc.org

David D.
Perlmutter
and
H. Denis Wu

THE AMERICAN POLITICAL CONSULTANT: A PROFILE

It is often said that doctors make poor patients; likewise, political practitioners have proven an elusive target for surveyors. Researcher Delbert C. Miller notes that historically the lowest return rates come from questionnaires sent to political leaders in Washington, D.C. (*Handbook of Research Design and Social Measurement*, 1991, p. 151). While this volume is an attempt to let political consultants and those who cover and study them talk about their craft, questions about who consultants are and what they do are not necessarily answerable by a few vocal members of the profession. To get a profile of American political consultants, therefore, we took two approaches. First, from August 1998 through January 1999, one of us (Perlmutter) conducted a series of interviews with political consultants. The list of interviewees was provided by the board of the American Association of Political Consultants, the profession's leading trade organization. The group consisted of about eighteen Democrats and twelve Republicans and several who worked with both parties. All were principals at major political consulting firms. Each was interviewed by phone or in person for about one-half hour to two hours. The interviews were completely open-ended but roughly structured around the state of the profession and its future.

The second approach to profiling consultants was a by-mail survey conducted by both authors in the last three months of 1998. The target population was *working* political consultants who were members of the AAPC. Of these 402 men and women, 236 completed and returned their surveys by the final deadline. (This response rate of 59 percent is considered high—according to Miller—for professionals involved in politics.) The survey consisted of a three-page questionnaire composed of thirty-seven questions, ranging from the respondents' demographic attributes, such as age or gender, to open-ended questions about ethical practices and the future of the business. The findings of both studies are discussed in brief here.

The AAPC is a trade organization, and although consulting firms will often purchase memberships for their middle-rank employees, there is a well-known bias toward the upper echelons of the trade. This bias was reflected in the respondents' descriptions of themselves, which mirror the profile of American white-collar executives: white, male, middle-aged, upper income. Despite the increasingly visible presence in political work of women and Hispanics, and to a lesser extent African Americans, the powers that be and "movers and shakers" still continue in the tradition of the American business place. Ninety-three percent of the respondents were white; about three percent were Hispanic; no respondent categorized him or herself as African American. Only two reported being of Asian and one of Native American descent. Eighty-four percent were male; 78.5 percent of the sample were between the ages of thirty-five and fifty-nine.

This profile of the profession is well recognized by the practitioners. One interviewee commented "When you go to conventions or meetings or get-togethers, you're seeing more and more women, and in fact a lot of the up-and-coming younger consultants, people coming out of campaign work and lobbying, are female. But the executives, the owners, are still overwhelmingly a bunch of guys." Another noted, "It's true that anyone can hang up a shingle and announce they're a political consultant, but to survive and make a living you have to have a preexisting reputation, and certainly many years of experience. There's just not a lot of women and minorities in the tunnel from ten or fifteen years ago working in politics with that kind of track record and cash. They're coming, but they haven't arrived yet, visibly." A senior consultant observed: "We don't look like the country—and that's true of both Republicans and Democrats." A female consultant added, "It's an old boys' club, but because everyone is so ruthlessly concentrated on winning, talent and merit end up counting much more than gender and ethnicity. Let's see what we look like ten years from now."

Nearly 40 percent of the respondents to our survey listed a bachelor's of art or sciences as their terminal degree, while 25 percent held a master's degree, and 6 percent had received a Ph.D. Only 13 percent reported not having graduated from college. To some extent, this finding was at cross purposes with the stereotype that is often held of political consultants—which they sometimes assume about themselves— that the typical consultant is an uneducated cowboy. In fact, as this response shows, consultants are much more likely to have been to college than the average American; only 55 percent of high school graduates even attend college, as of 1997.

While figures of previous years are not available, these findings do suggest that political consulting, like journalism and other former "crafts," is professionalizing, and that a college degree, even an advanced degree, is a prerequisite for acceptance as much as in any other profession. An interviewee commented: "It's not that the people who used to come into this business were illiterate. Many of them had journalism and political science backgrounds. But what's very new is the idea that you should study political work, campaigns and such, in college." Indeed, when asked about their recommendations for what courses college students interested in being political consultants should major in, the respondents were supportive of a broad liberal arts education, giving high ranks to advertising and marketing, public relations, political science, and psychology; but, interestingly, the strongest support was for a solid grounding in history. A senior consultant who employs many interns and young part-timers summarized: "I don't want young people who are just policy wonks or number crunchers. I want them to be able to *think*, and to understand social context and historical background."

At the same time, in the survey, a majority of consultants judged that anyone wanting to work for a political consulting firm should have at least a few—up to five—years working in some other aspect of politics. "A lot of kids don't want to hear this, but before you call yourself a consultant you should have done something," argued one respondent. The "something" reported by the interviewees was almost always working in an actual campaign, as a manager or an assistant to a manager. "Nothing gives you as much experience, wisdom, and understanding of political candidates and their problems as working every day in the trenches of a campaign," said one. The comment by the late Matt Reese that a consultant will "be a lot better after he loses a few campaigns" is the best précis of this view (see Napolitan, p. 20).

Political consulting, then, demands that its practitioners be both well-educated and at least moderately immersed in real-world experience. In other words, and this was the consensus in the open-ended interviews, most consultants did not see a Manichean division between school and real-life experience; both assisted the aspiring individual toward achieving excellence in the profession.

In other areas, consultants did not describe themselves out of line with characteristics of other upper-middle-class Americans. Forty-five percent reported themselves as belonging to a Protestant denomination, 26 percent Catholic, and 9 percent Jewish; several percents reported other religions, and about 14 percent asserted that they were not religious at all. About 40 percent of the sample reported that they attended a church or religious institution once a month or more; 16 percent are nonchurchgoers, while 43 percent attend church once or several times a year. (One wag added: "Midnight Mass—Election Eve.")

Politically, consultants are largely monogamous; 74.8 percent of the respondents work exclusively for either Democrats or Republicans. Of the remaining group, almost all work mostly for candidates of one party or the other. The consultants are also selective about their customers. Four out of five agreed or strongly agreed that they usually work for clients whose positions they endorse. This loyalty to party and ideology is another blow to the stereotype of the "gun for hire" mercenary interested only in the color of money.

The political consultants were very much unlike America's business elite in one important regard: almost all of them were small-business people. Nearly the entire sample reported that fewer than twenty employees worked for their firms during the 1998 campaign season. Sixty percent of the respondents reported having only one to five employees in their company. Only eight respondents claimed more than thirty employees. In tabulating the number of clients, the situation becomes more complicated. As we have seen, political consultants might just as likely be working for an industry as for an alderman. About half the sample, however, reported working for ten or fewer separate candidates per campaign season, and a similar number reported working for ten or fewer issue advocacy, referendums, or ballot measure campaigns. In this sense, the commonplace of the consultancy being a small-shop business with a few principals, a few secretaries, and a couple of interns, while the rest of the work is done by local freelancers, is largely confirmed.

The explanation for this business structure is simple. Until recently, political consultants were highly paid seasonal workers. Once the day after the election arrived, only residual checks came in and a one- to two-year famine began. Now, increasingly, as consultants turn to corporate work and as campaigns themselves lengthen, staffing is bound to increase. One consultant noted, "If all you do is political work, you have to keep a lean shop, contracting out almost everything that you don't directly do yourself." Another observed, "We're seeing a trend toward larger firms, as people more and more are crossing over into product advertising or corporate lobbying." Still another consultant added, however, that "it is still a very personality-linked business. Clients pick well-reputed consultants, not necessarily well-reputed firms. They want to work with *somebody*, not some company. So we'll never get too big because personal service is what they're purchasing." A senior consultant added a wrinkle to this equation: "Ego will always be important. Firms tied to individuals are gonna break up; people will retire. The Rolodex has to be redone every two years. I can't imagine it ever becoming a large, impersonal, corporate-type business."

Nevertheless, political consulting, at least for many of those who answered our survey, is a reasonably profitable enterprise. Nineteen percent of the sample reported that their annual personal income, before taxes and after overhead, including all politically related work, was over $310,000. More than half the sample reported earning over $150,000. The consultants earned this money largely from work related to media: among the top (over 50 percent) services offered by the respondents were media consulting, political advertising, and press relations. When we asked them to report the percent of their income they earned from various activities, "working with candidates" accounted for about 37 percent; the figure matched exactly the amount of *time* they reported actually working with candidates.

Political consulting is a profession in transition, or to put it more accurately, it is a craft that is professionalizing. *Campaigns & Elections* magazine at the time of this writing featured a list of the growing number of graduate programs offering campaign management or political campaign communication courses. As more and more Americans obtain degrees in political work, increasing standards and an inclination for self-regulation will be the inevitable result. As the writers here in the *Manship School Guide* generally emphasize, research, preparation, discipline, and experience are the requirements for political communication in the modern campaign era. That message is certainly welcome to educators, whatever criticisms we have about the state of the political process. It seems increasingly self-evident that these values will be learned by future generations of political consultants both in school and in the field.

This book is to some extent a recognition of those changes, of the need for the profession to systematize its knowledge, to move away from the cowboy era into the less glamorous but better understood and more mainstream world of American business. Consultants themselves realize that one age is fading and a new one is dawning; however, unlike the passing of many traditional societies, there is little sentimentality about the "good old days." Indeed, as is notable when consultants gather, the oldsters are the leading and loudest reformers.

Political consultants thus—who are only as reputable as their last election performance—know better than anyone that they must reinvent themselves. As one elder of the profession put it: "I'm pessimistic about some things. The more our numbers explode, the less quality control you have. On the other hand, I see the best and brightest in America's colleges wanting to work in our business. I'm not sure whether to be scared or happy, for the country or for myself." One aspect of the future is certain. Becoming more like businesses and less like fiefdoms will force the profession to become more "like America," that is, to build a work and executive force reflective of the nation as a whole; to endure and evolve, in reaction to public scrutiny and criticism; to develop and enforce standards of ethics and propriety. This book is an invitation for the reader, aspirant, pro, academic, or ordinary citizen to join in building that future.

CONTRIBUTORS

Rob Allyn runs an award-winning agency that for fifteen years has served more than 150 winning political campaigns, corporations, and causes. Allyn wrote the novel *Front Runner* (Crown, 1990) and is a regular commentator on PBS and Fox News.

Steven R. Avellino is a political consultant and publisher of the newsletter *Electoral[ly] Speaking: Republican Political Strategy.*

Dave Beattie is a principal partner of Hamilton Beattie & Staff, based in Washington, D.C., and Florida. He was elected to a board of education in 1998 and has managed or advised numerous campaigns from state representative to governor. He teaches campaign strategy in the political campaigning program at the University of Florida.

John Bovée is president and CEO of The Bovée Company, a California-based consulting firm that specializes in opposition research and fund-raising for Republicans and corporate clients. He has been involved in over 230 local and state campaigns. He has served in every capacity of campaign management ranging from fund-raiser to opposition research director, on-site coordinator, advance person, press spokesperson, volunteer recruiter, and political consultant.

Donna L. Brazile is chief of staff to Eleanor Holmes-Norton, the District of Columbia's delegate to the U.S. House of Representatives. She is also an at-large member of the Democratic National Committee and served as political consultant to the Democratic Congressional Campaign Committee on voter turnout and participation. In 1998, she designed the Voter/Campaign Assessment Program that was considered crucial in boosting black turnout in key congressional districts.

Anne E. Clinton is with The Clinton Group, Inc. She has been involved with campaigns, grassroots organizing, and political activism for ten years. She is currently studying law.

Walter D. Clinton is founder and president of The Clinton Group, Inc., which has provided direct mail and telephone-based persuasion pro-

333

grams for use in campaigns, issue referendums, and grassroots programs since 1971. A pioneer of campaign telecommunications techniques, he has participated in campaigns in every state in the United States and on three continents. He currently serves on the board of directors of the American Association of Political Consultants.

Charles H. Cunningham serves as acting director of federal affairs for the National Rifle Association. Previously, he served as the director of national operations for the Christian Coalition. He was honored as the first recipient of the annual Ronald Reagan Award for political activism and achievement at the 1998 Conservative Political Action Conference. He was also recognized by *Roll Call* on January 26, 1998, as one of the nation's fifty most influential and effective political operatives.

Diana Daggett worked from 1981 to 1996 as a campaign manager and political consultant. Among her campaigns were Pete Domenici for Senate (New Mexico), Kirk Fordice for governor (Mississippi), and Steven Schiff for U.S. House (New Mexico). She has also worked for the Republican National Committee, the Republican Governor's Association, and the National Republican Senatorial Committee. She is currently government relations manager for Texas at the Intel Corporation.

Louis A. Day teaches at Louisiana State University's Manship School of Mass Communication. He is the author of numerous articles on communications law and a widely used media ethics casebook, *Ethics in Media Communications: Cases and Controversies.*

Matthew Dowd is managing director of Public Strategies, Inc., an international public affairs firm based in Austin, Texas, working with companies and associations around the world. Before joining Public Strategies, Dowd served on the staffs of U.S. Senator Lloyd Bentsen (D-Texas) and Congressman Richard Gephardt (D-Missouri). In the spring of 1991, *Campaigns & Elections* magazine named Dowd a "Rising Star" on the national political scene, describing him as a "true scientist."

Thomas N. Edmonds is president of Edmonds Associates, a Washington, D.C.-based political consulting firm specializing in media campaigns for candidates at all levels of government as well as independent expenditure campaigns for major political organizations. He has also produced several acclaimed documentaries, including the award-winning television mini-series *Campaigns in American History* and *Ronald Reagan: An American President*. Edmonds has served as president of the American Association of Political Consultants and currently sits on the board of directors of the International Association of Political Consultants.

Bill Fletcher is president of Fletcher and Rowley Consulting, Inc., a political and media consulting firm based in Nashville. Fletcher is a writer, musician, photographer, and recovering newspaper reporter.

John Franzén, president of Franzén & Company in Washington, D.C., has produced media campaigns for Democratic candidates nationwide since 1978. He has extensive experience in ballot initiative campaigns and has produced issue advocacy media for the American Association of Retired Persons, the Sierra Club, and the California Teachers Association. He is a board member of the American Association of Political Consultants and has lectured widely in the United States and abroad on campaign strategy and techniques.

Robert V. Friedenberg is a professor of communication at Miami (Ohio) University, Hamilton. He is the author, co-author, or editor of five books, the most recent of which is *Communication Consultants in Political Campaigns: Ballot Box Warriors* (Praeger, 1998). With Judith S. Trent he has written *Political Campaign Communication: Principles and Practices*, the most widely used college-level text on political communication. He has also written approximately one hundred other articles, chapters, reviews, and convention papers and has worked in approximately seventy political campaigns.

Ronald Garay is professor and associate dean for undergraduate studies and administration in the Manship School of Mass Communication at Louisiana State University. Garay has written a variety of articles and book chapters on radio and television history and regulation and is the author of *Congressional Television: A Legislative History* (Greenwood, 1984) and *Cable Television: A Reference Guide to Information* (Greenwood, 1988).

Phillip L. Gianos, a professor of political science at the University of California, Fullerton, teaches courses in political behavior and politics and film.

Joseph A. Glick, a professor of psychology at the City University of New York, is president of Glick Associates: Strategic, which conducts focus groups for political campaigns.

Ben Goddard, president of Goddard Claussen, a California-based public affairs consulting firm, began his career in television news, moved into advertising, and then to political consulting working for Jimmy Carter, Gary Hart, Jesse Jackson, and Russian President Boris Yeltsin. He is often credited with creating the concept of advocacy advertising with the "Harry & Louise" campaign against the Clinton health care proposal. He has crafted campaigns on issues as diverse as Social Security reform, HMOs and the Y2K problem.

Armando Gutiérrez is president of A. Gutiérrez & Associates, Inc, a New Mexico–based political consulting firm specializing in outreach to Hispanic communities.

Bill Hamilton is a principal partner of Hamilton Beattie & Staff, based in Washington, D.C., and Florida. He has been a pioneer in political polling since 1966, past president and co-founder of the American Association of Political Consultants, and on the board of the International Association of Political Consultants. In 1999, he won the AAPC Life Achievement Award.

Carol Hess is president of Political Resources, Inc. She is publisher of the *Political Resource Directory*, now in its thirteenth year of publication. She also publishes a monthly newletter, *Political Web Notes*, in conjunction with her company's Web site.

Jon M. Hutchens is president of Media Strategies & Research, which he founded in November 1990. His company provides survey research and sophisticated broadcast media planning and placement services for Democratic political candidates, progressive initiative and referendum advertisers, and issue advocacy campaigns.

Bud Jackson is president of Jackson Communications, a Democratic political communication firm. Jackson Communications advises political candidates of every level in campaign strategy and message development. It also offers clients full television, radio, newspaper, and direct mail advertising services.

Lynda Lee Kaid is a professor at the University of Oklahoma and is director of the Political Communication Center.

Amy Keller is reporter at the Capitol Hill newspaper *Roll Call*. She covers politics, campaigns, the campaign consulting industry, and campaign finance reform.

Tom King is the former political director of the Democratic Congressional Campaign Committee and a partner at Fenn and King Communications, one of the country's leading political media consulting firms, specializing in electing Democratic candidates nationwide.

Kim Levine is a 1996 magna cum laude graduate of Lehigh University in Bethlehem, Pennysylvania, and works for Strother Duffy Strother.

Joseph Napolitan has been a political consultant since 1956. He is the founder of the American Association of Political Consultants and co-founder of the International Association of Political Consultants. He has served on the campaign staffs of Presidents John F. Kennedy and Lyndon Johnson, was director of media for Vice-President Hubert Humphrey, and has been a personal consultant to nine foreign heads of state. He is author of *The Election Game*.

Tony Paquin is the co-founder, president, CEO, and chairman of the board of directors of Netivation.com, an Internet products and services company. He has extensive background in technology and public policy and is currently writing a book about the use of technology and the Internet in political campaigns.

Wayne Parent, associate professor of political science at Louisiana State University, is co-editor of *Blacks and the American Political System* (University of Florida Press, 1995) and author of several book chapters and articles in scholarly journals, including *American Political Science Review* and other top journals in the field.

Trevor Parry-Giles was senior writer for the Campaign Performance Group, a political consulting firm in Washington, D.C. He is now a writer at Craver, Mathews, Smith & Company and teaches in the department of communication at the University of Maryland. He has published and taught extensively in the areas of political communication, legal communication, and presidential rhetoric.

David D. Perlmutter teaches political communication at Louisiana State University's Manship School of Mass Communication. His books include *Photojournalism and Foreign Policy* (Greenwood, 1998) and *Visions of War* (St. Martin's Press, 1999).

Jay Perkins is an associate professor at Louisiana State University's Manship School of Mass Communication and is a former Washington political reporter for the Associated Press.

Matthew M. Reavy, a former newspaper editor, teaches new media and computer-assisted reporting at the University of Scranton.

Lynn Reed, president of NetPolitics Group, was site producer of the Clinton/Gore '96 Campaign site. In 1998, in association with the media firm of MacWilliams, Cosgrove, Smith, Robinson, she designed www.missedvotes.com for the Brian Baird for Congress campaign and took over design of the Tammy Baldwin for Congress Web site during the general election. She was recently named one of the "Rising Stars of American Politics" by *Campaigns & Elections* magazine.

Sean Reilly served two terms in the Louisiana State House of Representatives. He is an adjunct professor at Louisiana State University's Manship School of Mass Communication. He is employed as director of mergers and acquisitions for Lamar Advertising Company, a nationwide provider of outdoor advertising.

Rick Ridder is president and co-founder of Ridder/Braden. He has been a senior consultant for the Clinton/Gore campaign, the national field director for two other presidential campaigns, and a staff member on two additional presidential bids. He has worked in Canada, Australia, Great Britain, Sweden, and Venezuela as well as other countries. He is also the current president of the International Association of Political Consultants.

Sheldon Smith is a former Republican Party leader and campaign manager. Today he is the most recognized "voice of the GOP," doing as many as eight-hundred radio and television commercials each election cycle.

Ann E. W. Stone is president of the Stone Group, a political consulting firm.

Dane Strother is a principal partner of Strother Duffy Strother. He has also worked as a journalist and as a creative director for television.

Raymond D. Strother has worked in politics for thirty years and is currently president of the American Association of Political Consultants. A novelist and a frequently published and quoted commentator on media and politics, he was described in *Campaigns & Elections* magazine as the "Poet of Democracy."

Luther Symons is senior associate at Ridder/Braden. He is a lawyer by training, and his major areas of expertise are organizational development, fund-raising, and media relations.

Gerald S. Tyson, a veteran of more than twenty-five years in the political consulting business, is president of The Tyson Organization, a Fort Worth–based voter contact and grassroots strategies firm. Tyson also heads TDM Research & Communications, which conducts field interviews for Democratic pollsters.

Don Walter is a former lawyer, Capitol Hill staffer, MSNBC and FOX television contributor, graduate school professor, and producer. Since forming his own firm, Creative Media Partners, Walter has produced direct mail, award-winning nonbroadcast videos, and television and radio ads for hundreds of Republican candidates for local, state, and federal office.

Darrell M. West is professor of political science at Brown University. He is author of *Air Wars: Television Advertising in Election Campaigns* (Congressional Quarterly Press, 1997) and co-author of *The Sound of Money: How Political Interests Get What They Want* (Norton, 1998). He is a frequent commentator on the national political scene for a variety of media organizations.

H. Denis Wu is assistant professor of mass communication at Louisiana State University. He teaches and conducts research in the areas of political communication and international communication.

Edward Zuckerman is the editor and publisher of the *Political Finance & Lobby Reporter*, a semimonthly newsletter devoted to campaign finance and lobbying issues. He also edits *The Almanac of Federal PACs*, a biennial reference work used by political fund-raisers and others who require background information about PAC-sponsoring organizations.

INDEX